Foreword

More effective public policies to assist in the reconciliation of work and family life can potentially have very desirable results – greater labour force participation of parents can contribute to the goal of reducing child poverty and thus to improving future outcomes for children. Higher labour force participation can also contribute to the future well-being of parents, in particular by reducing the risk of poverty in old age among those who may not otherwise have participated in the paid labour market. Increased labour force participation can also help in improving the sustainability of social protection systems in the light of population ageing, and well-designed policies may also help raise fertility rates from the exceptionally low levels that exist in some countries.

In recent years, the OECD Babies and Bosses reviews of policies to promote work and family reconciliation covered Australia, Denmark and the Netherlands (OECD, 2002a); Austria, Ireland and Japan (OECD, 2003a); New Zealand, Portugal and Switzerland (OECD, 2004a); and, Canada, Finland, Sweden and the United Kingdom (OECD, 2005a). This volume provides a synthesis of the analyses and policy recommendations contained in these four volumes and also extends the analysis to include other OECD countries, presenting indicators for all OECD countries for 2005, where possible. The report was prepared by Willem Adema and Peter Whiteford, with assistance from Janet Gornick, Annette Panzera and Maxime Ladaique, under the overall supervision of the Head of the Social Policy Division, Mark Pearson.

This OECD Babies and Bosses synthesis volume starts by summarising main findings and presenting broad policy recommendations for OECD countries building on existing family-friendly policy measures. Chapters 2 and 3 outline the demographic and labour market outcomes in OECD countries. The subsequent chapters try to relate the differences in parental family and labour market outcomes to differences in tax/benefit policies (Chapter 4), public child-related leave policies (Chapter 5), childcare policy (Chapter 6) and workplace practices (Chapter 7).

Babies and Bosses

RECONCILING WORK
AND FAMILY LIFE

A Synthesis of Findings for OECD Countries

OECD

ORGANISATION FOR ECONOMIC CO-OPERATION AND DEVELOPMENT

The OECD is a unique forum where the governments of 30 democracies work together to address the economic, social and environmental challenges of globalisation. The OECD is also at the forefront of efforts to understand and to help governments respond to new developments and concerns, such as corporate governance, the information economy and the challenges of an ageing population. The Organisation provides a setting where governments can compare policy experiences, seek answers to common problems, identify good practice and work to co-ordinate domestic and international policies.

The OECD member countries are: Australia, Austria, Belgium, Canada, the Czech Republic, Denmark, Finland, France, Germany, Greece, Hungary, Iceland, Ireland, Italy, Japan, Korea, Luxembourg, Mexico, the Netherlands, New Zealand, Norway, Poland, Portugal, the Slovak Republic, Spain, Sweden, Switzerland, Turkey, the United Kingdom and the United States. The Commission of the European Communities takes part in the work of the OECD.

OECD Publishing disseminates widely the results of the Organisation's statistics gathering and research on economic, social and environmental issues, as well as the conventions, guidelines and standards agreed by its members.

Also available in French under the title:
Bébés et employeurs : Comment réconcilier travail et vie de famille ?
Synthèse des résultats dans les pays de l'OCDE

Photo credit: Britt Erlanson and Peter Cade/Getty Images

Corrigenda to OECD publications may be found on line at: *www.oecd.org/publishing/corrigenda*.

Table of Contents

Charts

ISBN 978-92-64-03244-6
Babies and Bosses: Reconciling Work and Family Life
A Synthesis of Findings for OECD Countries
© OECD 2007

Chapter 1

Reconciling Work and Family Life in OECD Countries: Main Findings and Policy Recommendations

This chapter summarises the main findings of the Babies and Bosses reviews of work and family reconciliation policies in OECD countries. It introduces main issues and cross-national differences in policy objectives and approaches, and provides a concise overview of fertility trends and parental labour market outcomes. The chapter concludes with a discussion of the main policy recommendations which emerged from the reviews based on the analysis of tax/benefit policies, leave arrangements, childcare and out-of-school-hours care supports and workplace practices that affect the behaviour of families.

1.1. Introduction

Parents in all OECD countries face considerable challenges when they try to reconcile their work and family commitments. Many people manage to achieve their preferred work/family balance, but many others do not. Faced with such difficulties, some people either postpone having children, do not have as many as they might have intended, or even end up having no children at all. Other parents have the number of children they desire, but by taking time out to provide personal care to their children, they sacrifice their careers. Still others may struggle to support their children while holding down a job, but find that there is too little time in the day to provide the nurture that they would like to give their children. One way or another, as long as there are people who are constrained in their choices about work/family balance, the result may be both too few babies and too little employment and/or unsatisfactory careers.

There are families who have enough resources to be able to afford to choose the work/family balance they prefer. Some parents choose to work full-time and pay for formal childcare for their children, while others prefer to provide full-time personal care to their children, at least until school age, regardless of the employment opportunities open to them. Many parents are, however, constrained in their choices. Some working parents would like to reduce hours at work to spend more time with their children but either cannot afford this or workplace practices do not allow them to. Yet other parents, who are at home, would prefer to be in paid work, or work more hours to generate more family income, but cannot because they have limited access to affordable childcare for sufficient hours, or have difficulties resuming their careers after childbirth. The issue is critical for children as both poverty and a lack of personal attention can harm child development significantly. Finding a good work/family balance is an important element in getting good child development outcomes as well as helping parents to realise their labour market and family aspirations. Furthermore, a better reconciliation of work and family life can reduce health and stress risks, which can contribute to stronger parent-child and parent-parent relationships.

1.2. Policy objectives

All OECD governments want to enhance the well-being of parents and children and all say that they want to give parents more choice in finding their preferred work and family outcomes. To this end, public authorities invest in

---

Box 1.1. **What are family-friendly policies?**

Family-friendly policies are those policies that facilitate the reconciliation of work and family life, ensure the adequacy of family resources, enhance child development, facilitate parental choice about work and care, and promote gender equity in employment opportunities. Family-friendly policies include improved access to affordable and quality childcare, financial support for children, arrangements that allow working parents to take leave to care for children, and flexible workplace practices that allow a better reconciliation of work and care commitments. They also include financial incentives to work for families with children and employment support for jobless parents.

Parents whose primary activity is looking after their children and/or elderly relatives are working – they are just not paid for the work. Casual references to the desirability of increasing the number of, say, mothers who "work" are resented as not acknowledging the importance of this unpaid work. Nevertheless, to avoid making the discussion overly cumbersome and wordy, "work" is often confined in this report to encompass all *paid* work (employment and self-employment). Whenever this usage might be confusing, an explicit distinction is drawn between paid and unpaid work.

"Families" and "reconciliation policies" are defined as follows in this report:

- *Families*: "Each household of one or more adults living together with, and taking responsibility for the care and rearing of one or more children."

- *Reconciliation policies*: "All those measures that extend both family resources (income, services and time for parenting) and parental labour market attachment."

---

family-friendly policies (Box 1.1) to reduce barriers to both parenting (*e.g.* through time-related support) and employment (*e.g.* through formal childcare support).[1]

There are many different underlying reasons why governments invest in family-friendly policies, including enhancing equity between different income groups, family types, and men and women; promoting child development; and, ensuring future labour supply, thereby underpinning economic growth and future societal development:

- Declining birth rates have very significant implications for the shape of future societies. **Fertility rates** are the most important family policy concern in Japan and Korea – unsurprisingly, given that each woman of childbearing age averages below 1.3 children at present. Concerns about fertility rates are increasingly widespread, but most OECD countries do not consider the fertility rate a public policy objective.

- In many OECD countries, increasing **female (especially maternal) labour supply** is seen as being important to maintaining economic growth and ensuring sustainable pension and social protection systems more generally. Within the EU, this has been formalised as a target – the aim is for each member country to have a female employment rate in excess of 60% by 2010.

- In different ways **child development** is receiving increasing prominence in the public policies of most countries. Experience of poverty during childhood damages child development; consequently, reducing or even eliminating child poverty has become an explicit policy aim in some countries. This concern manifests itself in different ways. Maternal employment is an effective way of increasing family incomes, so policy aiming to increase parental employment is sometimes justified because of its effect on child poverty. Avoiding benefit dependency and persistent poverty of families with children motivate the development of policies to **promote autonomy** among (sole) parents on income support. Child development concerns also affect formal childcare policy development. For example, in the Nordic countries and New Zealand, childcare policy stresses the pedagogic role of participation in pre-school arrangements, whereas the system of childcare support payments to working parents in the Netherlands reflects the predominance of labour supply concerns.

- In the presence of young children, mothers withdraw from the workplace or reduce their hours to care for children whereas fathers do not (indeed, they often increase their hours of work once they become a parent). This contributes to the persistence of significant gender pay differences, and women having great difficulty climbing the career ladder. However, **gender equity** objectives appear to be incidental rather than serve as primary policy objectives in most OECD countries, with the exceptions of the Nordic countries and Portugal. With its largely individualised parental leave system, Iceland has the most comprehensive set of policies which aim to **enable fathers to spend more time with their children** and generate a more equal sharing of care responsibilities for young children.

These underlying policy objectives do not stand alone and there can be some tension between them which can complicate policy development. For example, parental leave allows parents to look after young children when they are most vulnerable, promoting good quality development without forcing parents to sacrifice their careers. But if parents remain on leave for too long a period, their human capital is diminished, costs to employers rise, and great damage can be done to their careers. The objective of policy has to be to allow parents to choose the appropriate trade-off between the various objectives, recognising that different parents will have different preferences.

More often than not, however, the various underlying policy objectives outlined above are compatible with one another. Childcare policy is a case in point. Changing female labour force behaviour over the past few decades increased the demand for formal childcare capacity to which policy responded for reasons related to the promotion of labour supply, gender equity and self-sufficiency among sole-parent families, while child development concerns are increasingly important as a factor encouraging greater investment in childcare systems.

1.3. Key family and work outcomes across OECD countries

It all used to be so simple. The male breadwinner model involved a clear allocation of responsibilities and time: men spent their time at work providing family income, while women spent their time caring for children at home. However, with changing female aspirations and female labour market behaviour since the late 1960s, the single-breadwinner model has lost much of its relevance. Female employment rates have increased across the OECD (Chapter 3), and nowadays only in a few countries, including Greece, Italy, Mexico, Spain and Turkey, are single-income couples nearly as common as dual-earner families. Otherwise, "dual-earnership" in couple families has become the norm in the majority of OECD countries.

The change in female labour force participation was accompanied by a decline in birth rates across the OECD. Looking at overall female employment rates and birth rates, work and parenthood seem to be particularly difficult to combine in many southern and central European and Asian OECD countries. With birth rates in excess of 1.7 children per women and with two-thirds of women in employment, it seems that Nordic countries and Australia, the Netherlands, New Zealand, the United Kingdom and the United States have the best employment and fertility rate outcomes, although generally below replacement levels (Chapter 2).

Notwithstanding the general upward trend in female labour force participation, considerable cross-country differences remain (Table 1.1). In 2006, female employment rates were highest at over 80% in Iceland, and were over 70% in Denmark, Norway, Sweden and Switzerland, well above the OECD average of 57%, while female employment rates are below 50% in Greece, Italy, Mexico, Poland and Turkey. The intensity of female labour market participation also differs, with part-time employment being very common in Australia, Germany, Japan, Switzerland, the United Kingdom, and nowhere more so than in the Netherlands where 60% of employed women work on a part-time basis. On the other hand, part-time employment is rare in the Czech Republic, Hungary and the Slovak Republic and concerns less than 15% of employed women in Finland, Greece, Korea and Portugal.

Table 1.1. **Key indicators on birth rates, female employment and child poverty**

	Total fertility rate	Employment/population ratio by group					Child poverty
	2005[1]	Women, 2006[2]		Mothers, 2005[3]		Sole parents, 2005 or latest year[4]	Around 2000[5]
	Children per woman	All	Part-time	Youngest child < two	Youngest child aged 3-5		Percentage
Australia	1.81	65.5	40.7	48.3		49.9	11.6
Austria	1.41	63.5	31.4	60.5	62.4	75.0	13.3
Belgium	1.72	53.6	34.7	63.8	63.3	62.0	4.1
Canada	1.53	69.0	26.2	58.7	68.1	67.6	13.6
Czech Republic	1.28	56.8	5.6	19.9	50.9	63.0	7.2
Denmark	1.80	73.2	25.6	71.4	77.8	82.0	2.4
Finland	1.80	67.3	14.9	52.1	80.7	70.0	3.4
France	1.94	57.1	22.9	53.7	63.8	70.1	7.3
Germany	1.34	61.5	39.2	36.1	54.8	62.0	12.8
Greece	1.28	47.5	12.9	49.5	53.6	82.0	12.5
Hungary	1.32	51.2	4.2	13.9	49.9	. .	13.1
Iceland	2.05	81.6	26.0	83.6		81.0	. .
Ireland	1.88	58.8	34.9	56.3		44.9	15.7
Italy	1.34	46.3	29.4	47.3	50.6	78.0	15.7
Japan	1.26	58.8	40.9	28.5	47.5	83.6	14.3
Korea	1.08	53.1	12.3	. .	. .	. .	. .
Luxembourg	1.70	53.7	27.2	58.3	58.7	94.0	. .
Mexico	2.20	42.9	27.6	. .	. .	. .	24.8
Netherlands	1.73	66.0	59.7	69.4	68.3	56.9	9.0
New Zealand	2.01	68.4	34.5	46.6		53.2	14.6
Norway	1.84	72.3	32.9	. .	. .	69.0	3.6
Poland	1.24	48.2	16.3	. .	. .	. .	9.9
Portugal	1.40	62.0	13.2	69.1	71.8	77.9	15.6
Slovak Republic	1.25	51.9	4.1	23.1	46.6	. .	. .
Spain	1.34	54.0	21.4	45.1	47.9	84.0	15.6
Sweden	1.77	72.1	19.0	71.9	81.3	81.9	3.6
Switzerland	1.42	71.1	45.7	58.3	61.7	83.8	6.8
Turkey	2.19	23.8	17.8	. .	. .	. .	21.1
United Kingdom	1.80	66.8	38.8	52.6	58.3	56.2	16.2
United States	2.05	66.1	17.8	54.2	62.8	73.8	21.6
OECD	**1.63**	**56.8**	**26.4**	**. .**	**. .**	**70.6**	**12.0**

1. Year of reference for total fertility rates – Canada: 2004.
2. Data for Luxembourg concern 2005.
3. Data for mothers in employment concern 1999 for Denmark; 2001 for Canada and New Zealand; 2002 for Finland and Iceland; and 2006 second quarter for Switzerland.
4. Data are for 2005 except for Denmark (1999), Belgium, Canada, Germany, Greece, Italy, Japan, Spain (2001), Finland and Portugal (2002), Iceland and Norway (2003), the Netherlands (2004), and 2006 second quarter for Switzerland.
5. The child poverty rate is defined as the share of children with equivalised incomes less than 50% of the median for the entire population.
Source: See Chapters 2 and 3.

BABIES AND BOSSES: RECONCILING WORK AND FAMILY LIFE – ISBN 978-92-64-03244-6 – © OECD 2007

The presence of children in households hardly affects male employment rates. By contrast, the presence of very young children generally reduces maternal workplace participation, especially when mothers have more than two children and/or when children are very young. Employment rates may not always pick up this effect because of long parental leave periods (during which women are recorded as employed), but for mothers with very young children in Australia, Canada, the Czech Republic, Germany, Hungary, Japan, New Zealand, the Slovak Republic, Spain, Switzerland, the United Kingdom and the United States, employment rates are significantly lower than for women in general. Employment rates for mothers with children over three years of age are highest in Nordic countries at close to 80%. On average across the OECD, seven out of ten sole parents, often mothers, are in paid employment, but sole-parent employment rates are considerably lower at below 60% in Australia, Ireland, the Netherlands, New Zealand and the United Kingdom (Table 1.1).

In general, all countries that enjoy very low rates of child poverty (under 5% of households with children as in Belgium, Denmark, Finland, Norway and Sweden) do so because they *combine* high levels of paternal and/or maternal employment with effective redistribution of resources through the tax-benefit system. Looking across OECD countries, around one in ten children live in poverty, but this is more than one in five in Mexico, Turkey and the United States (Table 1.1).

In many respects, the story of changing female labour market participation is one of success. More parents are working than before, and women and mothers who were denied the chance to pursue achievement through labour market careers, with the financial independence that work can bring, face vastly improved life chances than previously. However, despite the achievements in female and maternal labour force participation of the past few decades, women remain the dominant care-giver, gender employment gaps persist, gender wage gaps remain stubbornly wide, and women are at a greater risk of being "trapped" in jobs which do not give career progression (Chapter 3). In terms of paid and unpaid work outcomes, a gender-equitable society remains some way off.

1.4. The overall policy response

Given the importance of family-friendly policy objectives, it is not surprising that many countries have made considerable investments in family supports. Traditionally, one of the biggest sources of support for families with children is the provision of compulsory schooling, and public spending on primary and secondary education in the majority of OECD countries ranges from 3 to 4% of GDP (OECD, 2006a). However, spending on family benefits increased in the vast majority of OECD countries from 1980 to 2003 (Chart 1.1).[2] On average across the

Chart 1.1. **Public spending on families has increased in many countries since 1980**

Public social spending on family benefits, 1980 and 2003, as a percentage of GDP

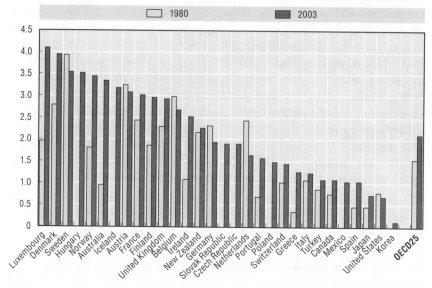

Countries are ranked from left to right in terms of the highest to the lowest spending ratios in 2003. Data for Turkey concern 1980 and 1999.
Source: OECD (2007a).

OECD, *gross* (before-tax) public spending on family benefits increased from 1.6% of GDP in 1980 to 2.2% in 2003, amounted to more than 3% of GDP in Australia, Austria, Denmark, France, Norway, Sweden and was highest at over 4% of GDP in Luxembourg (OECD, 2007a).

1.4.1. Public support to sustain both employment and fertility

Systems, which provide a continuum of work/family reconciliation supports, help avoiding very low birth rates...

In general, since female labour market aspirations have changed, all policies which enhance female labour force participation may also help to avoid very low fertility rates. The *Babies and Bosses* reviews found that systems which provide a continuum of support to families – support for parents at home when the child is very young, leading on to a childcare place, pre-school, school and out-of-school-hours care activities – perform best in helping parents reconcile work and family life. Such an approach stimulates birth rates as parents can realistically plan their work and family commitments. At the same time, employers can be reasonably certain about whether and when employees will return to work.

Only a minority of OECD countries provide such a continuum of work/ family support throughout childhood to families on a comprehensive basis. In many countries, there are gaps in support at some point *e.g.* when leave expires, childcare support may not yet be accessible. Policy in the Nordic countries, Hungary and to a lesser extent France and the Canadian province of Québec[3] does provide a coherent system of supports. While systemic logic differs, all policy models include parental leave (9 to 18 months in Iceland, Denmark and Sweden) and/or home-care supports until children are three years of age (Finland, Hungary and Norway), followed by early childcare, kindergarten and other pre-school services, and primary education. In Denmark and Sweden (and to a lesser extent France and the Canadian province of Québec), these supports are complemented by a comprehensive system of out-of-school-hours care services, while parents in Sweden are also entitled to reduce working hours until children go to primary school.

... but they can be very expensive.

There is a price to pay for such comprehensive supports. Nordic countries and Hungary spend at least 0.6% of GDP or more on income support during leave *and* more than 0.9% of GDP on childcare and early education, to cover the period up to primary school. Not all OECD countries are prepared to tolerate Nordic public spending and tax levels (in Denmark and Sweden the tax-to-GDP ratio is close to 50%). Rather than building universal support systems, most countries try to restrict spending (and the burden of taxation) by focusing public support more on some areas of social policy than others and/ or by targeting resources at low-income families more generally.

1.4.2. Tax/benefits systems

Public policy has to strengthen financial incentives to work for parents...

Financial incentives to work do matter. Differences in the tax and benefit systems are found to have an effect on the decision of parents to participate, and whether they work part-time or full time. The majority of OECD countries now have individualised tax systems, but nearly all OECD countries either have some form of tax relief for non-employed spouses or some form of family assistance that aggregates incomes of spouses to determine levels of assistance. These arrangements potentially produce weak financial incentives to work (more) for (potential) second earners, as the effective marginal tax rate of the second earner is close to that of the primary earner.

In view of budgetary considerations, family-friendly policy priorities are often pursued by targeting scarce public resources at those most in need. Unfortunately, such an approach has its own problems, because of the effects of withdrawing help as family income rises. When tax/benefit support is targeted at low-income households, incentive effects are worst for those who are likely to have the most significant difficulties in entering the labour force and/or work more hours, *e.g.* women with low-paid husbands and families receiving welfare payments. Low effective tax rates on paid work are desirable, and tax/benefit systems should be so designed as to give both parents in couple-families equally strong financial incentives to work.

... including sole parents, who should be helped back to work as children get older.

Policy clearly affects the proportion of sole parents who end up relying on benefit support. Low levels of public benefits (*e.g.* in southern Europe) in effect force sole parents to work for a living, often while relying on informal networks for care support. At the other extreme, the comprehensive formal care support system in Nordic countries enables *all* parents to work, regardless of their marital and/or partnership status: upon the expiry of child-related leave, parents on income support are required to look for employment and/or be available for participation in labour market support measures like any other job-seeker. Particular problems arise when adequate benefits are provided without having at the same time both the sort of support services, especially childcare, that sole parents require, and a clear policy signal that work is expected of sole parents. For example, in contrast to other OECD countries which require parents on income support to look for work when children are of pre-school or primary school age, tax/benefit systems in Australia, Ireland, New Zealand, and the United Kingdom provide categorical income support for sole parents for a prolonged period without, until recently, any job search or work requirement as the quid pro quo for receiving a benefit. As a result, in these countries expectations on a return to work among sole parents receiving benefits are weak.

It is not in anybody's interest to see sole parents becoming dependent on benefits for many years – the sole parents themselves, their children and the taxpayer all pay the cost in one form or another. There is a need for earlier and more active interventions to support work by (sole) parents on income support, including childcare support, while for the existing long-term clientele comprehensive measures to upgrade their skills may be necessary. The countries with the best outcomes for sole parents combine a system of employment and good-quality childcare supports with requirements for sole parents to take advantage of the opportunities open to them, like for other unemployed people. With public investment in employment and childcare supports, a system of mutual obligations should be embraced and enforced, and include the threat of moderate benefit sanctions if benefit recipients do not take active steps to find work or improve their employability.

1.4.3. Parental leave

Paid leave policies should be of moderate length...

Maternity, parental and childcare leave with employment protection enhances child development and can also contribute to raising employment rates of parents, particularly mothers. Good leave schemes give parents choice in their return-to-work decision, and allow flexibility in taking leave entitlements, *e.g.* allow a parent to return to work after a shorter period, possibly on a part-time basis, without loss of overall entitlements.

From a narrow labour market perspective, the optimal period of leave seems to be around four to six months (measured in full-time equivalents), and employers report that leave for about four to five months after childbirth causes less disruption than longer leave periods. If leave periods are shorter, mothers are often not ready to go back to work, while the use of longer leave periods by mothers can permanently damage their labour market position, leading to lower employment rates and lower earnings. In terms of child development, the available evidence seems to suggest that child development is negatively affected when an infant does not receive full-time personal care for the first 6-12 months of a child's life. Cognitive development of a child benefits from participation in good-quality formal care (and interaction with its peers) from age 2-3, with the evidence being ambiguous regarding the intermediary period. If both parents were to take their individual leave entitlements consecutively where these are available (or take their leaves simultaneously on a part-time basis, as, for example, is allowed in the Netherlands), this would go some way towards covering this period.

... and policy should encourage fathers to take more advantage of leave arrangements

As long as women rather than men take advantage of care provisions, there are employers who will perceive women as less committed to their career than men, and are therefore less likely to invest in female career opportunities, depressing female earnings a whole. To some extent this is a vicious circle: since female workers have limited incentives to pursue a career if they perceive the likelihood of advancement is more limited than for men, they are indeed more likely to withdraw from the labour force, only to return, if at all, in jobs that are often low in job-content compared with their potential. However, if fathers also take leave, in principle it becomes possible to ensure that one or other parent can spend time with their young children without such deleterious effects. Increasing the amount of parental leave taken by fathers can also reduce the demand for (expensive) formal care arrangement for very young children, and whilst increasing female labour supply generate more gender equitable employment and care outcomes.

Policy in many European countries tries to stimulate fathers to spend more time with their children by legislating periods of paid parental leave exclusively for their use. There is some success, as many fathers use these short (two to four weeks) periods of paid leave. However, taking a few weeks of leave after childbirth or around summer and Christmas holidays does not reflect a fundamental behavioural change. Paternal attitudes are not the only issue, as mothers frequently seem reluctant to give up leave in favour of their partner. Except in Iceland (see Chapter 5), the debate about *individualisation* of the entire paid parental leave entitlement which could contribute to a more equal sharing of care responsibilities has yet to start in earnest. Countries are encouraged to introduce measures aimed at reducing the differences in the use of parental leave between men and women by, for example, increasing information to both parents about fathers' rights to parental leave and/or increasing the duration of paid leave entitlements that are non-transferable between the parents.

1.4.4. Childcare and out-of-school hours care

Policy should ensure that childcare issues do not establish a barrier to parental employment…

The absence of affordable, good-quality formal child and out-of-school-hours (OSH) care can be a major barrier to being in paid work and/or working more hours. In Nordic countries, subsidies to parents using quality childcare centres are generally so high, that one is almost "a thief of one's own wallet" if one does not use public childcare facilities and engage in paid work. In other countries, the story is rather different. Parental fees are often high, and formal childcare support may not be universally accessible for (working) parents. In Ireland and the United Kingdom, the costs of childcare can be so high, that in the short term work does not pay for many second earners in couple families and this applies to sole-parent families in the Canadian province of Ontario, Ireland, France, and the city of Zürich in Switzerland.

… and the Nordic model provides affordable, quality childcare to all…

Both demand and supply-side funding can be effective in achieving the more-or-less general drive across the OECD towards more investment in childcare capacity and quality. The *Babies and Bosses* reviews appreciated the supply-side-funded childcare systems in Nordic countries because the quality of care is good, because it is provided on a full-time basis and because coverage of the population is high. Apart form the high tax burden this involves, other OECD countries do not have a strong tradition of good-quality local public service delivery or considerable taxing powers for local government (Chapter 4). The Nordic model is therefore not directly exportable to other OECD countries which are in the process of building up childcare capacity and quality. Furthermore, notwithstanding a growing awareness that participation in childcare serves a child-development purpose, many countries still consider formal childcare as a service for which working parents and employers (see below and Chapter 7) should largely pay themselves.

... but a different mix of public support and providers can also help parents find childcare solutions that match their needs...

The *Babies and Bosses* reviews advocated the use of a mixture of financing tools. Direct supply-side subsidies should be made towards capital investment, providers in deprived and/or scarcely populated areas and/or concerning the provision of services to children with special needs. In addition, as in Australia and the Netherlands, the private sector can be relied upon to provide childcare and when combined with demand-side funding to parents which is earmarked (vouchers), relatively high coverage of the population can be achieved. A further advantage of this approach is that parental choice is promoted, potentially leading to more variety in types of services and service providers, and efficiency can be promoted as well through competition between providers. Budgetary costs can be controlled through income testing and targeting of public supports on families which need it most. To contribute to the long-term financial viability of childcare systems, the role of family day-care services should be maintained as such services are often less costly than centre-based care services. Finally, fee support for childcare can also be linked to working hours, to pursue employment policy objectives.

... although public support should always be tied to compliance with standards of good quality.

Regulation of providers has been found to be necessary in order to ensure good-quality childcare, and public funding of (private) providers should be strictly tied to compliance with pre-set quality standards. Such quality standards should not merely cover health and safety aspects, rules on the number of certified staff among personnel, and staff-to-child ratios, but should also include child developmental goals and involvement of parents in the supervision of childcare facilities.

Policy should expand out-of-school-hours care services

At first sight it is somewhat surprising that it has taken so long for out-of-school-hours (OSH) care to emerge as a policy priority. In theory, costs of providing such care should be relatively low because existing infrastructure (schools) could be used for OSH-purposes (and use of schools would avoid the need to ferry children from one location to another), and, as child-to-staff ratios for this older age group are relatively high compared to childcare for pre-school children, operational costs can be low. However, in many countries there is a long-standing reluctance among education authorities to allow schools to be used for this purpose. In Denmark and Sweden (the countries with the most comprehensive system), educational authorities are happy with the use of schools for after school "leisure activities". Recent reforms in the Netherlands which require schools to help organise OSH-care services and Extended Schools in the United Kingdom are policy initiatives moving in the same direction. The development of out-of-school-hours services deserves a higher priority than it currently gets in many OECD countries.

1.4.5. Workplace practices

Family-friendly workplace measures are key to work/family reconciliation…

Family-friendly workplaces are essential for the reconciliation of work and family life. Even where countries have good public policies, if the workplace is not family-friendly, they will have little effect. Arguably, this is the case in Japan and Korea, for example, where public policies are similar to those in many other countries, but where workplace practices (long hours and seniority-based remuneration systems that punish any worker who takes time off to care for children) make it very hard to balance work and caring activities (Chapter 7). The most common types of family-friendly work practices are part-time work, flexible workplace, granting days to care for sick children, and to a lesser extent employer-provided parental leave support. Teleworking, school-term working and employer-provided childcare support are generally less widespread.

… but the business case for such measures alone will not make all workplaces family-friendly…

There is potentially a "business case" for family-friendly workplace support. Having a family-friendly workplace can motivate current staff, reduce staff turnover, help attract new staff, reduce workplace stress and generally enhance worker satisfaction and productivity. Companies that have introduced family-friendly measures often report significant reductions in staff turnover, absenteeism, and an increased likelihood that mothers return to the original employer upon expiry of maternity leave. However, hard-nosed statistical evidence that providing family-friendly measures will improve profitability of companies introducing such measures is scarce. There are some such studies, but there are as many which show that there is no such effect.

... externalities to the bargaining process can lead to government intervention...

Access to family-friendly workplace support provided by employers on a voluntary basis or after agreement with unions is unequal. There is no reason to override these outcomes, unless there are "externalities" to the bargaining process which hamper the pursuit of public policy objectives to achieve wider social and economic goals. For example, policy makers may be concerned about the decline in birth rates and demographic trends, but as these issues are not of immediate interest to employers and employees they did not determine workplace outcomes. Policy may wish to intervene to ensure that parents have sufficient time to spend at work and with their children, as, amongst other things, this helps to sustaining birth rates and strengthens future labour supply. Equity concerns about limited access among low-income workers to workplace supports may be another driver of government intervention.

... encouraging enterprises to provide workplace supports...

Governments remain reluctant to intervene in the workplace because of the fear of increasing labour costs and in the belief that this is an area best left to employers and employees to negotiate. In many countries therefore, public policy limits itself to encouraging enterprises to make more family-friendly supports available. The *Babies and Bosses* reviews found that publicly supported "consultancy" initiatives which provide tailored advice to companies are an innovative way of fostering family-friendly workplaces, especially when they included re-assessment to ensure long-term enterprise commitment. However, there is not much evidence that such initiatives have become widespread.

... or legislate to extend coverage of some family-friendly measures to all workers.

On the other hand, some countries have introduced legislation entitling employees to flexible workplace practices. For example, in the Netherlands employees of enterprises with ten workers or more can change their working hours for whatever reason, unless the courts uphold employer-objections, and in Sweden working parents are entitled to reduce working hours until their youngest child enters primary school. However, legislation is not always needed in flexible labour markets: many female employees in the Netherlands were working part-time before legislation was introduced, and many mothers in Australia and New Zealand find it possible to work shorter hours when children are young, increasing their working time when children turn five, without any recourse to legal entitlements.

Policy in the United Kingdom has granted parents with children under age six the right to request flexible working hours (which includes reduced working hours). This initiative can also involve costs for the employer, but, as both the employee has to motivate his/her request and employers have to justify why they would turn it down, it at least forces both key actors to think and communicate about the family-friendly nature of their workplace. The right to ask approach is a middle way which emphasises employer and employee involvement, is flexible enough to focus on measures that suit the workplace and the worker, and extends access to many low-income workers whose bargaining position is relatively weak. This approach of strengthening the position of employees with children in negotiations with their employers, without imposing a "one-size-fits-all" solution, may be worth introducing in other OECD countries as well.

Notes

1. The *Babies and Bosses* reviews did not focus on the reconciliation issues that parents with long-term sick and/or disabled children have to face, nor did the reviews address issues related to elderly care. The *Babies and Bosses* reviews did address child development issues, but future work will address issues related to child well-being and developmental outcomes in depth (OECD, 2008, forthcoming).

2. The most notable exceptions to the upward trend in public spending on family benefits over the 1980-2003 period are the Netherlands (reform of child allowances in the late 1980s) and Sweden (budget cuts in the aftermath of the economic crisis in the early 1990s).

3. In France, there remains a certain ambiguity about supporting working parents with children under three years of age, while in the Canadian province of Québec, which models its policy on Scandinavian countries, there remain gaps in its childcare policy (OECD, 2005a).

ISBN 978-92-64-03244-6
Babies and Bosses: Reconciling Work and Family Life
A Synthesis of Findings for OECD Countries
© OECD 2007

Chapter 2

The Demographic and Family Environment

This chapter compares demographic, family and social outcomes across OECD countries, and illustrates changing patterns in family formation, fertility behaviour and its relationship to employment trends and desired fertility outcomes.

2.1. How have family structures changed?

Changing family structures, ageing populations and shifting fertility patterns (see below) have led to a growing share of households without children, a decline in the average size of households and a decline in the proportion of couple families. Table 2.1 shows that in many OECD countries (not including Canada, Ireland, New Zealand, Poland, Portugal and the Slovak

Table 2.1. **Households with more than two children are uncommon**

	Households by number of children, 2005[1]				Sole-parent households as a proportion of all households with children
	No children	With one child	With two children	With three or more children	
Australia	66	..	..	..	22
Austria	70	15	11	4	12
Belgium	66	14	14	6	18
Canada	55	19	18	8	25
Czech Republic	64	17	16	3	13
Denmark	74	11	12	4	16
Finland	76	10	9	5	10
France	66	14	13	6	14
Germany	75	13	9	3	16
Greece	68	15	14	3	5
Hungary	64	17	14	5	11
Iceland	60	17	15	8	27
Ireland	45	17	16	14	22
Italy	68	17	13	3	6
Luxembourg	64	14	15	7	9
Netherlands	69	12	14	6	13
New Zealand	65	14	13	8	28
Norway	70	12	12	6	17
Poland	53	22	18	8	9
Portugal	58	24	14	3	7
Slovak Republic	54	19	19	8	6
Spain	61	20	16	3	6
United Kingdom	68	14	12	5	24
United States	68	13	12	7	33

1. Source: Australia, Family Characteristics, June 2003; Canada, Census, 2001; Iceland, NOCOSCO, 2004 ; Ireland, Census, 2002; New Zealand, Census, 2006; Norway, Population and Housing Census, 2001; and US Census Bureau, 2005. All data refer to children aged less than 18 living within the household and still dependent with the exception of New Zealand where children are classified as dependent if not in full-time employment. For all other European countries, data are taken from EU LFS, Spring 2006 (except for Denmark and Finland, 2004). Data refer to children aged less than 24 and still dependent (inactive with at least one parent in the household).

Republic) at least 60% of households do not include children. Moreover, while most children live in households with one or two children, the proportion of households with at least three children is below 10% in all countries for which information is available, except Ireland. At one point in time, most children are in families with two adults, but the incidence of sole-parent families has increased markedly, and in 2005 sole-parent families in Australia, Canada, Iceland, Ireland, New Zealand, the United Kingdom and the United States constituted over 20% of all households with children (Table 2.1).

2.2. Changing patterns of family formation

Family life and the nature of partnerships between adults have changed in most OECD countries. Fewer marriages are taking place than in the past; on average across the OECD marriage rates have fallen from 8.1 marriage per 100 000 persons in 1970 to 5.1 in 2004 (Chart 2.1). There is considerably variation across countries; marriage rates remain highest in Turkey, Denmark and the United States and lowest in Belgium, Greece and Italy. In contrast to other countries, since 1970, there has been little change in the marriage rate in Denmark and Sweden.

Over the same period, most OECD countries recorded significantly higher divorce rates, except Australia, Luxembourg and the United States (Stevenson and Wolfers, 2007). In 2004, on average across the OECD the crude divorce rate was 2.3 per 100 000 people, twice the level recorded in 1970 (Chart 2.1), and this upward trend has led to an increase in the number of sole-parent families and the number of children living in reconstituted families. In 2004, on average across the OECD, there were just over four divorces per ten marriages. In Belgium, there were three divorces for four new marriages; at the other extreme, in Mexico there was only one divorce per ten new marriages.

The decline in the marriage rate has been accompanied by a tendency to defer the age at which the first marriage occurs. On average, the mean age of women at first marriage has increased from 23.3 in 1980 to 27.7 years in 2004, and nowhere more rapidly than in Iceland where the mean age increased by more than seven years over the period. In Denmark, Iceland and Sweden, a woman who gets married for the first time is on average over 30 years of age (Table 2.2). In many Nordic and continental western European countries, Australia and New Zealand, cohabitation is increasingly regarded as an alternative to marriage rather than merely a trial leading up to formal marriage, and in Norway and Sweden there are now more adults in the age group 20-40 who are cohabiting than in a formal marriage (OECD, 2007b).

In fact, across the OECD the mean age of women at first marriage is now higher than the mean age of women at first childbirth (Table 2.2). Therefore, it is not surprising that the number of children being born out-of-wedlock has increased rapidly to on average about three in ten children across the OECD. At

Chart 2.1. **There are fewer marriages which are more likely to end up in divorce**

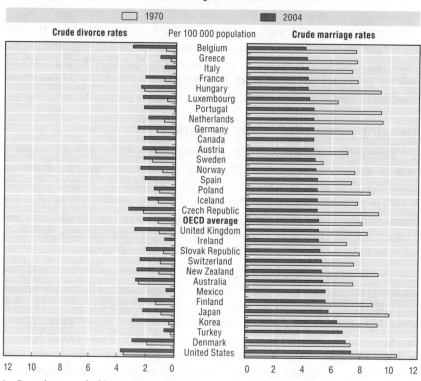

1. Countries are ranked in ascending order of crude marriage rates in 2004.
Source: OECD (2007b).

least four out of ten children are born outside marriage in Denmark, Finland, France, New Zealand and the United Kingdom, whereas the rate is over half in Norway and Sweden and concerns two out of three children in Iceland.

Family life has changed in most OECD countries over the past 30 years. Total Fertility Rates (TFRs) have fallen in all countries; marriage rates have fallen whereas divorce rates have gone up. There is an increasing share of births outside marriage, and an increase in the incidence of sole-parent families in the majority of OECD countries. Teenage motherhood has become relatively rare in most countries, but teenage birth rates remain relatively high in Mexico, Turkey and the United States (Table 2.2).

Table 2.2. **Selected family statistics, OECD countries**

	Total fertility rate		Mean age of women at first birth		Mean age of women at first marriage		Births out-of-wedlock		Teenage birth rate[1]
	1970	2005[2]	1970	2004	1980	2004	1980	2004	2004
Australia	2.89	1.81	23.2	..	..	..	12.4	32.2	14.9
Austria	2.29	1.41	..	27.0	23.2	27.9	17.8	35.9	12.7
Belgium	2.25	1.72	24.3		22.2	27.1	4.1	31.0	8.1
Canada	2.33	1.53	23.1	26.3	..	..	..	27.6	13.8
Czech Republic	1.90	1.28	22.5	26.3	21.5	26.0	5.6	30.6	11.5
Denmark	1.95	1.80	23.8	28.4	24.6	30.4	33.2	45.4	6.8
Finland	1.83	1.80	24.4	27.8	24.3	29.0	13.1	40.8	10.0
France	2.47	1.94	24.4	28.4	23.0	28.5	11.4	46.4	9.3
Germany	2.03	1.34	24.0	29.0	22.9	28.4	11.9	27.9	10.1
Greece	2.40	1.28	..	28.0	23.3	27.5	1.5	4.9	9.1
Hungary	1.98	1.32	22.8	26.3	21.2	26.2	7.1	34.0	21.2
Iceland	2.83	2.05	21.3	26.2	23.7	30.9	39.7	63.7	17.6
Ireland	3.87	1.88	..	28.5	24.6	28.2	5.0	32.3	14.0
Italy	2.43	1.34	25.0	..	23.8	28.0	4.3	14.9	7.0
Japan	2.13	1.26	25.6	28.9	25.2	27.8	0.8	2.0	5.7
Korea	..	1.08	28.2	28.9	23.2	27.5	..	1.3	3.5
Luxembourg	1.97	1.70	24.7	28.6	23.0	28.1	6.0	25.8	8.9
Mexico	6.82	2.20	..	..	..	..	..	..	67.3
Netherlands	2.57	1.73	24.8	28.9	23.2	28.7	4.1	32.5	4.8
New Zealand	3.28	2.00	23.4	28.0	..	28.8	21.5	44.8	24.4
Norway	2.50	1.84	..	27.6	23.5	29.1	14.5	51.4	9.6
Poland	2.26	1.24	22.8	25.6	22.7	24.9	4.8	17.1	14.7
Portugal	3.01	1.40	..	27.1	23.2	26.3	9.2	29.1	18.9
Slovak Republic	2.41	1.25	22.6	25.3	21.9	25.0	5.7	24.8	20.5
Spain	2.88	1.34	..	29.2	23.4	28.6	3.9	23.4	9.3
Sweden	1.92	1.77	25.9	28.6	26.0	30.7	39.7	55.4	6.9
Switzerland	2.10	1.42	25.3	29.3	25.0	28.6	4.7	13.3	4.6
Turkey	5.68	2.19	..	..	20.7	22.6	2.9	..	41.4
United Kingdom	2.43	1.80	..	29.5	23.0	28.1	11.5	42.3	25.8
United States	2.48	2.05	24.1	25.1	23.3	25.1	18.4	35.7	50.3
OECD	**2.70**	**1.63**	**24.2**	**27.5**	**23.3**	**27.7**	**11.2**	**30.9**	**15.8**

1. Adolescent fertility rate; births per 1 000 women aged 15-19.
2. Year of reference for total fertility rates – Canada: 2004
Source: D'Addio and Mira d'Ercole (2005); and OECD (2007b).

2.3. Changing fertility behaviour

Low fertility rates, combined with increased life expectancy, imply rapid ageing of the population and declines in its size in the future. The most immediate consequence of population ageing is the loss of reproductive potential, measured in terms of women at childbearing ages. Population ageing has, however, other financial and economic consequences. Growing public spending on pensions and health care as a percentage of GDP, due to population ageing, may put pressures on public budgets, compromising financial stability and crowding out other expenditure programmes (*e.g.* those devoted to families with children). An older labour force may be less willing or capable to adapt to changes, in terms of both geographical and occupational mobility. In turn, changes in the size and structure of the population may affect economic growth: as younger cohorts shrink, the number of people holding jobs falls, the pool of domestic savings in the economy gets smaller, with negative consequences on productive investments (Oliveira Martins *et al.*, 2005). The growing number of older people may also imply risks of greater tensions between generations. Finally, with only two, one or perhaps no children at all, questions about the availability of family carers for adults in their old age are set to become more important over time (Ogawa *et al.*, 2004).

Patterns of family formation are changing such that fertility trends contribute to concerns about future labour supply and the financial sustainability of social protection systems. At an individual level, there is concern about to what extent parents are able to have as many children as they desire.

2.3.1. Birth rates have fallen in most countries

Total fertility rates declined dramatically over the past few decades, falling from an average of 2.7 children per women of childbearing age in 1970 to 1.6 in 2004 (Chart 2.2 and Table 2.2 for data on individual countries). On average across the OECD, the total fertility rate has been below its "replacement" level,[1] since the early 1980s. Table 2.2 showed that in 2004 only Turkey and Mexico had fertility rates well above replacement level, with birth rates above 1.9 children per woman being close this replacement in Iceland, Ireland, France, New Zealand and the United States. The timing and pace of decline, however, varies widely from country to country. In Nordic countries, for example, the decline started early, but came to a halt in the early 1990s, stabilising at a level of around 1.8. Southern European countries, conversely, have shown a decline in fertility rates beginning in the mid-1970s, but have now reached an extremely low level of 1.3 children per women, the same level as recorded in Japan and Korea, although this has fallen even further in more recent years.

The postponement of marriage and childbearing are among the key reasons for the fall of fertility rates across OECD countries. On average across the OECD, in most countries the mean age of childbirth has increased to 27.5 years, and at almost 27 years the mean age of first marriage is not far behind (Table 2.2). In fact, in Austria, Finland, Denmark, Iceland, New Zealand and Sweden (countries where cohabitation is frequently seen as an alternative to marriage), the mean age of first marriage is at least one year above the mean age of mothers at first childbirth.

Chart 2.2. **Fertility patterns differ across the OECD**

Total fertility rates, 1970 onwards

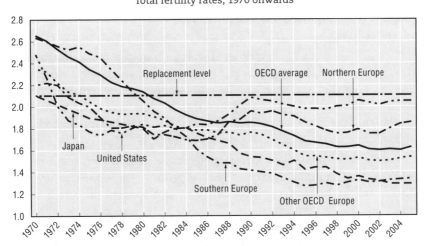

Table 2.2 showed that in many countries the decline in the marriage rate has contributed to a significant proportion of children being born out of wedlock. By contrast, in Greece, Italy, Japan, Korea and Poland, the decline in fertility is closely related to the postponement of marriage and the decline in marriage rates. In Japan, the proportion of 20-34-year-olds who are not married and live at home, the so-called "parasite singles", has grown to 45%, up from 30% in 1980 (Nishi and Kan, 2006). Regardless of marital status, the increase in the age of first childbirth has led to a concentration of childbearing in ever narrower age-intervals (Kohler and Ortega, 2002) and a declining incidence of large families in many OECD countries.

Although there are significant cross-country differences, there are some common trends in the process of childbearing postponement to later ages (D'Addio and Mira d'Ercole, 2005):

- In the period between 1970 and 1980, fertility rates declined for both younger and older women. In most countries, the decline of age-specific fertility rates of younger women is larger than that of older women. In this period, most countries were at the onset of large-scale childbearing postponement.

- Between 1980 and 1990, the fertility rates of younger and older women moved in different directions in most countries: the fertility rates of women aged 30-49 increased, while those of women aged 15-29 continued to fall. This suggests the onset of childbearing recuperation in most countries.

- Between 1990 and 2000, the fertility rates of younger and older women kept moving in opposite directions for most countries. This suggests that recuperation continued, but at a lower pace.

The childbearing patterns observed for these birth cohorts confirm that, in all countries, recent generations of women have fewer children at early stages of their reproductive cycle and more children at later ages. In general, however, the higher number of children that women have when older does not fully compensate for the fewer children that women have when young. This suggests that the low level of fertility rates is not a temporary phenomenon, but one that could well persists in the longer term.[2]

At the individual level, increasingly many women (and men) remain childless, and in many countries this appears to be related to levels of educational attainment, earnings capacity, and opportunities to combine work and family commitments (Sleebos, 2003; and d'Addio and Mira d'Ercole, 2005). In Germany, combining work and family life is perceived as difficult for women: about 36% of all women aged 41-44 remain childless, which is just below the proportion of childless women with a tertiary degree (Statistisches Bundesamt, 2005). In Switzerland, for example, on average 15 to 20% of women remain childless around age 40, while this was around 40% for women with tertiary education (OECD, 2003a). By contrast, in Sweden, with its longstanding policy emphasis on giving both parents the opportunity to maintain employment relationships, women with relatively high education do not appear to have significantly less children than on average (Batljan, 2001).

2.3.2. Children and paid maternal employment: are they more compatible than in the past?

The male-breadwinner model involves a clear allocation of responsibilities, with men providing family income, and women providing care at home. Female employment was incompatible with caring for children, but, as long as both parents generally accepted this gender division of responsibilities, fertility rates remained stable and high. However, female aspirations have changed as, for example, reflected in changing patterns in participation in education and labour market behaviour while fertility rates have declined.

The relation between female employment and fertility rates is complex. At the level of individuals, several studies have postulated theoretically and documented empirically the existence of an inverse relationship between fertility rates and labour market participation of women.[3] However, the relation between these two variables differs when observed across countries. Several authors have stressed that, in recent years, the sign of the cross-country correlation between female employment rates (or labour force participation rates) and total fertility rates may have changed (Ahn and Mira, 2002; and del Boca, 2003). Others suggest that while the relationship is still negative, the degree of incompatibility between paid work and caring for children has diminished (Engelhardt *et al.*, 2001; and Kögel, 2001). This, in turn, has led many more women to confront the difficulty of combining professional and family life.

To the extent that getting a foothold in the labour market is important before women consider having a child, unemployment is also likely to play a role. The effects of unemployment on the timing of births and number of births are, however, ambiguous. Unemployment may increase fertility rates, as each woman may expect a lower probability of finding jobs and lower wages, both of which reduce the opportunity costs of childbearing (Adsera, 2004; and Gauthier and Hatzius, 1997). On the other hand, when unemployment is high, youth may decide to remain in their parent's home and/or to continue their education, both of which contribute to postponing partnership formation and childbearing.[4]

Chart 2.3 shows that across OECD countries the relationship between female employment and fertility has changed significantly over the last 35 years. Apart from the general increase in female employment (note the different scales on the horizontal axes of the panels), in 1980 there was a clear negative correlation between female employment and fertility rates, while in 2005, OECD countries with higher rates of female employment also had

Chart 2.3. **Countries with high female employment rates now also have the highest fertility rates**

Total fertility rate and female employment rate, 1980 and 2005

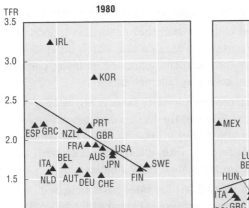
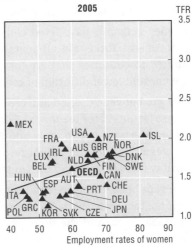

Source: OECD (2007b).

relatively high fertility rates (OECD, 2005b). Clearly, the degree of incompatibility between paid work and having children has diminished, but there are substantial cross-country differences: combining childrearing and being in employment is most incompatible in the Mediterranean countries, Japan and Korea.

With birth rates in excess of 1.75 per woman and with two-thirds of women in employment, it seems that Nordic countries and Australia, the Netherlands, New Zealand, the United Kingdom and the United States have the best outcomes. Sometimes the compatibility of paid work and childrearing is due to the existence of comprehensive public support systems (as in Nordic countries), or largely related to parents making use of flexible workplace practices. In general, since female labour market aspirations have changed, all policies which enhance female labour force participation also help countries to have fertility rates that are close to those needed to assure the future stability of their populations.

2.3.3. A widening gap between desired and observed fertility rates

Changes in work and living environments and life styles have contributed to men and women postponing parenthood, and having fewer children than previous generations. However, to what extent does this reflect their preferences rather than constraints imposed by, for example, labour market insecurity, education and housing costs, and difficulties in reconciling work and family life. Indications about the potential role of these constraints on women's childbearing decisions can be derived from answers to questions about the "desired" or "ideal" numbers of children provided from opinion surveys. While interpreting answers to these questions is not straightforward, the evidence summarised in Chart 2.4 highlights a number of consistent patterns:[5]

- Women generally have fewer children than they desire. Exceptions to this pattern – in Turkey (in all years) and Mexico and Korea (in 1980s) – are limited to countries that are (or were) characterised by lower per capita income and lower diffusion of contraceptive methods.

- The gap between desired and observed fertility rates is higher in countries where fertility rates are lowest. Some of the OECD countries where fertility rates are lowest (Japan, Italy and Spain) in 2000 recorded the largest gaps between desired and actual fertility rate, while countries with higher fertility rates (France and the United States) show smaller gaps.

- The gaps between desired and actual fertility rates have increased over the past ten to twenty years. On average, across the countries for which data are available in each of the three years shown, the gap between desired and actual fertility rates grew from 1980 to 1990 and from 1990 to 2000.

Chart 2.4. **Desired fertility has fallen, but remains above observed levels in most countries**

Desired and observed fertility rates, 1981, 1990 and 2000

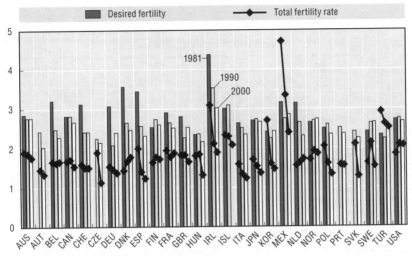

Note: The observed fertility rate is measured by the total fertility rate of each country in that year. The three bars shown for each country refer to data for 1981, 1990 and 2000, with the exceptions of Austria, and the Czech Republic where data refer to 1990 and 2000, and of Switzerland, Poland and Turkey, where data refer to 1990, 1995 and 2000.

Source: D'Addio and Mira d'Ercole (2005).

Information about changes in desired and observed fertility rates among different cohorts of women can be obtained by looking at women of the same age (29 to 39, and 39 to 49) at ten-year intervals. Chart 2.5 shows that among younger women the gap between desired and observed fertility rates increased strongly over time, as postponement of childbearing led to sharp falls in observed fertility rates. Among older women the gap between desired and observed fertility rates also widened, but by a smaller amount:[6] most women in this group, who in several OECD countries in the 1980s had more children than they desired, declared in 2000 that they desired more children than they actually had. For women who are close to the end of their reproductive cycle, postponement of childbearing is a less plausible explanation of this widening gap: despite the effects of medical advances in extending childbearing until higher ages, women in this age group are unlikely to realise fully their childbearing intentions.

Chart 2.5. **In many OECD countries women in their 40s have fewer children than they would like**

Desired and observed fertility rates among women of different ages in selected OECD countries

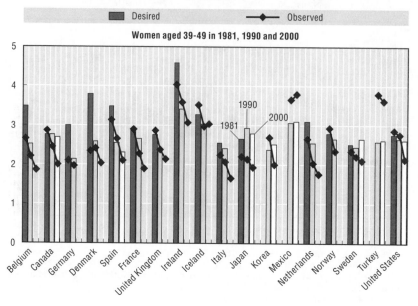

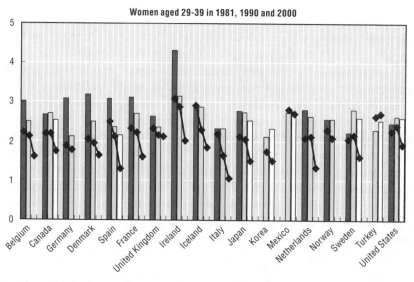

Note: Observed fertility rates are measured by the number of children that women of different ages declared in the survey. Data for Germany refer to western *Länder* only.

Source: D'Addio and Mira d'Ercole (2005).

BABIES AND BOSSES: RECONCILING WORK AND FAMILY LIFE – ISBN 978-92-64-03244-6 – © OECD 2007

Notes

1. In fertility statistics the "fertility replacement" level is defined as the cohort fertility rate of 2.1 children per woman which would ensure the replacement of the previous generation, and therefore population stability, under assumptions of no immigration and of no change in mortality rates.

2. Nordic countries took the lead in adapting family policies to facilitate parental labour force attachment; policy models now provide a continuum of support with parental leave, child and out-of-school hours care support as well as facilitative workplace practices. Rather than fertility rates declining to 1.2 to 1.5 children per women, the Nordic policy model is credited with contributing to birth rates oscillating around 1.8 children per mother, and that when family policies in other countries mature to levels comparable to what is sustained in Nordic countries, birth rates could well rebound from very low levels. For example, Roy and Bernier (2007) suggest that family policy in the Canadian province of Québec now is comparable to levels of support found in Nordic countries around 1985-1990, and that preliminary data on total fertility rates in Québec for 2005-06 show an increase that is in line with the recent development of a comprehensive family support policy in this jurisdiction.

3. The seminal papers, at the theoretical level, are those by Becker and Lewis (1973) and Willis (1973). A negative relation between paid employment and childbearing has been empirically documented by Butz and Ward (1979) for the United States and by Mincer (1985) on a cross-country basis.

4. In most OECD countries fertility rates are higher in periods of low unemployment and lower when unemployment is high. There are some exceptions: in Korea both fertility and unemployment rates have declined over the past twenty years; in Canada, Australia and New Zealand, as well as several Nordic countries, swings in unemployment rates are not associated with significant changes in fertility rates. Conversely, in southern European countries, higher unemployment strongly reduces fertility, as the low female participation in the labour market implies that the substitution effect arising from a decrease in the opportunity cost of the woman's time is small compared to the income effect from the loss of male income (Ahn and Mira, 2002). The negative association between unemployment and fertility rates seems to hold also when considering the female unemployment rate instead of the overall unemployment rate (Adsera, 2004).

5. Survey evidence about *desired* fertility, as available for most OECD countries, is based on data from the various waves of the *World Values Survey*, 1981, 1990, 1995-97 and 2000 (World Values Survey Association, 2004), as well as from the EFILWC (2004). Data on "desired fertility" need to be interpreted with care, given differences in the wording of the questions in the two surveys. The question in the *World Values Survey* is: "What do you think is the ideal size of the family – how many children, if any?"; the question in EFILWC (2004) Eurobarometer is: "For you personally, what would be the ideal number of children you would like to have or would have liked to have had?"

6. Changes in the demographic composition of women also affect changes in the gap between desired and observed fertility rates; Chart 2.5 suggests that a growing share of older women *ceteris paribus* is likely to lead to smaller aggregate differences between desired and observed fertility levels.

ISBN 978-92-64-03244-6
Babies and Bosses: Reconciling Work and Family Life
A Synthesis of Findings for OECD Countries
© OECD 2007

Chapter 3

Parents in Employment – Achievements and Challenges

This chapter discusses parental employment patterns in OECD countries. The presence of children in households has little effect on how much men work, but it can profoundly affect maternal labour force behaviour. In general, mothers have strengthened their labour market attachment in recent decades, but there are considerable differences in employment patterns across countries. Apart from the discussion of employment trends and how maternal employment outcomes vary with the age and number of children, this chapter also considers gender wage gaps and gender differences in the contribution to household earnings, as well as joblessness among families and the related issue of family poverty.

In many OECD countries, female and maternal employment patterns have changed radically since the late 1960s, with a rapid increase in female employment. However, notwithstanding the enormous improvement in the labour market position of women, significant challenges remain. Female employment remains concentrated in certain occupations and sectors, and in terms of hours in work, employment contracts of fixed duration, earnings and hours in unpaid work, gender differences remain substantial. To a considerable extent these gender differences are related to the presence of children in families: while children affect female employment patterns noticeably, they seem to have little impact on male labour force behaviour.

This chapter illustrates the different labour market outcomes for men and women, and how parental work and family reconciliation solutions differ among fathers and mothers. It starts with an overview of trends, followed by a more in-depth look at maternal employment outcomes. In view of stubbornly persistent gender pay gaps, the chapter then considers remaining challenges in improving the labour market position of mothers and fathers, and concomitantly reducing the risk that children grow up in poverty, which is particularly high in households where no one works.

3.1. Key labour market achievements

3.1.1. Trends in female labour force participation

Changing female aspirations have led to increased female labour market participation in many OECD countries – and the biggest change in behaviour was among married mothers.[1] The timing of the increase varied across countries, for example, in Australia, the Nordic countries, New Zealand and the United States, the increase started in the early 1960s (OECD, 1999a), while in the past two decades the largest increases have been observed in Ireland, the Netherlands and Spain (Chart 3.1).

Increasing female employment is associated with a number of factors, including the shift from agriculture and manufacturing to services. By 2005, two-thirds of all OECD employment was in the service sector, and with four out of five women in service sector employment, the importance of this sector's growth in fostering female labour participation can hardly be exaggerated.

Supply-side factors have, however, also played a key role in developing female employment, among them women's rising educational levels, higher

Chart 3.1. **Women participate increasingly in paid work**
Female employment population ratios (age 15-64), 1980-2005

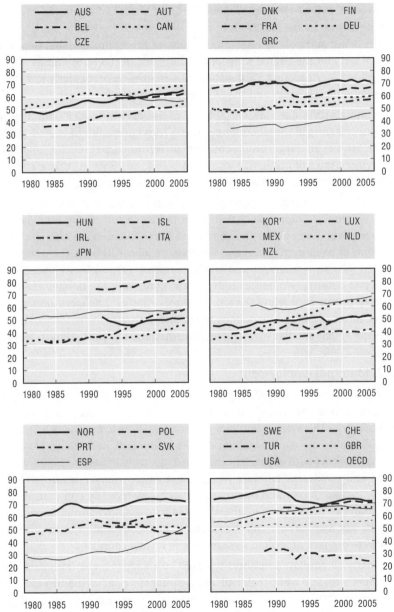

1. For Korea, data refer to ages 15-59 prior to 1989.
Source: OECD database on Labour Force Statistics.

real female wages, changing preferences for paid work as well as other factors such as a greater reliance on two incomes to sustain family spending patterns.

Around 25% of all employed women and a third of employed mothers work part-time in the OECD area, with the rates of part-time work among women being particularly high (around 40% or more) in Australia, Germany, Switzerland and the United Kingdom and highest in the Netherlands at over 60% (Table 3.1). At around 5% the share of part-time is particularly low in the Czech Republic, Hungary and the Slovak Republic.

Among prime-age women (aged 25 to 54 years old), 69.8% on average were participating in the labour force and 65.7% were employed in 2006 (OECD, 2007c). However, large cross-country differences persist. In 2006, the employment rates of prime-age women ranged from 26.6% in Turkey, and 50% in Mexico to above 80% in Denmark, Iceland, Norway and Sweden (Table 3.1).

Compared to men, the position of women in the labour market remains weak. Women are more likely than men to have a temporary employment contract, particularly in Finland, Japan and Korea. Women are also less likely then men to be in managerial and supervisory jobs. Although the number of reported jobs with management and supervisory responsibility varies from country to country, women in Italy, Japan, Korea and Spain have the most difficulty getting through to the top. The proportion of managers among men is three times as high as for women in Finland, Italy and Switzerland, and the gap is not much smaller in Germany, Luxembourg, the Netherlands, Norway and Spain (Table 3.1).

3.1.2. Maternal employment

On average across OECD countries in 2005, more than six out of ten mothers with dependent children were in paid employment, while for the EU19 countries the average was two percentage points lower (Table 3.2). There is considerable cross-national variety. At below 50% in 2005, employment rates for mothers with dependent children (0-16) were lowest in Hungary, Italy, Poland and the Slovak Republic, while these employment rates in Germany, Greece, Ireland, Japan and Spain were also below 55%. By contrast, in 2005 more than two out of three mothers were in paid employment in Canada, the Netherlands, Switzerland and the United States while maternal employment rates were highest, at around 75% or more in Nordic countries.

Nearly all employed mothers typically take a short break from paid work just before birth and while their children are infants, i.e., a few months old. After this period, differences in national parental leave and childcare support arrangements (Chapters 5 and 6) contribute to different labour force behaviour of mothers. Whereas in some countries, e.g., Portugal or the Netherlands, mothers frequently return to the workplace after a few months of paid maternity leave, in many other countries combined paid maternity and

Table 3.1. **Selected labour market statistics by gender, OECD countries, 2006**

	Employment rate (age 25-54)		Share of part-time employment in total employment		Share of service sector in civilian employment, 2005		Management and supervisory jobs, 2000			Share of temporary employment in dependent employment	
	Men and women	Women	Men and women	Women	Men and women	Women	Managers among male workers	Managers among female workers	Proportion of managers who are female	Men and women	Women
Australia	79.2	71.4	27.1	40.7	75	87.9	..	..	..	5.2	5.9
Austria	83.5	77.0	17.3	31.4	66.9	81.5	6.5	3.7	31.1	9.1	8.8
Belgium	78.2	70.8	19.3	34.7	73.3	87.2	7.3	3.9	29.4	8.9	10.8
Canada	81.6	77.1	18.1	26.2	75.3	87.9	9.3	6.1	37.8	13.0	13.7
Czech Republic	82.5	81.3	3.3	5.6	56.4	70.6	5.4	2.7	30.0	8.7	10.1
Denmark	85.5	81.7	18.1	25.6	72.6	85.8	4.7	2.2	23.4	9.6	11.2
Finland	82.5	79.7	11.4	14.9	69.1	84.5	7.3	2.2	29.8	16.4	20.0
France	80.0	73.4	13.3	22.9	..	..	5.9	3.3	33.6	12.9	13.4
Germany	78.8	72.7	21.9	39.2	67.6	82.2	4.7	1.7	23.4	14.2	14.0
Greece	75.3	60.6	7.5	12.9	65.2	76.1	2.9	1.4	24.4	12.1	14.7
Hungary	74.2	67.6	2.7	4.2	62.2	75.9	6.4	4.3	38.3	6.7	6.0
Iceland	89.1	83.8	16.0	26.0	71.7	86.3	9.2	4.2	31.1	9.6	9.7
Ireland	78.4	68.1	19.9	34.9	65.5	85.8	5.5	4.3	38.8	4.2	4.9
Italy	73.3	59.3	14.9	29.4	64.6	79.3	3.7	0.8	12.8	13.0	15.3
Japan	79.6	66.6	24.5	40.9	66.4	76.8	..	..	9.6	14.0	22.3
Korea	73.9	60.0	8.8	12.3	65.2	74.4	..	..	7.8	29.4	32.5
Luxembourg	80.7	68.4	12.7	27.2	..	..	5.5	2.1	20.4	5.3	5.8
Mexico	69.9	50.0	15.1	27.6	57.2	75	..	..	..	20.3	11.9
Netherlands	82.0	75.1	35.5	59.7	..	..	10.8	4.2	23.0	16.2	17.6
New Zealand	82.1	74.4	21.3	34.5	70.7	84.3	..	..	38.0	..	..
Norway	84.4	81.0	21.1	32.9	75.7	90.3	14.3	5.5	26.6	10.1	12.6
Poland	71.8	65.3	10.8	16.3	53.4	66.2	5.1	3.6	38.2	27.3	26.0
Portugal	81.3	75.3	9.3	13.2	57.3	68.5	1.9	0.9	28.3	20.2	21.5
Slovak Republic	77.2	70.2	2.5	4.1	56.3	72	4.7	3.2	38.2	5.1	5.2
Spain	75.8	63.7	11.1	21.4	64.8	84	2.9	1.0	17.2	34.4	37.3
Sweden	84.7	81.5	13.4	19.0	75.7	89.6	5.6	2.5	31.6	16.8	18.7
Switzerland	85.2	77.6	25.5	45.7	72.5	85.4	8.1	2.6	21.2	13.6	14.1
Turkey	54.2	26.6	7.9	17.8	45.8	33.3	..	..	..	12.7	12.0
United Kingdom	81.2	74.9	23.4	38.8	76.2	89.6	18.4	10.2	33.4	5.6	6.3
United States	79.8	72.5	12.6	17.8	78.6	90.0	7.6	3.9	30.0	4.2	4.2
EU19	**78.0**	**69.8**	**16.6**	**29.0**	..	..	..	..	..	..	..
OECD	**76.5**	**65.7**	**16.1**	**26.4**	**66.3**	**79.2**	..	..	..	**13.1**	**14.0**

Data on employment rates in Luxembourg concern 2005; data on part-time employment concern 2004 for Mexico; part-time employment in Japan refers to less than 35 hours per week: data for Australia, Japan and Korea concern actual hours worked per week and not usual hours as for the other countries. Data for the United States concern dependent rather than total employment.

Data on temporary employment concerns 2002 for Iceland, 2004 for Korea and Mexico, and 2005 for Austria, Greece, Japan, Luxembourg and the United States.

Source: OECD database on Labour Force Statistics – employment rates, and part-time employment; OECD, Annual Labour Force Statistics database – service sector employment, except for the United States with data taken from Bureau of Labor Statistics, Current Population Survey Statistics, Household Data, Annual Averages, Table 17, Employment by Industry, Sex, Race and Occupation; ILO, Laborsta (women and management); and the OECD database on Temporary Employment, except for Korea where data on the incidence of non-regular employment was taken from Grubb *et al.* (2007).

Table 3.2. **Most mothers are in paid work, especially when children go to school, 2005**

Maternal employment rates, women aged 15-64

	By age of youngest child				By number of children under 15		
	0-16	<2	3-5	6-16	One child	Two children	Three children
Australia	63.1	48.3		70.5	63.3	58.1	
Austria	64.7	60.5	62.4	67.5	67.7	60.1	46.5
Belgium	59.9	63.8	63.3	56.9	58.3	58.5	39.4
Canada	70.5	58.7	68.1	71.1	70.1	73.2	66.3
Czech Republic	52.8	19.9	50.9	67.6	57.4	52.5	34.4
Denmark	76.5	71.4	77.8	77.5	. .	. .	. .
Finland	76.0	52.1	80.7	84.2	71.2	70.9	60.1
France	59.9	53.7	63.8	61.7	62.2	57.6	38.1
Germany	54.9	36.1	54.8	62.7	58.4	51.8	36.0
Greece	50.9	49.5	53.6	50.4	48.4	44.4	37.4
Hungary	45.7	13.9	49.9	58.3	53.7	48.3	24.6
Iceland	84.8	83.6		86.5	88.5	82.3	
Ireland	57.5	55.0		59.9	55.4	52.5	42.3
Italy	48.1	47.3	50.6	47.5	48.3	41.0	27.4
Japan	52.4	28.5	47.8	68.1	. .	. .	. .
Luxembourg	55.4	58.3	58.7	52.7	56.0	49.8	33.8
Netherlands	69.2	69.4	68.3	69.4	70.1	70.6	59.9
New Zealand	64.6	45.1	60.6	75.3	64.1	64.5	56.7
Poland	46.4	. .	. .	. .	42.7	35.6	28.5
Portugal	67.8	69.1	71.8	65.4	63.5	59.2	46.1
Slovak Republic	48.4	23.1	46.6	60.4	56.4	49.4	31.5
Spain	52.0	52.6	54.2	50.9	51.1	44.7	38.5
Sweden	82.5	71.9	81.3	76.1	80.6	84.7	75.6
Switzerland	69.7	58.3	61.7	77.0	69.5	65.4	58.0
United Kingdom	61.7	52.6	58.3	67.7	67.1	62.4	42.3
United States	66.7	54.2	62.8	73.2	. .	. .	. .
EU19	**59.5**	**51.1**	**58.2**	**63.2**	**59.4**	**55.2**	**41.2**
OECD average	**61.5**	**51.9**	**61.3**	**66.3**	**60.6**	**57.0**	**44.0**

Source: Australia, Australian Bureau of Statistics (2005); 6224.0.55.001 FA2 Labour Force Status and Other Characteristics of Families; Statistics Canada (2001 data), Statistics Denmark (1999 data), Statistics Finland (2002 data), Statistics Iceland (2002 data for women age 25-54), Japanese authorities (2001 data), Swiss LFS (2006 second quarter data), UK Office of National Statistics (2005 data), and the US Current Population Survey (2005 data); all other EU countries, European labour Force Survey (2005 data), except for Italy which concerns 2003.

parental leave schemes cover an employment-protected period of absence from work for about one year (Chapter 5).

Table 3.2 shows that in the Czech Republic, Hungary, Japan and the Slovak Republic women often withdraw from the labour force upon childbirth (for Korea, see OECD, 2007d), it is not uncommon that women resign from their job upon marriage). In some countries, mothers often withdraw from work during the first three years of their children's lives – via paid leave schemes or career breaks or both – and then return to paid work. This practice is common in for example, Austria and Finland, but whereas women with home care payments in Finland are frequently not counted as employed in the national statistics, their counterparts in Austria are. Institutional differences regarding parental leave arrangements (Chapter 5) and recording practices in labour force surveys complicate comparisons of employment rates of mothers with very young children (Box 3.1).

Table 3.2 shows that in many countries maternal employment rates rebound when children are three to six years of age, and maternal employment rates often increase further when children enter primary school around age six. Table 3.2 masks considerable cross-national differences in the dynamics of the nature of employment relationships. For example, in Australia and New Zealand (OECD, 2002a and 2004a), mothers often reduce hours of work per week to care for young children and increase hours when children go to primary school at age five, in contrast to the Netherlands and Switzerland where part-time employment is a more permanent feature for mothers with children throughout childhood (OECD, 2002a, 2004a). The employment position of "mother returners" in Japan and Korea is relatively weak as they frequently cannot go back to regular employment but have to make do with non-standard employment conditions of a relatively unfavourable nature (OECD, 2003a and 2007d).

Employment rates tend to be lower for mothers with a greater number of dependent children. In 2005, on average almost 60% of mothers with one child were in paid employment, while this was about 55% of mothers with two children, while in Greece, Hungary, Italy, Luxembourg, Poland, the Slovak Republic and Spain, less than half of mothers with two or more children were in paid employment in 2005. Maternal employment rates tail off even further in the presence of a third child, to below 30% in Hungary, Italy and Poland (Table 3.2).

Looking across the OECD, the increase in female and maternal employment has led to an increase in the share of couple families where both adults are in paid employment. By the early 2000s, in most countries the male-breadwinner household had been replaced by the dual-earner couple: 60% of couples are now dual-earner families, and this proportion exceeds 80% in Nordic countries (Chart 3.2).

However, while "dual earnership" has become the norm among couple families, in Australia, the Netherlands, Switzerland and the United Kingdom fathers in most couple families tend to work full-time, while many mothers work part-time. In Denmark, Canada, Finland, Portugal and Sweden, both parents work on a full-time basis in most couple families (OECD, 2002a, 2003a, 2004a and 2005a).

Box 3.1. **Mothers in employment are not always at work**

Cross-country comparisons of data on mothers in employment have to be made with care, as differences in parental leave arrangements and the way these are treated in labour force statistics vary. In principle, all women on maternity leave are counted as employed. EU guidelines stipulate counting parents as employed when they are on parental leave for less than three months or with continual receipt of a significant portion of previous earnings (at least 50%). However, national treatment of parental leave varies widely. For example, many parents on parental leave in Austria (up to two years) are counted as employed, while leave is technically unpaid (there is an income support benefit for all parents with a child not yet 30 months old, Chapter 5). By contrast, many of the parents in Finland on home-care leave (which is often taken when the child is one to three years of age) are often not included in the employment statistics; instead they are classified as inactive.

The effect is shown in the chart below. Considering employment rates for mothers with a child not yet three years of age, these are highest in Austria and Sweden at about 72%. However, when we look at mothers with young children at work (and not on leave) employment rates are high in Australia, Ireland and Sweden

The majority of mothers with very young children are not at work

Employment rate and the proportion of mothers at work and on leave by age of youngest child, 1999-2003[1]

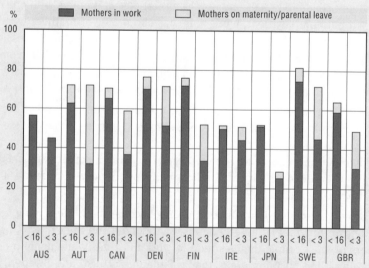

1. Years of reference: Australia (2000); Austria, Canada and Japan (2001); Denmark (1999); Finland and Ireland (2002); and Sweden and the United Kingdom (2003).

BABIES AND BOSSES: RECONCILING WORK AND FAMILY LIFE – ISBN 978-92-64-03244-6 – © OECD 2007

Box 3.1. **Mothers in employment are not always at work** (*cont.*)

at around 45%, and highest in Denmark at over 50%, where mothers generally work on a full-time basis (around 38-39 hours per week). In contrast to what employment data seem to suggest, in terms of mothers at work Austria and the United Kingdom appear to be rather similar, at just over 30%, with the majority of mothers working part-time. By comparison, in Japan, there are not many mothers with young children on maternity leave; many Japanese women still withdraw from the labour force upon childbirth.

Chart 3.2. **Most couples are dual-earner families**

Distribution of paid employment among couple families, 2000-02

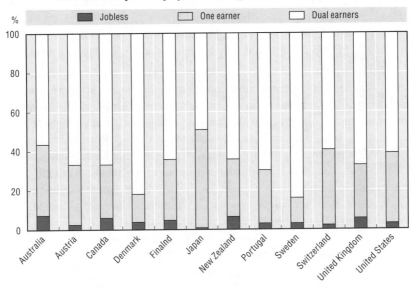

Source: OECD (2002a, 2003a, 2004a and 2005a); Denmark (1999), United Kingdom (2003). For the US: Bureau of Labor Statistics, Current Population Survey (2005 data).

3.2. Remaining challenges

In many respects, the story of changing female labour market participation is one of success. More parents are working than before, and women and mothers who were denied the chance to pursue achievement through labour market careers, with the financial independence that work can bring, face vastly improved life chances than previously.

Notwithstanding the high proportion of women and mothers in employment, they still face considerable labour market challenges. In general, labour market outcomes for women are not as good as those of men; maternal employment conditions lag behind those of their husbands/partners, in terms of working hours, pay and career opportunities.

There also remains a significant group of households without earnings, and many of these households are sole-parent families. Sole mothers have worse outcomes than sole fathers, and most single parents are women; labour market losses associated with sole parenting are experienced almost exclusively by women, and this population group faces particular challenges in trying to cope with work and family commitments.

3.2.1. Gender differences in labour market outcomes

Despite the undoubted improvements in the labour market situation of women in recent decades, in all OECD countries there remain significant differences in employment outcomes for men and women. Many of these differences can be related to the period of family formation. Chart 3.3 shows that employment rates for men and women tend to be similar between the ages of 20 and 24 years, but that they diverge in the period of family formation.

The sharp increase in female employment since 1980 (Chart 3.1) and the slight decline of male employment rates over the same period has led to a narrowing of the gender gap in employment. Female employment has grown among women of all ages, and also because many women in younger cohorts, for example, in Ireland, increasingly seek to combine paid work with raising children. Employment gains for women in Greece, Italy and Spain, however, have not been sizeable enough to generate an appreciable narrowing of the gender gap in employment. Consequently, in 2004-05, gender differences in employment rates for prime-age workers remained largest in Greece, Italy, Japan, Korea, Luxembourg, Mexico, Spain and Turkey.[2] At very high employment rates, gender employment gaps are smallest in the Nordic countries. The overall gender employment gap is narrower in Canada and the United States than in many European OECD countries.[3]

OECD (2002b) showed that maternal employment gaps differ in the way they arise. For example, in Greece, Italy, Luxembourg and Spain employment rates for women without children are already about 30 percentage points lower than for men (the "pure gender gap"), and make up about three-quarters of the difference in employment rates between men and mothers with one child (the "maternal employment gap"). By contrast, in Canada, the Czech Republic, France and Germany, the "pure gender gap" is less than half the "maternal employment gap".

In the absence of longitudinal data that follow a cohort of workers over the life-cycle, the chart presents cross-sectional data for on employment rates by age and gender for 2005.

Chart 3.3. **Age-employment profiles, men and women**
Employment rates by age, 2005

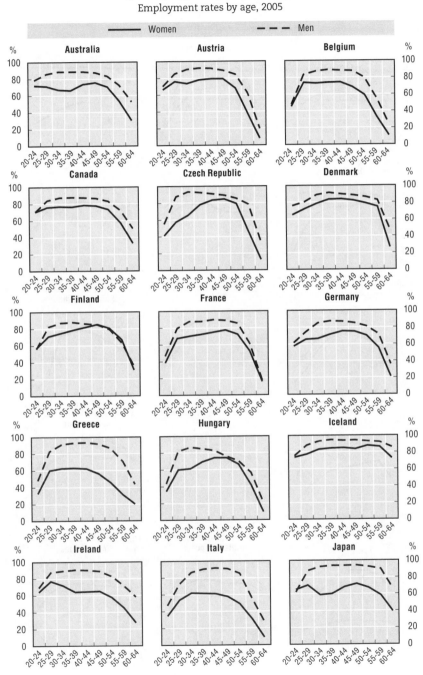

Chart 3.3. **Age-employment profiles, men and women** *(cont.)*

Employment rates by age, 2005

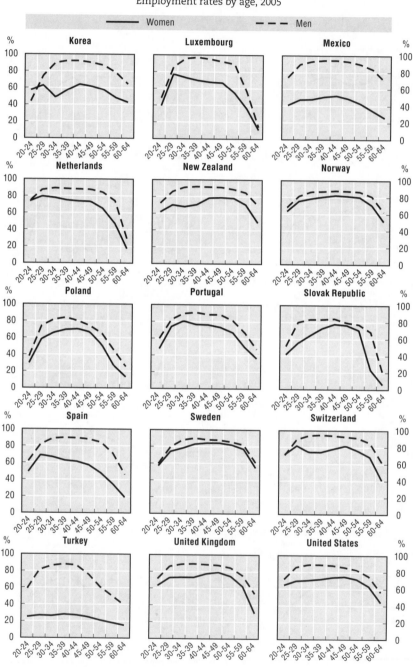

Source: OECD Labour Force Statistics database.

The impact of education

Employment rates are generally much higher for women with tertiary qualifications than among low-educated women, and gender employment gaps are lower. Higher education is likely to give women access to more interesting and well-paid occupations, making paid employment more attractive and formal childcare arrangements more affordable.

Table 3.3 shows that across the OECD the employment rate of women aged 25-64 was about 20 percentage points lower than for men in 2004. Employment rates for women who have not completed secondary education were more than 30 percentage points lower than for men in Ireland, Italy and Spain, more than 40 percentage points lower in Greece and Mexico, and more than 60 percentage points lower in Turkey.

Other than in Japan and Korea, the gender employment gap for women with tertiary education is lower than for women who have attained less than secondary education. For women who have completed tertiary education, the employment gap is only 10 percentage points, and in Nordic countries, Portugal and the United Kingdom it is less than 5 percentage points. Education thus proves to be an important instrument in helping women to find employment, except in Japan and Korea, where women have caught up with men in terms of participating in education (Box 3.2), but not in terms of workplace opportunities.

The differences in current and past educational practices contribute to employment outcomes that are gender-segmented by occupation or sector. The large majority of employed women and men are concentrated in a small number of occupations that tend to be either female or male-dominated, but in general women are concentrated in far fewer occupations than men; about ten occupations account for half of female employment compared with about 20 for men. Men are predominant in manual and production jobs (Chart 3.4, p. 58). By contrast, women are over-represented in clerical occupations, sales jobs, childcare, health and teaching professions, and domestic and personal care services (Chart 3.4). As health, childcare and education in Nordic countries are within the public domain, this contributes to about half of female employment in these countries being in the public sector (Table 3.1). However, it cannot be said that the degree of occupational segmentation tends to be higher, when female employment rates are higher; countries with high and low female employment rates can be found at both ends of the spectrum of occupational concentration.

Gender pay differences

Reflecting the rise in educational attainment and training and work attachment for women relative to men, the size of the gender wage gap has tended to decline over the past two or three decades in all countries for which

Table 3.3. **Gender employment gaps are smaller at higher levels of educational attainment**

Female employment rates (aged 25-64), as related to male employment rates (aged 25-64), by level of educational attainment, 2004 or latest year available

	All levels of education		Less than upper secondary education		University/tertiary education	
	Employment rate	Gender gap[1]	Employment rate	Gender gap[1]	Employment rate	Gender gap[1]
Australia	64	20	51	23	79	11
Austria	63	15	45	19	79	10
Belgium	59	17	45	28	81	8
Canada	71	11	52	20	80	6
Czech Republic	63	19	39	14	79	13
Denmark	74	9	55	17	85	2
Finland	71	5	59	11	83	6
France	64	13	59	17	77	7
Germany	62	13	43	18	79	8
Greece	51	32	43	43	76	13
Hungary	57	15	35	11	79	9
Iceland	83	8	76	11	93	3
Ireland	60	23	46	38	83	9
Italy	49	28	44	35	77	11
Japan	60	29	53	26	67	26
Korea	56	30	59	24	57	32
Luxembourg	57	26	43	28	75	16
Mexico	46	46	47	47	73	18
Netherlands	66	17	51	28	83	6
New Zealand	71	17	55	22	80	11
Norway	77	7	55	16	88	3
Poland	55	13	31	14	80	6
Portugal	68	14	74	12	87	1
Slovak Republic	56	17	20	9	79	9
Spain	52	29	48	36	78	9
Sweden	78	4	66	13	87	1
Switzerland	86	8	59	20	82	13
Turkey	26	51	18	61	63	18
United Kingdom	73	10	47	13	86	4
United States	69	12	47	21	78	11
OECD average	**63**	**19**	**49**	**23**	**79**	**10**

1.   Percentage point difference between the employment rates for men and women 25-64 years old.
Source: OECD Education at a Glance, 2006.

data are available (OECD, 2002b; and Weichselbaumer and Winter-Ebmer, 2005 and 2007). Since the early 1980s, the largest declines have occurred in the United States from a relatively high level and in France from a lower level.

BABIES AND BOSSES: RECONCILING WORK AND FAMILY LIFE – ISBN 978-92-64-03244-6 – © OECD 2007

Box 3.2. **Despite marked progress, gender differences in education persist**

The population structure in terms of levels of educational attainment is very different across the OECD. In Mexico, Turkey and Portugal, less than 40% of the 25- to 34-year-olds have completed secondary education compared with over 95% in Japan, Korea and Norway (see chart below). However, in all OECD countries younger generations are doing better than previous generations, and nowhere more so than in Korea, where 97% of those aged 25-34 have completed secondary education as opposed to about half of those in the age group 45-54.

In terms of educational attainment women are overtaking men

Percentage of population that has attained at least an upper-secondary education, by gender and age group, 2004

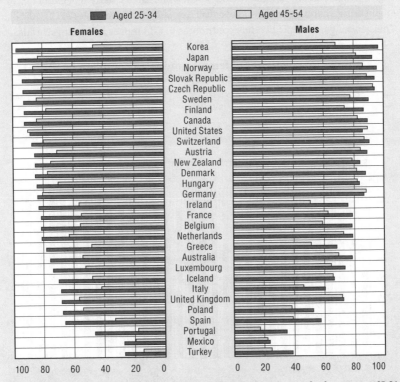

Countries are ranked in descending order of female educational attainment for the age group 25-34.

Source: OECD Education database.

Box 3.2. **Despite marked progress, gender differences in education persist** (*cont.*)

Furthermore, on average across the OECD women have made bigger gains than men; in fact, they are overtaking men in terms of educational attainment. In 2004, on average 61% of women in the age group 45-54 had completed secondary education compared to 66% of men. However, for the younger age group 25-34, 76% of men had completed secondary education, compared with 78% of women. A considerable improvement in labour market outcomes for women can thus be expected, if the labour market allows women to cash in on their (and their parents) investment in their education.

Levels of educational attainment may have become similar, but there remain profound gender differences in chosen areas of study (see chart below). On average across the OECD, almost three-quarter of women who "majored" had a degree in a health and welfare field of study, while three-quarters of graduates in engineering, manufacturing and construction subjects were male (OECD, 2006b). This gender gap in topic of study contributes to differences in earnings' levels.

Almost three-quarter of female graduates complete health and welfare subjects of study

University graduates in health and welfare subjects, by gender, 2004 or latest year available

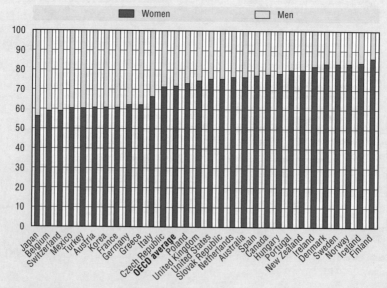

Source: OECD Education database.

Box 3.2. **Despite marked progress, gender differences in education persist** (cont.)

OECD (2004b) found that the levels of mathematical literacy at age 15 (or the end of compulsory schooling) were higher among boys than girls in all countries except Iceland (see chart below), so gender differences are present before compulsory schooling is finished. However, the differences in performance were fairly modest, ranging from over 20 points difference in Korea to just 5 percentage points difference in Australia and the Netherlands. By comparison, girls far outperform boys on the equivalent reading literacy scale.

Boys are slightly better than girls in maths, but are outclassed in reading literacy skills

Gender differences (boys-girls) in student performance in reading and mathematical literacy

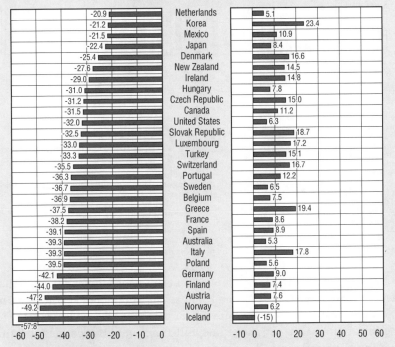

Source: OECD (2004b).

The relatively low entry rates of women into maths and science courses are more likely to be related to attitude than aptitude. OECD (2006b) shows that there are marked differences between males and females in their interest in and enjoyment of mathematics. As these differences help shape student's education choices and career patterns, policy needs to focus on changing attitudes towards mathematics among students at an early age (OECD, 2006b).

Chart 3.4. **Female employment is concentrated in a relatively small number of occupations**

Number of occupations that account for half of total employment, 2004 or latest year available

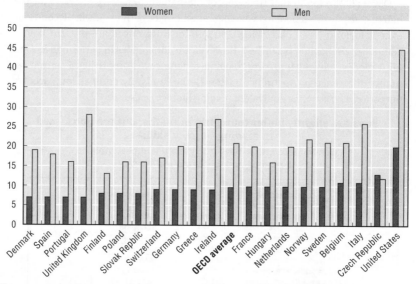

Many more women than men work as:
Pre-primary education teaching associate
    professionals (14.5)
Nursing and midwifery professionals (10.1)
Secretaries and keyboard-operating clerks (9.8)
Nursing and midwifery associate professionals (9.5)
Personal care and related workers (9.3)
Primary education teaching associate professionals (6.2)
Shop, stall and market salespersons
    and demonstrators (5.8)
Special education teaching professionals (5.6)
Domestic and related helpers, cleaners
    and launderers (5.4)
Primary and pre-primary education teaching (5.3)

Many more men than women work as:
Miners, shot firers, stone cutters and carvers (80.2)
Building frame and related trades workers (64.8)
Ships' deck crews and related workers (52.9)
Building finishers and related trades workers (35.4)
Mining and construction labourers (35.3)
Agricultural and other mobile plant operators (30.5)
Mining and mineral-processing-plant operators (24.5)
Metal moulders, welders, sheet-metal workers,
    structural-metal preparers, and related trades
    workers (23.1)
Machinery mechanics and fitters (21.7)
Power-production and related plant operators (15.9)

Source: *European Labour Force Survey* and March *Current Population Survey* for the United States.

Nevertheless, in terms of employment outcomes, a gender equitable society is some way off (Box 3.3) and women are still more likely to work in temporary employment relationships and/or part-time jobs where wages tend to be lower than in permanent and full-time jobs. Hence, despite the narrowing trend women still earn, on average, 16% less than men per hour worked (OECD, 2006c). In the United States, the gap is around 23%, while among EU countries the wage gap ranges between 10 and 25%; in Japan and Korea, the gender wage gap is highest as women on average earn one-third less than men.

A substantial part of the gender wage gap in each country, and part of the differences between countries, can be accounted for by gender differences in the composition of the workforce. The overall degree of wage inequality in

Box 3.3. **Fathers and families**

There are two main reasons why some policy makers are concerned about the amount of time that fathers spend with their children. The first is that getting fathers to take their parental responsibilities seriously is good for the child and even, possibly, good for the relationship between the parents. Keeping fathers in contact with their children following break-up of the relationship between parents is an objective of policy in many countries. Encouraging fathers to play a more prominent role in the care of their children can be motivated by such concerns.

The second reason for being concerned about the amount of time fathers spend with their children is because this makes it easier to meet other public policy objectives. For example, governments may wish that parents spend an extended period with their very young children without using formal childcare which, especially for very young children can be costly to provide (Chapter 6). Moreover, the key to a more gender equitable employment outcomes requires men to act upon the notion that work and family reconciliation is also their concern. As long, as mothers rather then fathers reduce labour force participation in the presence of children, and make use of parental leave provisions, are of course employers who perceive women as less committed to their career than men, and are therefore less likely to invest in female career opportunities. However, if fathers also take leave (and individualization of paid leave in Iceland has led to a marked increase in use by fathers, see Chapter 5), reduce working hours or start using flexitime arrangements when children are young, then in principle it becomes possible to ensure that both fathers and mothers fathers have sufficient time to spend at work and with their children. In turn, this would help to sustain birth rates, strengthen future labour supply and reduce child poverty risks.

each country also underpins, and possibly accounts for much of, the cross-country variation in the size of the gender wage gap (Blau and Kahn, 2001).

The interruptions to women's working careers associated with motherhood also contribute to the wage gap (Box 3.4). Despite equal pay for equal work provisions and anti-discrimination legislation in most OECD countries, part of the gender gap in earnings in each country may also reflect discrimination against women in the labour market. However, given that discrimination is rarely directly observable and because of other measurement problems, it is difficult to pin down precisely its contribution to the size of the gender wage gap within and across countries.

Box 3.4. **Lower female earnings: the costs of children**

There are different reasons why mothers earn less over their lifetime than other women, or men. One is that women with children are less likely to work in the labour market than other women, or men. A second is that women with children, when they do work, tend to work fewer hours. Third, they tend to earn lower wages. Fourth, due to foregone employment and lower pay, income in retirement also tends to be low.

In one of the first studies of the "indirect" costs of children (by which is meant lost earnings, as opposed to direct costs which are those arising from increased consumption needs), Calhoun and Espenshade (1988) derived estimates of the impact of children on hours of market work and earnings for American women aged 15 to 55. Using panel data from the National Longitudinal Survey of Labour Market Experience, potential earnings (based on a human capital wage model) were combined with the working-life histories implied by the life-table analysis to estimate opportunity expenditures (i.e. the money value of foregone employment opportunities) associated with different childbearing patterns. The findings included that opportunity expenditures on children have been declining over time and were roughly proportional to the number of births, for women of similar background and labour market experience. Furthermore, labour supply reductions immediately following each birth contributed most to observed opportunity expenditures, whereas the marginal effect of total family size is small by comparison.

Using British data from the 1980 *Women and Employment Survey*, Joshi (1990) found that a woman who had two children would give up nearly half the lifetime earnings that she otherwise might have had, with these lost earnings due, in roughly equal parts, to reduced participation in the labour market, shorter hours of work, and lower wages. For the 1990s, using data from the British Household Panel Survey, analyses again showed that the typical woman, with a medium level of education, gave up roughly half the earnings she otherwise would have had upon having children. However, they also indicated that the earnings costs of motherhood were now much lower for the highly educated women, who had become increasingly likely to return to their jobs post-childbirth and on a full-time basis (Joshi and Davies, 2002).

Using data from the *Australian Negotiating the Life Course Survey* (NLCS), Gray and Chapman (2001) find that for women who have completed secondary education, having one child decreases after-tax lifetime earnings by around AUD 162 000 (additional earnings losses from second and third children are relatively small). Women with one child are estimated to earn 63% of what they would have earned had they remained childless. Because Australian mothers are more likely to return to the workforce and do so more quickly after childbirth than previously, the family gap in lifetime earnings between

Box 3.4. **Lower female earnings: the costs of children** *(cont.)*

childless women and those with children while remaining considerable had more than halved between 1986 and the end of the 1997 (Chapman *et al.*, 2001).

Cross-national studies suggest that institutional differences in family-friendly policy stances can have a significant impact on the opportunity costs of children. Joshi and Davies (1992) compared foregone earnings in West Germany, France, Britain and Sweden due to lost years of employment, lower hours when the mother returns to the labour force, and lower rates of pay after childbearing. They estimated that the hypothetical West German mother in 1980 lost 49% of her undiscounted lifetime earnings if she embarked on the employment and earnings path typically associated with a two-child family, and the hypothetical British mother lost more, 57%. Swedish and French women's earnings are less affected by childrearing, the former losing 12% and the latter 6%, due to widely available public childcare in these two countries. Datta Gupta and Smith (2002) also found that children do not on average seem to have any long-term effect on their mother's wages compared to non-mothers.

Sigle-Rushton and Waldfogel (2006) use cross-section data from the Luxembourg Income Study to compare the earnings of women with children relative to childless women and to men in eight countries – Canada, Finland, Germany, the Netherlands, Norway, Sweden, the United Kingdom and the United States. They find that in the Nordic countries, mothers at age 45 have earned between 82 and 89% of what non-mothers have earned. At the other extreme, mothers in the Netherlands and Germany have earned only 56 to 74% of non-mothers' earnings by age 45. The story for women in the Anglo-Saxon countries is more complicated. Comparing mothers to non-mothers, women in the United Kingdom are similar to women in the Netherlands and Germany, earning between 67 and 75% of non-mothers' pay. Mothers in Canada do better, earning only 17 to 19% less than childless women, and mothers in the United States do even better, earning only 11 to 19% less than non-mothers in the long-term. In terms of family gaps, the United States is more similar to the Nordic countries than to the other Anglo-Saxon countries. However, when comparing the earnings of mothers to men, they find that the story changes, particularly for Canada, the United States and Norway, where both mothers' and non-mothers' earnings lag considerably behind men's.

Chart 3.5 shows that in most countries, gender wage gaps are wider for high-income workers (at the 80th percentile) than they are for low-income workers (at the 20th percentile). Exceptions exist, including Portugal, Switzerland and the United Kingdom, while in Belgium and Denmark the

Chart 3.5. **In many countries gender pay gaps are largest at higher earnings**

Gender pay differences at the top and bottom of the earnings distribution,
2003 or latest year available

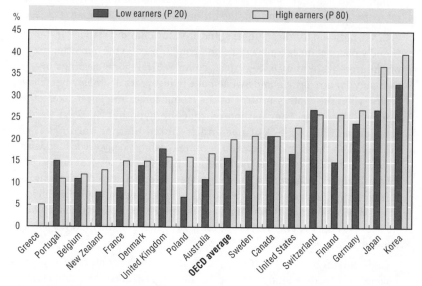

Source: OECD Distribution of Earnings database.

differences are not significant. The higher degree of gender wage equity towards the bottom of earnings distributions is likely to reflect institutional factors such as the influence of minimum wages and the coverage of collective bargaining (Blau and Kahn, 2001), while the wider gap at higher earnings levels is often taken as an indicator of the existence of the so-called "glass ceiling" (Arulampalam *et al.*, 2006).

Gender wage gaps at higher earnings levels are higher in Nordic countries than on average across the OECD. Long periods of child-related leave taken by mothers rather than fathers do not help female career progression. The high cost of domestic services in Nordic countries deters many female career workers in these countries from working long hours, thereby limiting their competitive edge with male counterparts.[4] Women in countries where domestic services are relatively cheap, such as in North America, find it less costly to work long hours to pursue their career (Datta Gupta *et al.*, 2003; and OECD, 2005a).

In view of the persistent gender pay gap, it is no surprise that across the OECD, on average mothers in dual-earner couple families contribute less to household income than men. This also applies to (Nordic) countries where female employment rates have been high for a relatively long time, although the gap is relatively small. In Denmark and Sweden, the spousal contribution to income of dual-earner families is relatively high at 70 and 63% respectively, but it is highest in Portugal at 81% (Chart 3.6). In general, the spousal contribution to household income of dual-earner families ranges from 40 to 60% of partners earnings, but in the Netherlands this is only about one quarter; in 2004, earnings of about half of all women age 25-44 amounted to less than 25% of all household earnings (Hagoort *et al.*, 2007). This is because many among this group of workers work less than 20 hours per week (Chapter 7).

Chart 3.6. **Wives contribute far less to household income than their husbands**

Average contribution of wives to the income of couple families as a percentage of their husband's earnings, early 2000s

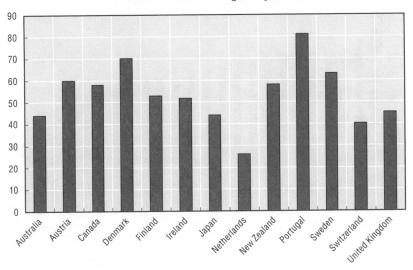

"Wives" refer to female spouses in couple households regardless of marital status.

Source: OECD Babies and Bosses reviews, various issues.

3.2.2. Joblessness among households

The most disadvantaged families with children are those where no adults are in paid employment. In many OECD countries there has been a shift in patterns of employment within households with children, away from the male single-earner model toward more dual-earner families. Joblessness among households with children increased between the 1980s and the 1990s, but tended to decrease in the second half of the 1990s (Förster and Mira d'Ercole, 2005). Rates of non-employment are quite diverse across OECD countries. Less than 3% of couples with children were jobless in 2001 in

Austria, Luxembourg, Portugal and the United States, but more than 6% were jobless in Australia, Belgium, Hungary, New Zealand, the Slovak Republic and the United Kingdom (Förster and Mira d'Ercole, 2005). Joblessness is generally much higher for sole-parent families than for couples with children, and the growth in the incidence of sole-parent families (Chapter 2) has been a significant contributor to trends in family joblessness. Sole-parent employment rates are highest (and rates of joblessness lowest) at over 80% in Denmark, Greece, Luxembourg, Iceland, Japan, Spain, Sweden and Switzerland, but around 55% or below in Australia, Ireland, the Netherlands, New Zealand and the United Kingdom (Chart 3.7).

Chart 3.7. **Sole-parent employment rates are lowest in Australia, Ireland, the Netherlands, New Zealand and the United Kingdom**

Sole-parent employment rates, 2005 or latest year available

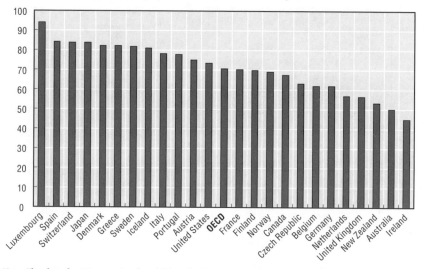

Note: The data for EU countries for which only 2001 Eurostat data are available (see below), concern sole-parent employment rates for the age group 25-49, and as they do not include groups for which employment is typically lower (very young sole parents and older women), they are not fully comparable with data for the other countries. More cross-nationally consistent data is being collected for the OECD Family database.

Source: Australia, Australian Bureau of Statistics; 6224.0.55.001 FA2 *Labour Force Status and Other Characteristics of Families*; Statistics Austria (2005 data); Statistics Canada (2001 data); Statistics Czech Republic; Statistics Denmark (1999); Statistics Finland (2002 data); INSEE, Statistics Ireland; Japanese authorities (2001 data); Statistics Netherlands (2004 data); Portuguese authorities (2002 data); Swiss authorities (2006 data); UK Office of National Statistics; and the *US Current Population Survey*; all other EU countries, Eurostat (2001 data). Unless stated otherwise, data are for 2005.

3.2.3. Child poverty

In most OECD countries, poverty risks (as measured with respect to half median disposable household income) have shifted over the past 20 years towards families with children (Förster and Mira d'Ercole, 2005). In many countries, families with children are disproportionately likely to be poor; only in Belgium, Denmark, Finland, Greece, Norway and Sweden do children face lower risks of poverty than the national average (Förster and Mira d'Ercole, 2005). After Mexico, the United States has the highest rate of child poverty, which is also high in Turkey, New Zealand, the United Kingdom, Portugal and Italy (Table 3.4).

Table 3.4. **Children in sole-parent families face a relatively high poverty risk**

Poverty rates for children and for families by employment status, percentages, around 2000

	Children[1]	Sole parent		Two parents		
		Not working	Working	No worker	One worker	Two workers
Australia	11.6	58.7	11.7	43.3	5.4	3.3
Austria	13.3	67.6	23.3	35.6	12.7	8.6
Belgium	4.1	22.8	11.4	16.1	2.8	0.6
Canada	13.6	89.7	27.7	75.3	22.9	3.5
Czech Republic	7.2	53.7	5.5	35.7	3.7	0.6
Denmark	2.4	22.2	4.0	19.0	6.4	0.7
Finland	3.4	25.0	7.2	25.8	5.4	1.3
France	7.3	61.7	9.6	37.9	6.3	1.6
Germany	12.8	55.6	18.0	51.5	6.4	1.9
Greece	12.5	18.8	20.0	13.4	16.8	4.8
Hungary	13.1	..	..	33.1	10.0	6.7
Ireland	15.7	88.7	22.1	74.8	17.4	1.6
Italy	15.7	76.8	13.4	61.1	23.9	1.6
Japan	14.3	52.1	57.9	46.0	12.3	10.6
Mexico	24.8	45.6	32.6	37.9	26.2	15.4
Netherlands	9.0	42.8	17.7	50.7	7.8	1.7
New Zealand	14.6	63.5	18.6	45.5	13.9	4.8
Norway	3.6	24.7	2.8	38.0	2.8	0.1
Poland	9.9	60.0	6.1	28.4	9.0	3.0
Portugal	15.6	84.8	20.3	50.6	32.4	4.8
Spain	15.6	68.2	32.8	64.7	18.1	4.7
Sweden	3.6	34.2	5.6	13.7	8.2	1.2
Switzerland	6.8	..	2.3	..	9.6	4.7
Turkey	21.1	51.6	65.4	25.2	17.2	15.7
United Kingdom	16.2	62.5	20.6	37.4	17.6	3.6
United States	21.6	93.0	39.9	77.7	30.5	8.3
OECD	**12.0**	**56.2**	**20.0**	**41.4**	**13.3**	**4.4**

1. The child poverty rate is defined as the share of children with equivalised incomes less than 50% of the median for the entire population.

Source: OECD Income Distribution Study. Data is collected about every five years, and more up-to-date information will become available at the end of 2007 or in the beginning of 2008.

On average, sole parents are represented three times as often in the poor population as in the working-age population as a whole. This over-representation has been decreasing over time in about half the countries, especially in Australia, Canada, Germany and the Nordic countries. Poverty rates of sole parents, however, remain high almost everywhere. In some (Canada, Denmark, Germany, the Netherlands, United Kingdom), their poverty rates are as much as four times higher than for the total working age population. An exception is Sweden, where the poverty rate for persons living in sole-parent households fell significantly during the past 10 to 20 years, and is today at the same low level as for the entire population, and slightly lower than for the working-age population.

The economic vulnerability of families is linked to parents' capacity to reconcile employment and parenthood. Child poverty rates vary across household types, but it is the employment status of parents' that has the strongest influence on the extent of child poverty. In most OECD countries child poverty rates are nearly three times higher on average for lone parents who are not working than for those in paid employment. Among couples with children, child poverty rates are around three times higher for families where neither parent is in paid employment than where one parent is employed, which in turn are three times higher than for families where both parents are in paid employment. The heightened risk of child poverty associated with joblessness can be as high as 50 to 1 compared to families where both parents are in paid employment (Czech Republic and Ireland) or even higher, as in Norway.

Working sole parents have poverty rates exceeding 20% in Austria, Canada, Germany, Greece, Ireland, Japan, Mexico, New Zealand, Portugal, the United Kingdom and the United States. Similarly, poverty rates among single-income couples are over 20% in Italy Mexico, Portugal and the United States, and are even substantial for two-earner families in Austria, Japan, Mexico and Turkey. Benefit support may be needed in addition to policies that help parents find a match between work and care commitments in order to combat child poverty effectively.

3.3. Conclusions

Changing female aspirations have led to increased female labour market participation which, as in the past, will be pivotal to economic growth in the future. There are substantial differences across countries, but on average across the OECD over 60% of mothers with dependent children are in work, and this is around 75 to 80% in Nordic countries. The intensity of female labour market participation also differs, with part-time employment being rare in the Czech Republic, Hungary and the Slovak Republic, but very common in Australia, Germany, Japan, Switzerland, the United Kingdom, and the Netherlands where almost two-thirds of employed women work part-time.

Despite the increases in female and maternal labour force participation of the past few decades, there remain considerable labour market challenges. The presence of children in households hardly affects male employment rates, but can profoundly change female labour force behaviour, especially when children are very young. Gender employment gaps persist and are highest in Greece, Italy, Japan, Korea, Mexico, Spain and Turkey and smallest in Nordic countries; gender employment gaps are generally smallest among workers with tertiary education.

Gender pay differences also persist: across the OECD women on average get paid less per hour than men: at median earnings women earn about one-sixth less then men. At average earnings, gender pay differences are largest in Japan and Korea and smallest in the Nordic countries, where gender segregation in public service employment (health, education and childcare) remains strong. Long periods of child-related leave that are taken by mothers rather than fathers do not help female career progression. Gender wage gaps at higher earnings levels are higher in Finland and Sweden than on average across the OECD, and there are proportionally more women in management positions in Canada, New Zealand and the United Kingdom than in these two Nordic countries.

Clearly, in terms of employment outcomes, a gender-equitable society is some way off because women currently adapt their labour market behaviour after childbirth, whereas men's behaviour changes little if at all. The key to a more gender-equitable outcome requires men to act upon the notion that work and family reconciliation is also their concern. There are exceptions but men generally still work the standard full-time working week, while many women work part-time (and take leave to care for children).

Maternal employment often has a significant impact on the poverty risk that children face, and children in dual-earner families are least likely to face poverty risks. The most disadvantaged families with children are those where there is no adult in paid employment, and on average around one-third of all poor families with children live in jobless families. Sole parenthood is often associated with joblessness, and in Australia, the Netherlands, New Zealand, Norway and the United Kingdom, all countries with relatively low sole-parent employment rates, more than half of the jobless families are headed by sole parents.

Joblessness among families with children increased in the 1980s and 1990s in a number of OECD countries, and while the extent of this problem has lessened since the middle of the 1990s, it remains significant in a number of countries. On average across the OECD, around one in ten households with children live in poverty, but this is less than one in twenty in

Belgium, Denmark, Finland, Norway and Sweden and close to one in five in Mexico, Turkey and the United States. In general, all countries that enjoy very low rates of child poverty (under 5% of households with children) do so because they *combine* high levels of parental employment with effective redistribution of resources through the tax-benefit system.

Notes

1. The labour force participation decision of a parent is affected by, for example, parental preferences (*e.g.* Jaumotte, 2003), net family income in and out of work of the parent(s) concerned, access to and the costs of childcare and the prevalence of convenient working-hour arrangements. Given resource constraints parents balance work and time for caring considerations in view of the cost of alternative behaviour.

2. There are also significant differences in unemployment rates between men and women in a number of countries. In the Czech Republic, Greece, Italy, Luxembourg, and Spain, the female unemployment rate is at least 1.5 times as high as the male unemployment rate; in contrast, in Canada, Ireland, Japan, Korea, Norway, Sweden and the United Kingdom, female unemployment rates are lower than those of men (OECD, 2007c).

3. Comparisons of headcount measures of employment by gender overstate the degree of women's presence in employment, as they take no account of the higher incidence of part-time employment among women.

4. To assist working women, a large Swedish insurance firm arranged a personal assistant "butler" service for its employees to compensate for the expensive domestic work market. The company subsidised butler performs employees' household chores such as laundry, running errands, fixing household appliances and buying birthday presents.

ISBN 978-92-64-03244-6
Babies and Bosses: Reconciling Work and Family Life
A Synthesis of Findings for OECD Countries
© OECD 2007

Chapter 4

Tax and Benefit Systems and the Work Choices by Parents

This chapter discusses key characteristics of tax and benefit systems across the OECD, and the support they provide to families and children. The chapter looks at spending on family benefits and its implications for the reconciliation of work and family life, and the degree of targeting of public support on low-income groups. It then considers how tax/benefit systems alter financial incentives to work for second earners in couple families and how they affect the distribution of paid work in these families. The chapter also discusses how tax/benefit systems may provide sole parents with financial incentives to work, and how differences in the general policy stance towards sole parents contribute to marked differences in benefit dependency among these families across OECD countries.

4.1. Concise overview of the scope and nature of tax/benefit systems and support for families

Across the OECD, there is wide variety in the scope of public social protection systems. In 2003, public social spending was about 21% of GDP on average; it exceeded 25% in Austria, Belgium, Denmark, Germany, France, Norway; and was highest in Sweden at over 30% (Table 4.1). However, governments in these countries levy significant income taxes on cash transfers and indirect taxes on the consumption out of benefit income, so that net (*after-tax*) public social spending is at least 3 percentage points lower in these countries (except for Germany where benefit income is generally not subject to taxation, see Adema and Ladaique, 2005; and OECD, 2007a).

In most OECD countries, public social spending generally constitutes about 40 to 50% of total government spending, except in Korea, where this was only 20% in 2003 (Table 4.1). Cross-national differences in gross public social spending are mirrored in tax burdens across countries. In 2005, tax-to-GDP ratios were highest in Denmark and Sweden at around 50%, compared with around 30% in Australia and just below that in Japan and the United States. In 2005, the tax wedge on labour (see note to Table 4.1) was highest in Belgium, France, Germany and Hungary at over 50% (OECD, 2006d).

Tax/benefit systems across the OECD all provide support for families with children. Indeed, families with children have always been an important client group for social policies, although spending on family benefits such as, for example, child allowances, parental leave benefits and childcare support, is considerably lower than spending on pensions; it amounted to one-tenth of all public social spending in 2003 (OECD, 2007a).

Available historical information on the tax/benefit position of employees in the OECD (OECD, 1984, 1997 and 2007e) suggests broad stability in the ratio of cash benefits and tax assistance provided to couple families to earnings of an average worker.[1] Since 1997, cash and tax support for families with average earnings has increased markedly in the United Kingdom and the United States.[2]

Traditionally, one of the biggest sources of support for families with children is the provision of compulsory schooling, and public spending on primary and secondary education in the majority of OECD countries ranges from 3 to 4% of GDP (OECD, 2006a). However, spending on family benefits is catching up. On average across the OECD, public spending on family benefits

Table 4.1. **Public social spending exceeds a quarter of GDP in Austria, Belgium, Denmark, France, Germany, Norway and Sweden**

	Tax burden in 2005		Public social expenditure, 2003		
	Tax-to-GDP ratio	Tax wedge	Percentage of general government spending	Percentage of GDP	
				Gross	Net
Australia	31.2	28.3	50.9	17.9	17.2
Austria	41.9	47.4	51.2	26.1	20.6
Belgium	45.4	55.4	51.8	26.5	22.9
Canada	33.5	31.6	42.3	17.3	17.2
Czech Republic	38.5	43.8	39.5	21.1	19.5
Denmark	49.7	41.4	49.9	27.6	20.3
Finland	44.5	44.6	44.1	22.5	17.7
France	44.3	50.1	53.5	28.7	25.5
Germany	34.7	51.8	56.3	27.3	26.2
Greece	35.0	38.8	43.1	21.3	..
Hungary	37.1	50.5	45.6	22.7	..
Iceland	42.4	29.0	39.2	18.7	16.6
Ireland	30.5	25.7	47.7	15.9	14.0
Italy	41.0	45.4	50.1	24.2	20.6
Japan	26.4	27.7	46.9	17.7	17.6
Korea	25.6	17.3	18.4	5.7	5.9
Luxembourg	37.6	35.3	49.3	22.2	..
Mexico	19.8	18.2	..	6.8	7.6
Netherlands	37.5	38.6	43.9	20.7	17.9
New Zealand	36.6	20.5	50.2	18.0	15.1
Norway	45.0	37.3	51.8	25.1	20.2
Poland	34.4	43.6	50.0	22.9	..
Portugal	34.5	36.2	48.6	23.5	20.8
Slovak Republic	29.4	38.3	43.6	17.3	16.1
Spain	35.8	39.0	53.0	20.3	17.6
Sweden	51.1	47.9	53.8	31.3	24.3
Switzerland	30.0	29.5	55.9	20.5	..
Turkey	32.3	42.7	..	..	..
United Kingdom	37.2	33.5	48.4	20.6	18.9
United States	26.8	29.1	43.6	16.2	17.3

Tax-to-GDP data are for 2004 for Australia, Greece, Japan, the Netherlands, Poland and Portugal.
Tax wedge is defined as the gap between total labour costs to the employer and the corresponding net take-home pay to single workers without children at average earnings. Labour costs are defined as gross wages paid to employees plus employer social security contributions and payroll taxes.
Source: OECD (2006d, 2006f and 2007a).

increased from 1.6% of GDP in 1980 to 2.2% in 2003, and gross (before-tax) public spending on family benefits amounted to more than 3% of GDP in Australia, Austria, Belgium, Denmark, Germany, Finland, France, Hungary, Norway, Sweden and was highest at over 4% of GDP in Luxembourg (Chart 4.1).

Chart 4.1. **Family spending has the greatest focus on childcare services in France and the Nordic countries**

Family spending in cash, services and tax measures, in percentage of GDP, in 2003

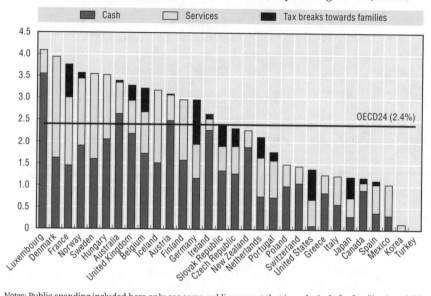

Notes: Public spending included here only concerns public support that is exclusively for families (*e.g.* child payments and allowances, parental leave benefits and childcare support). Spending recorded in other social policy areas as health and housing support also assists families, but not exclusively, and is not included here.

OECD24 does not include Greece, Hungary, Luxembourg, Poland, Switzerland and Turkey where relevant tax data are not available.

Source: OECD (2007a).

The composition of family spending varies widely. Financial support delivered through the tax system is an important component of family assistance in many OECD countries. Trend data are not available, but Chart 4.1 shows that in 2003 tax breaks for families were significant in the Czech Republic, Japan, the Netherlands, the Slovak Republic, the United Kingdom and were particularly important in Germany, France and the United States, at 1.0%, 0.8% and 0.7% of GDP, respectively.

In the vast majority of OECD countries, cash transfers (either income-related or universal child allowances, leave payments) constitute the dominant component of gross public spending directed towards families, accounting for around 70% of all such spending on average. Australia, Austria, Hungary, Ireland, and Luxembourg all spend more than 2% of GDP on cash transfers to children. Public spending on family services is around 1.5% of GDP or more in the Nordic countries, France and Hungary (OECD, 2007a). In all, Chart 4.1 shows that about one-third of OECD countries spend more than 3% of GDP on family benefits, and that the focus in most countries is on financial transfers rather than earmarked spending on childcare measures that facilitate families to combine work and care commitments.

4.1.1. A continuum of work and care supports

It is one thing to spend a lot of money on family policies; it is quite another to spend it sensibly. In contrast to some of the other countries where public spending on family benefits exceeds 3% of GDP, policy in the Nordic countries, Hungary (OECD, 2007d) and to a lesser extent France and the Canadian province of Québec (OECD, 2005a) *does* fit together in something like a coherent system of supports for families trying to combine work and family life through childhood. While systemic logic differs, common elements are parental leave (9 to 18 months in Iceland, Denmark and Sweden) and/or home-care supports until children are three years of age (Finland, Hungary, and Norway) followed by childcare, kindergarten and other pre-school services, and primary education. In Denmark and Sweden (and to a lesser extent France and the Canadian province of Québec[3]), these supports are complemented by a comprehensive system of out-of-school-hours care services, until around age 12, while parents in Sweden are also entitled to reducing working hours until children got to primary school.

To support effective use of parental leave and formal childcare supports, Nordic countries and Hungary spend 0.6% of GDP or more on income support during maternity, paternity, parental and home-care leave periods *and* more than 1% of GDP on childcare and early education, to cover the period up to primary school. Public support for childcare is highest in Denmark, Iceland and Sweden where children at age two are very likely to participate in formal care (Chapter 6). In France, there remains a certain ambiguity about supporting working parents with children not yet three years of age and there remain gaps in public childcare support for very young children. Public childcare and early education support is largely focused on "maternelles" and care services for children aged three years and over.

4.1.2. Targeting public support

One of the tendencies to which comparative analysts of social policy are particular prone is to call for reforms to make such-and-such a country more like some other country. In family policy during the first decade of the 21st century, the model countries usually held up as deserving of emulation are most often the Nordic countries, especially Denmark and Sweden. There is much in the family policies of these countries worthy of copying, but there are limits to their use as role models. Nordic family policies are expensive. Nordic countries are relatively small, cohesive and egalitarian societies where populations have a high degree of trust in their local governments to deliver high-quality childcare, health and education services. Because of this, they are willing to bear a relatively high tax burden to sustain a universal social policy approach (and the associated high tax-to-GDP ratios, Table 4.1). However, electorates in many other OECD countries are not willing to sustain a tax burden of similar magnitude, and ways and means are sought to curtail public spending. Rather than building universal support systems, policy makers try to curtail spending (and the burden of taxation) by putting in place relatively inexpensive policy measures and/or focusing public support more on some areas of social policy than others and/or by targeting resources at low-income families more generally. As a result in many OECD countries, there are significant gaps in public family support, including unpaid parental leave periods, lack of childcare support for very young children, and lack of out-of-school-hours care support.

Formal centre-based childcare for young children (say those aged from 12 months, or even younger) as provided on a comprehensive basis in, for example Denmark and Sweden (OECD, 2001a and 2005a) is particularly expensive. Child-to-staff ratios are much lower for the care of two-year-olds than for, say, five-year-olds, and the costs of childcare are therefore higher for younger than for older age groups (Chapter 6). This is one of the reasons why Finland, Norway and Hungary focus public resources on supporting parents, usually mothers, to provide home care for very young children up to around age three (see Chapter 5 for more detail), rather than focusing support on centre-based childcare. Although cheaper, this approach weakens the mother's labour market position (Chapter 3), and particularly in Hungary, the resultant barriers to the fulfilment of female labour market aspirations contribute to downward pressure on birth rates (Chapter 2).

In many other OECD countries, costly childcare for the very young is not replaced by supporting comparatively cheaper parental care, but support systems for parental leave, childcare, or out-of-school-hours care are not comprehensive, and parental leave policy is often not coherently integrated with childcare policy, leading to significant gaps in support.

Available data on public spending on cash and tax-based support for families with children, income support during leave, spending on child- and out-of-school hours care services, and spending on primary education for New Zealand and Sweden illustrate the issue. Chart 4.2 shows that in New Zealand in 2004/05 (i.e. before the introduction of free early education for three-four year old children, which is rolled out in 2007-08) public spending on children is relatively low in the first three years of their life, with limited use of childcare facilities by children in this age group. When children start to make greater use of kindergarten and childcare (age three and four, i.e. their fourth and fifth year, respectively), spending increases, going up still more when children enter primary school (Adema, 2006a).

Chart 4.2. **Sweden frontloads public spending during the early years**

Public spending on education and family benefits per age of children

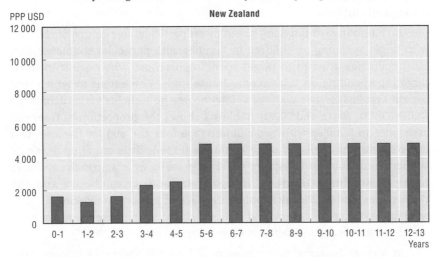

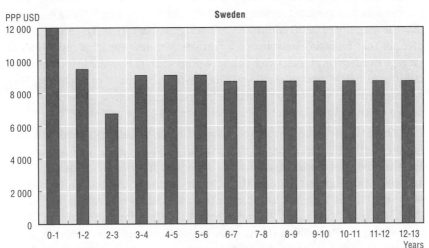

Note: Public spending in US dollars adjusted for the cost of living on basis of purchasing power parities (PPP). Data do not include public spending on health and/or housing. Spending items include, public child benefits (cash allowances, family credit, etc.), income support during leave, subsidised childcare, pre-school and primary school expenditure. For New Zealand, all income support during leave is allocated to children age 0-1, while for Sweden such payments are here assumed to be paid during the first 17 months of a child's life (periods of parental leave can be taken until the child goes to school in Sweden), and is thus allocated over years 0-1 and 1-2; the "dip" in spending for year 2-3 is related to low childcare participation rates compared to other ages (unlike for the year 1-2, no leave spending is included).

Source: OECD (2007a) and Education database.

It thus appears that in New Zealand support for families with children is least intensive from when paid parental leave expires (14 weeks) until age three, when child and early education support become available on a comprehensive basis. By contrast, Swedish policy seems to *frontload* its support: it is highest in the first year, but otherwise is fairly constant in value throughout childhood.

An alternative to targeting spending on particular age groups of children is to target spending on children in families with particular characteristics. Most countries attempt to target spending on those who need it most by targeting spending on low-income households. The extent to which tax/benefit systems target resources at low-income households varies across the OECD (OECD, 2007e and 2007f). Table 4.2 shows the proportion of financial assistance to families with two children (age four and six) for families with different earning levels. In some countries there is little targeting of family support, and financial assistance to families varies little across the earnings range in Belgium, Germany, Hungary, Ireland, Luxembourg and the Netherlands, and the Slovak Republic. The lack of support for working families with low earnings in Greece and Italy is related to the absence of national social assistance support systems in these countries (OECD, 2007f).

In general, however, the proportion of financial assistance in household income falls as household earnings increase.[4] The last column in Table 4.2 shows that the majority of OECD countries have designed tax/benefit systems in such a manner that financial assistance for families with low earnings (up to 25% of average earnings) is at least twice as high a proportion of household income as for families at twice average earnings. The Australian, Canadian, Japanese, New Zealand, Polish, and Korean tax/benefit systems involve a particularly high degree of targeting support at families with limited earnings (Table 4.2).

The effective redistributive power of tax/benefit systems towards families with children depends not only on the progressivity of income tax systems and the income-tested nature of benefit programmes (Adema, 2006b) and their take-up, but also on the absolute amount of social spending for families. This is high in Nordic countries and higher in Australia than in Canada, Japan, Korea and Poland (Chart 4.1). Whiteford and Adema (2007) found that tax/benefit systems play a significant role in reducing child poverty: on average across 19 OECD countries for which data are available, public transfers and taxes lifted out of relative poverty around 40% of all households with children in 2000. The extent of this reduction ranged from around 70% or more in the Nordic countries, Belgium, the Czech Republic and France, around 60% in Australia to being negligible in Italy, Japan, Portugal, and Switzerland. Innovatively, Mexican policy has moved to make receipt of family support conditional on children participating in health and education programmes; this approach reflects the multifaceted nature of effective anti-child-poverty policies (Box 4.1).

Table 4.2. **Financial support for families with children varies with income level**

Financial assistance to families as a percentage of earnings of an average worker, 2004

	Earnings as % of the average wage (AW)									Ratio AW = 0/ AW = 200
	0	25	50	75	100	125	150	175	200	
Australia	19.1	16.6	15.8	20.2	14.8	9.4	7.5	4.4	2.9	6.6
Austria	17.4	17.8	17.8	12.8	12.8	12.8	12.8	12.8	12.8	1.4
Belgium	10.9	7.7	10.0	10.1	10.1	10.1	10.1	10.1	10.1	1.1
Canada	17.0	22.7	21.4	16.4	8.7	5.8	4.7	3.7	2.6	6.5
Czech Republic	23.7	23.7	18.4	20.7	14.3	10.6	7.8	8.9	9.0	2.6
Denmark	21.6	21.6	21.6	14.0	11.1	8.6	7.5	7.5	7.5	2.9
Finland	17.9	17.9	17.9	12.3	8.1	8.1	8.1	8.1	8.1	2.2
France	12.9	14.0	14.0	6.0	5.1	6.3	7.5	8.6	9.1	1.4
Germany	9.2	9.2	9.2	9.7	9.4	9.6	9.5	9.5	9.7	0.9
Greece	1.9	1.9	1.9	1.9	2.4	3.5	5.1	5.1	5.1	0.4
Hungary	9.0	9.0	9.0	13.4	14.7	14.7	14.7	14.7	14.7	0.6
Iceland	17.1	17.1	17.1	15.4	13.9	12.3	10.6	8.8	7.1	2.4
Ireland	16.3	16.3	18.4	11.9	13.0	13.0	13.0	13.0	13.0	1.2
Italy	0.0	3.7	5.6	13.6	10.8	9.1	6.8	6.1	4.2	0.0
Japan	19.2	19.2	19.2	7.2	4.2	4.6	2.4	3.3	3.8	5.0
Korea	17.2	17.2	8.3	0.4	0.9	1.8	1.8	1.8	1.8	9.5
Luxembourg	18.0	19.9	19.7	19.6	14.4	16.8	17.5	17.5	17.5	1.0
Netherlands	4.9	4.9	7.3	6.5	5.0	5.0	5.0	5.0	4.7	1.0
New Zealand	11.2	11.1	10.7	7.9	0.0	0.0	0.0	0.0	0.0	. .
Norway	14.5	14.5	8.1	6.4	6.4	6.4	6.4	6.4	6.4	2.3
Poland	25.8	23.3	9.1	9.3	6.6	3.5	0.0	0.0	0.0	. .
Portugal	26.3	26.3	19.5	20.3	19.0	11.0	7.1	6.7	6.7	3.9
Slovak Republic	12.1	13.3	11.2	11.5	11.5	11.7	11.9	12.1	12.3	1.0
Spain	10.3	10.3	2.9	2.2	3.5	3.5	3.9	4.1	4.1	2.5
Sweden	12.4	12.4	12.4	8.0	7.4	7.4	7.4	7.4	7.4	1.7
Switzerland	11.7	11.7	11.7	8.0	9.8	5.4	5.6	6.1	6.4	1.8
United Kingdom	18.6	18.6	23.9	20.0	11.5	7.0	7.0	7.0	7.0	2.7
United States	29.7	24.6	24.7	16.5	11.2	10.6	10.6	10.6	10.6	2.8
Average	**15.2**	**15.2**	**13.8**	**11.5**	**9.3**	**8.2**	**7.6**	**7.5**	**7.3**	**2.1**

Note: Assistance for children is calculated as the difference between the net incomes of a single-income couple without children and a single-income couple with two children, at different levels of earnings, expressed as a percentage of the average worker's earnings.

Source: Calculated from OECD tax-benefit models.

4.2. Financial incentives to work for couple families without childcare costs[5]

4.2.1. Moving into work

Tax/benefit systems play a key role in parental work and care decisions. For potential employees, the financial gain from taking up a job is affected by the amount of tax (including social security contributions) and other mandatory charges due on earnings. Furthermore, those entitled to receive social benefits

Box 4.1. "Oportunidades" in Mexico, conditional support for low-income families

Oportunidades – introduced in 1997 as *Progresa* – aims to combat malnutrition, promote regular health checks and enhance participation in education (*www.oportunidades.gob.mx*). Cash payments made to poor families are *conditional* on children staying in school and undertaking regular health checks. In 2006, the programme reached 5.8 million families, around 25% of the total national households with coverage about 75% among households in rural areas (INSP, 2006), with an annual budget of over 31 billion pesos in 2005 (about 0.4% of GDP). Cash subsidies are paid periodically and can reach 22% of the recipients' total income; they are slightly higher for girls than for boys (about 10% for girls in secondary school); and they increase with children's school level.

Transfers are made directly to mothers are also responsible for adhering to reporting requirements. This reflects the notion that when child payments are made to mothers such spending is most likely to benefit children. For Canada, Woolley (2004) finds that particularly when child payments aim to cover basis needs, such payments should be made to mothers since they make the spending decisions on food, household supplies and children's clothing.

In addition to cash-transfers, the programme provides basic health services to all family members and special care services for pregnant and nursing women and to children not yet two years of age. Targeting is accomplished by first selecting (using an index based on census-data) communities with a high concentration of the population below the poverty line or inadequate coverage of public services and basic infrastructure (56.3% of households taking part in the Oportunidades live in the eight states with the lowest degree of human development) and is then based on a proxy means-test of each household in these selected localities. In all, 90% of programme spending was focused on the 40% of poorest households (INEGI, 2002).

In terms of *health and nutrition*, INSP (2006) showed that outcomes improved:

● The most extreme form of malnutrition "emanciacion" (*i.e.* low weight for a given height) concerned 1.6% of children not yet five years of age, down from around 3% in 1999.

● The prevalence of malnutrition among children over five decreased during this period from 16% to 10.4% for males and from 16% to 9.5% for females.

As those with any level of *educational attainment* are 2.7 times less likely to live in poverty than those without (INEGI, 1996 and 2004), improving educational outcomes is a key policy objective:

● Between 1996 and 2004, school attendance among children from households in extreme poverty aged 12 to 14 increased by 21.6%, and that of those aged 15 to 17 increased by 71%

> ### Box 4.1. **"Oportunidades" in Mexico, conditional support for low-income families** (cont.)
>
> - Between 1996 and 2004, the risk among children aged 12 to 15 from a household in extreme poverty of leaving school without degree decreased by 34.1%.
> - Parker (2003), found that the Oportunidades programme increased secondary school registration in rural areas by 24%, among girls the increase was of 32%.
>
> Increased participation in education has also been instrumental in the fight against child labour: Behrman et al. (2005) found that between the year 1997 and 2003 the Oportunidades programme decreased the probability of children aged 10 and 14 being in employment by 35% and 29%, respectively.

while not in work, may experience a loss of benefit payments once they are. The reduction of benefit income can significantly reduce the net payoff from work, in certain circumstances so much so that it does not pay to work (at least in a short-term perspective.[6] As being in work opens up new career opportunities, there may be long-term gains from accepting low-paid jobs in the short term). Given that many social transfers are specifically targeted towards low-income households, especially if children are present, parents in these households are most likely to face weak financial incentives to work.

The question as to what part of in-work earnings is effectively taxed away for somebody moving into work can be addressed by looking at the average effective tax rate (AETR). This indicator measures the proportion of any increase in earnings which is lost either to taxation or loss of benefit income.

Table 4.3 shows the average effective tax rates parents face when contemplating transitions into work. These depend on prospective earnings, non-employment income and income of the partner.[7] Note that the costs of childcare are not accounted for here (see Chapter 6), so it is implicitly assumed that employed parents have access to free informal childcare. Parents living in a jobless couple family with two children whose income support levels (from social assistance and housing payments) are relatively high and which is rapidly withdrawn[8] face high average effective tax rates (over 90% Denmark, Finland and Sweden; column 1, Table 4.3) when moving into work, and thus make only very small income gains from moving into a job at two/thirds of average earnings, and none at all in Oslo, Norway and the city of Zürich in Switzerland.[9] In general, parents who move into employment with higher earnings face lower AETRs (columns 3 and 1, Table 4.3), except for Greece (no benefit withdrawal, but progressive income tax) Italy (where family benefits

Table 4.3. **In general, moving into work pays for parents in dual-earner couple families**

Average effective tax rates for parents in couple families entering employment, 2004

	0 >> 2/3 of AW		0 >> of AW	
	One-earner married couple (1)	Two-earner married couple (2)	One-earner married couple (3)	Two-earner married couple (4)
Australia	72	49	66	46
Austria	82	31	69	35
Belgium	65	47	60	50
Canada	54	46	57	45
Czech Republic	79	45	71	42
Denmark	92	63	82	57
Finland	94	34	84	37
France	82	25	63	27
Germany	75	49	66	51
Greece	16	17	19	20
Hungary	55	35	62	42
Iceland	87	48	74	48
Ireland	88	31	72	29
Italy	−9	40	11	42
Japan	89	22	66	21
Korea	71	8	51	9
Luxembourg	89	18	65	23
Netherlands	88	38	71	37
New Zealand	83	43	74	37
Norway	101	30	79	33
Poland	65	49	63	44
Portugal	57	20	60	23
Slovak Republic	41	24	33	26
Spain	58	17	47	21
Sweden	98	32	79	33
Switzerland	104	28	83	28
United Kingdom	77	41	74	38
United States	41	43	44	39

Note: In the initial situation, social assistance and any other means and/or income-tested benefits (e.g. housing support) are assumed to be available subject to the relevant income conditions. Children are aged four and six and neither childcare benefits nor childcare costs are considered. For married couples the percentage of AW relates to one spouse only; the second spouse is assumed to be "inactive" with no earnings in a one-earner couple and to have full-time earnings equal to 67% of the AW in a two-earner couple. The average wage reflects the earnings an average worker (OECD, 2007e).
Source: OECD Tax/Benefit Models.

increase with the number of days worked) and the United States, because of the phasing out of the Earned Income Tax Credit.

Compared to their counterparts without partners who have their own earnings, parents whose partner is already in paid employment at two-thirds of average earnings, face considerably lower AETRs and relatively strong financial incentives to move into work (compare columns 2 with 1, and 4 with 3, Table 4.3). Exceptions are countries without national social assistance support – Greece and Italy. Because of the earnings of the partner, any entitlement to social assistance in the initial situation is likely to have been small, if any, so that when the non-employed parents move into work, withdrawals of income-related transfers are largely not relevant.

With AETRs generally well below 50% (Table 4.3), work pays for potential second-earners in families who are not on income support themselves, *e.g.* mothers with a working partner, who choose to provide personal care for children on a full-time basis for a number of years. However, in some OECD countries, including Australia, Belgium, Denmark, Germany, Iceland, and Poland, financial incentives to move into work for spouses appear to be weak. Chapter 6 considers whether that observation still holds after accounting for the cost of childcare.

4.2.2. Working more hours

The mix of tax increases and benefit withdrawals also affects the financial incentives for increasing working hours or work effort for those already working. Marginal effective tax rates (METRs) can be used to measure these disincentives for a range of working-hours transitions. Changes in net incomes are evaluated for the household as a whole since any additional earnings by a member of the household affects taxes paid and benefits received by other household members. Results for different working-hours transitions are shown in Table 4.4, for parents in couple families whose partners is either in full-time employment at two/thirds of average earnings, or who is in receipt of income support.

Table 4.4 shows that METRs for parents in couple families are low in countries where tax burdens are small (for example, in Korea) or where means-tested benefits play less of a role (for example, Greece, Italy and Spain). For short working hours, METRs can be very low in cases where some benefit payments are conditional on having employment income of a certain minimum level or are conditional on working a certain minimum number of hours. For example the METR in Italy for a transition from 1/3 to 2/3 of full-time hours in the case of families with children is very low, as family benefits increase in line with the number of days worked (Table 4.4).

The highest METRs (close to or in excess of 100%) are observed for working parents in single-earner couple families who double their hours from 1/3 to 2/3 of full-time hours (equivalent to an increase in earnings from one-third to two-thirds of average earnings) in Denmark, Finland, Japan, Luxembourg and Switzerland. In these countries, it hardly pays for parents in

Table 4.4. **Increasing part-time working hours may not pay for parents in couple families**

Marginal effective tax rates for parents couple families who work part-time, 2004

	1/2 of AW >> AW		1/3 of AW >> 2/3 of AW		2/3 of AW >> AW	
	One-earner married couple (1)	Two-earner married couple (2)	One-earner married couple (3)	Two-earner married couple (4)	One-earner married couple (5)	Two-earner married couple (6)
Australia	58	43	75	53	52	38
Austria	44	44	65	38	44	44
Belgium	52	57	47	61	51	55
Canada	59	41	50	40	65	42
Czech Republic	42	31	58	39	54	34
Denmark	70	49	93	59	59	43
Finland	75	42	99	34	63	44
France	34	32	57	31	23	30
Germany	51	53	63	51	48	54
Greece	23	24	16	17	26	26
Hungary	83	50	59	35	77	55
Iceland	44	48	70	48	48	48
Ireland	50	30	76	29	41	26
Italy	26	46	−13	59	50	47
Japan	47	24	97	26	20	20
Korea	31	11	70	9	11	12
Luxembourg	49	30	110	19	18	34
Netherlands	52	40	78	43	37	36
New Zealand	76	23	88	27	66	24
Norway	52	36	92	32	36	37
Poland	57	35	78	45	57	35
Portugal	39	29	75	25	24	31
Slovak Republic	15	30	34	34	16	30
Spain	23	27	15	15	24	29
Sweden	57	35	97	35	38	35
Switzerland	65	27	108	39	39	27
United Kingdom	74	33	84	33	66	33
United States	50	29	47	37	50	29

Note: Hourly earnings correspond to the AW level throughout so that a half-time employee would have earnings equal to 50% of AW. Social assistance and any other means-tested benefits are assumed to be available subject to the relevant income conditions. Children are aged four and six and neither childcare benefits nor childcare costs are considered. In-work benefits that depend on a transition from unemployment into work are not available since the person changing working hours is already in employment prior to the change. For married couples, the percentage of AW relates to one spouse only; the second spouse is assumed to be "inactive" with no earnings in a one-earner couple and to have full-time earnings equal to 67% of AW in a two-earner couple.

Source: OECD, Tax/Benefit Models.

single-earner couples to increase hours worked as income-tested support is withdrawn at about the same rate as earnings increase.

Employment-conditional benefits are generally targeted towards low-income families with children and are reduced at higher earnings levels. This helps explain why in the United Kingdom METRs for parents in single-earners families tail off at higher earnings ranges (columns 3 and 5 in Table 4.4) and are much higher than for second earners in households without children (OECD, 2007f).

When one parent in the couple family earns two-thirds of average earnings (columns 2, 4 and 6 in Table 4.4), it generally pays for their partners to increase earnings, with METRs generally being around 40% or less. However, in Denmark, Belgium, Germany and Italy, METRs are close to or above 50% across the earnings range of one-third to average earnings. In these countries financial incentives to work more hours for second earners in couple families are relatively weak (again, this is before accounting for formal childcare fees, Chapter 6).

Tax/benefit systems also have a significant impact on the earnings and labour market behaviour of parents when systems are discontinuous. Often a clustering of earnings outcomes occurs at low earnings levels, as these earnings are not taxed and/or subject to social security contributions and benefits above these points are often cut off rather than withdrawn on a gradual basis. For example, in Austria and Germany earnings from small-hours jobs are not taxed and under certain conditions benefit recipients can engage in these jobs without losing entitlement (Adema *et al.*, 2003; and OECD, 2007a). In Japan, the social security system has a significant effect on maternal labour force behaviour since as long as spouses earn approximately just below one-third of average earnings, they do not have to pay health and pension insurance contributions (while benefiting from their employed partner's contributions). Above this level, payments are *not* gradually phased in, but are a sizeable lump-sum, which increase with earnings.

4.2.3. Tax/benefit systems and the distribution of earnings within families

Couple families can choose a range of possible labour supply options to procure a desired level of disposable family income: the single-breadwinner approach, a combination of full-time and part-time work, or both partners earning equal amounts. If tax/benefit systems are largely neutral between these choices, public policy has little effect on how paid work is distributed within couple families. More commonly, however, public policy gives financial incentives to structure household earnings in a particular way. Whether it is the one-earner model that is favoured or the equal-sharing approach varies across countries.

The nature of the tax unit is an important factor determining the extent to which tax and benefit systems favour either single-earner or dual-earner couples. Other things being equal, tax systems that assess tax liabilities on *individual* income as opposed to taxation on basis of *all* household income provides greater incentives for partners of already-employed people to work. Under *joint* or *family-based* taxation systems, the marginal tax rate of the second earner – most commonly the female spouse – will be the same as the marginal tax rate of the primary earner, and if the taxation system is progressive, this will be higher than the marginal rate for a single person at the same level of earnings, with possible adverse incentives for female partners to participate in the paid labour market. Moreover, with progressive tax rates, individual taxation means that a second earner will be taxed less heavily than the primary earner for the same level of additional earnings, implying that couples can achieve higher levels of disposable income by becoming a dual-earner family. Individual tax systems with progressive income tax schedules include a certain bias towards spreading earnings across different household members.

During the past three decades, most OECD countries have moved towards individual taxation, partly in recognition of the positive externalities that increased employment of second earners can bring, partly out of a concern for gender equality. In 2003, nineteen OECD countries had separate income taxation of spouses, five had joint systems and six had either optional separate or joint taxation, or required joint taxation over certain income levels (OECD, 2003b). The only countries with joint taxation, or where couples with average earnings were likely to opt for joint taxation, were the United States, Portugal, Poland, Ireland, Germany, Switzerland, France, Luxembourg and (for all but very small incomes) Turkey (OECD, 2003b).

However, the nature of the tax unit is only part of the story. Tax reliefs and credits are frequently related to family composition, as indeed, are most income-tested cash benefits. Many "individual" tax systems exhibit other "joint elements" aimed at lowering tax burdens for families with only one earner. When the previously non-employed partner takes up employment, these tax concessions are withdrawn, reducing the income gain from participation in the labour market. For example, unused tax-free allowances are often transferable between partners, as in Denmark, Iceland and the Netherlands. If the second spouse finds employment, a part of this allowance is no longer available to the first earner. Since the first earner's income – and marginal tax rate – is higher, employment of the second earner can then lead to relatively large income tax increases for the family as a whole.[10] In sum, when the second adult in a couple family starts earning, these earnings first off-set the value of the tax allowance and lead to a (often equivalent) loss of benefit income (*e.g.* housing benefit). As a result, such income-tested benefits, family-based tax credits and transferable tax allowances introduce a bias towards single-earner couples in tax/benefit systems (*e.g.* Dingeldey, 2001), and to understand tax incentives and their implications for employment

Table 4.5. **Tax/benefit systems often favour dual earnership among couple families**

Average payments to governments as a percentage of gross earnings, at different earning distributions for a couple with two children aged four and six with family income equal to 133% of average earnings, 2000-03

Earnings level (first earner-second earner)	Total tax (incl. social security contribution) payments to government less family benefits		
	133-0 (%)	100-33 (%)	67-67 (%)
Australia	19.9	16.2	15.4
Austria	18.5	13.4	10.2
Canada, province of Québec	20.3	18.8	17.1
Denmark	37.2	35.6	35.6
Finland	27.6	21.9	19.4
Ireland	3.6	2.5	1.2
Japan	13.6	13.6	13.6
Netherlands	23.5	23.6	21.4
New Zealand	23.7	19.7	18.9
Portugal	9.1	6.1	5.9
Sweden	33.4	29.5	28.7
Switzerland			
Canton Ticino	8.0	6.4	7.0
Canton Vaud	13.3	11.5	12.1
Canton Zürich	12.1	10.4	11.0
United Kingdom	19.4	12.9	8.5

Source: OECD Babies and Bosses reviews, various issues.

patterns, it is necessary to look beyond a simplistic characterisation of tax systems as "individual" or "joint".

Table 4.5 illustrates how tax/benefit systems may affect the distribution of earnings among spouses in a couple family (results will be different at different levels of household income). It looks at how couple families with an income of 133% of average earnings may best allocate earnings among themselves. Three alternatives are considered: i) the single breadwinner (first earner with 133% of average earnings); ii) the dominant breadwinner (first earner with average earnings, second earner with one-third of average earnings); and iii) "equal partnerships" where both spouses earn the same. In each of these three cases, the table reports how much net transfers (the difference between taxes paid and family benefits received) would be from the household to the government. For example, in 2000, at 133% of average earnings net transfers for an Australian single breadwinner family amounted to about 20% of gross earnings, while this was 15% for couples in which both partners had the same level of earnings. In sum, at the selected level of earnings, the Australian tax/benefit system favours a dual-earnership split of earning responsibilities rather than a single-breadwinner approach.

Regardless of the nature of the tax system (joint assessment as in different cantons in Switzerland, splitting the tax base in Portugal, and individual assessment in the other countries presented in Table 4.5), single-breadwinner families pay more net tax than do "equal partnership" families (with "dominant earner families" paying slightly less than "equal partnership" couples in Switzerland only). Table 4.5 shows that tax/benefit systems are virtually neutral between dual and single-earner couple families in Ireland, Japan and the Netherlands (at least when part-time earnings are small); have a small but significant bias towards dual-earner families in most countries, and are most favourable to dual-earner families in Austria and Finland (both being countries which encourage one parent to stay at home when children are very young) and the United Kingdom.

4.3. Policies to help sole parents to combine work and care commitments

In the absence of a partner with whom caring and earnings responsibilities can be shared, sole parents face particular challenges when trying to combine work and family commitments. In order to prevent children in sole-parent families growing up in poverty, it is essential that the sole parent can earn a living. However, in many countries employment rates for sole parents are well below those of mothers generally, and, children in sole-parent families are more likely to grow up in poverty which hampers child development.

What type of policy helps sole-parent families balance work and care commitments? The next sections consider the general policy stance towards sole parents, their financial incentives to work, and review recent policy experiences in countries where sole-parent employment rates are relatively low.

4.3.1. The policy stance towards sole parents on income support

While recent years have seen falling levels of joblessness among families with children, improvements have been relatively modest for sole-parent families. Non-employment among sole parents ranges from around 25% in Austria, Portugal and Nordic countries to close to 50% in Australia, Ireland, the Netherlands, New Zealand and the United Kingdom.

The general policy approach towards sole parents in social protection policy is critical in determining the extent of benefit dependency among this client group. At first sight, it might appear paradoxical that in Austria, Iceland, Finland, Denmark, Norway and Sweden – all countries where financial incentives to work are not very strong (see below) – sole-parent employment rates are nevertheless relatively high. This is because the policy approach towards sole parents is the same as for any other parent. Parents who are no longer entitled to parental leave (Denmark and Sweden) or home care or childrearing allowance (Austria, Finland and Norway) are work-tested for benefit receipt (either unemployment insurance or social assistance). This policy stance towards sole parents is made possible by comprehensive childcare systems that provide formal care support when leave benefits expire (around 9 to 17 months in Iceland, Denmark and Sweden; around age three in Austria, Finland and Norway – see Chapters 5 and 6). In addition, in Nordic countries these are supported by a comprehensive system of employment supports including job-matching, training and other skill-upgrading programmes, that are made available to clients from an early stage of benefit receipt. In 2004, public spending on active labour market policies (not including those targeted at the disabled) in Denmark was 1.3% of GDP. In Nordic countries, comprehensive employment and childcare support lets parents on income support focus on their labour market (re-)integration even when they are caring for a young child.

Some other countries have specific benefits arrangements for sole parents. Employment rates of sole parents in these countries are often low, and many sole parents are in receipt of income support.[11] In Australia, Ireland, New Zealand and the United Kingdom, the entitlement to income support plays a key role in explaining low employment levels. In these countries benefit durations are not limited and parents can receive benefits without a work test until their youngest child is a teenager (Table 4.6). The signal being given to sole parents on income support has been that dependency is expected. Little effort was made in the past to tell sole parents that work is desirable and beneficial to the family as a whole.

4.3.2. Financial incentives to work

In most OECD countries financial incentives to work are stronger for sole parents than for potential primary earners in couple families on social assistance (who face even higher AETRs when moving of benefit into work). However, AETRs for sole parents are often considerably higher than for secondary earners in couple families (compare Table 4.7 with Table 4.3).

Relative to two-thirds of average earnings, benefits tend to be highest in Denmark, Norway and the city of Zürich in Switzerland, while in the vast majority of OECD countries net payment rates are in the range of 60 to 80% of the reference wage of two-thirds of average earnings. Income support to sole parents is below this level in Canada (the province of Ontario), Hungary, Korea, Poland, the Slovak Republic, Spain and the United States. Sole parents in countries without a uniform social assistance system (Greece and Italy) by definition have very strong financial incentives to work full-time in a job at two-thirds of average earning. In Denmark, Norway and the city of Zürich in Switzerland, financial incentives to work for sole parents are relatively weak.

Table 4.6. **Sole parents in Australia, Ireland, New Zealand and the United Kingdom can potentially remain on benefit for a long period of time**

Work tests for sole parents, selected countries, 2005-06

No work test	Work test	
	Independent of child age	Dependent on child age *(age limit in years)*
Portugal	Belgium[1] *(discretion)*	Ireland *(18 or 22 if child in full-time education)*
Spain	Denmark *(subject to childcare)*	New Zealand[3] *(18)*
	Finland	United Kingdom[4] *(16)*
	Japan *(discretion)*	Australia[5] *(16/7)*
	Netherlands[2]	Luxembourg *(6)*
	Sweden	Canada[6] *(0.5-6)*
		Czech Republic *(4)*
		Austria *(about 3)*
		France *(3)*
		Germany *(3)*
		Norway *(3)*
		Switzerland *(3)*
		United States[7] *(0.25-1)*

1. All social assistance beneficiaries, including single mothers, are in principle required to be looking for work and to be ready to take up employment. However, in the case of sole parents with young children, this requirement is not enforced very strongly.

2. Under national guidelines until 2004, municipalities did not require availability for work when the youngest child was aged less than five. Since 2004, municipalities are free to determine work-availability requirements for all clients in view of individual circumstances.

3. Clients are required to attend planning meetings and preparing a Personal Development and Employment Plan that covers goals for the future and steps to reach those goals.

4. Clients are required to attend a Work Focused Interview with a Personal Adviser on application for Income Support and at intervals during receipt of it.

5. Until 2006, parenting payment recipients with a youngest child aged less than six years had no participation requirement; those with a youngest child aged 6 to 12 years were required to attend an annual Personal Adviser interview; those with a youngest child aged 13-15 years had to undertake 150 hours of approved activities each 26 weeks. From 30 June 2006, single parents still receiving the parenting payment when their youngest child turns seven must seek at least part-time work; sole parents with children aged 8 and more making a new benefit application will instead qualify for unemployment benefit (Newstart) with a similar work requirement. There are some exemptions for large families and parents with a child with a disability ("Changes to Parenting Payment from 1 July 2006", *www.centrelink.gov.au/internet/internet.nsf/services/welfare_parents.htm*).

6. Participation requirements depending on the age of the youngest child are as follows: Alberta from six months; British Columbia from three years; Saskatchewan two years; Manitoba six years; New Brunswick, Prince Edward Island, Nova Scotia and Yukon, no formal requirements; Ontario, school age; Quebec five years; Newfoundland and Labrador two years; Northwest Territories and Nunavut under three years, or under six years if two or more children.

7. Varies from State to State. Some States have no exemption. The maximum age exception is four years, but the majority of States have exceptions which are between three months and 12 months (though often this will be on a lifetime basis).

Source: Adapted from Bradshaw and Finch (2002).

Table 4.7. **Financial incentives to work for sole parents are relatively weak in Denmark, Norway and Switzerland (city of Zürich), 2004**

	Net replacement rate		Average effective tax rate		Marginal effective tax rate		
	At 2/3 of AW	At AW	0 >> 2/3 of AW	0 >> AW	1/2 of AW >> AW	1/3 of AW >> 2/3 of AW	2/3 of AW >> AW
Australia	64	55	55	55	61	71	55
Austria	69	53	71	62	44	44	44
Belgium	69	54	71	66	58	59	56
Canada	56	49	48	53	59	41	64
Czech Republic	71	58	69	64	57	38	54
Denmark	85	72	85	77	59	75	61
Finland	67	57	64	62	61	62	58
France	71	49	75	58	35	57	24
Germany	72	56	78	70	52	69	54
Greece	3	2	16	19	23	16	26
Hungary	48	39	48	50	62	45	55
Iceland	77	63	74	65	48	48	48
Ireland	68	59	25	36	72	61	59
Italy	0	0	−4	16	33	−6	55
Japan	75	56	76	62	40	86	20
Korea	57	39	60	44	12	48	12
Luxembourg	71	52	69	54	20	60	24
Netherlands	76	56	78	65	51	57	38
New Zealand	79	64	78	71	79	86	70
Norway	87	64	88	71	36	69	36
Poland	70	56	75	69	88	93	57
Portugal	55	41	58	50	29	34	33
Slovak Republic	47	35	35	33	29	23	29
Spain	49	35	52	43	23	16	24
Sweden	67	54	66	61	52	52	49
Switzerland	91	67	92	73	45	84	34
United Kingdom	71	61	70	68	71	84	62
United States	45	36	39	41	47	44	45

Note: Social assistance and any other means-tested benefits are assumed to be available subject to the relevant income conditions. Children are aged four and six and neither childcare benefits nor childcare costs are considered. In-work benefits that depend on a transition from unemployment into work are not accounted for in the calculation of METRs presented here, since these concern "within-employment transitions" only.
Source: OECD Tax/Benefit Models.

4.3.3. Policy experiences and evidence on reform effects

The drawback of the comprehensive support provided in Nordic countries is that employment supports and (in particular) childcare support is expensive (Chapter 6). In an attempt to keep costs down, many countries have sought to target formal childcare support on low-income families, including sole parents. Apart from this, the policy package which most countries have been using in order to support lone parents includes an emphasis on strengthening financial incentives to work, introducing elements of compulsion into benefit receipt, and a greater focus on re-employment in benefit delivery.

Increasing financial incentives to work have sometimes had a substantial effect on the employment rates of lone parents. For example, Canada (see also Box 4.2) is one of the few OECD countries which experienced a huge reduction in the number of social assistance recipients (including many sole parents): the proportion of the Canadian population in receipt of social assistance support halved from 10.8% at its peak in 1994 to 5.5% in 2003. Sole-parent employment rates increased from 59% in 1996 to 68% in 2001, and this increase can be related to improved economic conditions as well as a tightening in the generosity of the provincial social assistance programmes through narrowing eligibility criteria and curtailing payment rates, often through non-indexation (OECD, 1999c; and Sceviour and Finnie, 2004).[12]

Rather than cutting benefits, an alternative approach to improving work incentives involves paying cash benefits to low-wage employees. A number of countries have introduced such wage supplements to strengthen work incentives for the population as a whole, but in practice it is often sole parents in particular who have benefited (Box 4.1). In the United States, one of the first countries to introduce this type of benefit, the Earned Income Tax Credit (EITC) is now the largest anti-poverty programme at the national level. In other countries (Ireland, the United Kingdom and, more recently, France, the Netherlands and New Zealand), employment-conditional benefits are operated alongside comprehensive "safety-net" benefits seeking to ensure acceptable living standards for workless households.

In-work benefits will partly offset the adverse work incentives associated with the loss of out-of-work benefits. However, their effectiveness at increasing employment depends on the specific structure of labour markets and the resources governments are willing to commit to this type of measure (except for the United States and the United Kingdom, the size of in-work benefits is still very small compared to other social transfers; a detailed analysis of relevant policy rules in OECD countries is in OECD, 2007f).

OECD (2004a) recommended that an employment-conditional benefit be introduced in Portugal, but not in order to increase employment rates; in Portugal, the sole-parent employment rate is around 80% and almost nine out of ten sole parents in work are employed on a full-time basis. Benefit income is low (Table 4.7) and many sole parents simply cannot afford to stay out of work. However, earnings are not high either, and in-work poverty is a key challenge in Portugal. The introduction of an employment-conditional

Box 4.2. **The Canadian Self-sufficiency Project**

Arguably, one of the most cited research projects looking at incentives to work for sole parents is the Canada Self-sufficiency Project (SSP). This federally funded research project involved experimental studies over a ten-year period to establish the effects of financial incentive structures on the labour market behaviour of sole parents in receipt of social assistance.

SSP was launched in 1992 and included three main studies: the Recipient SSP study involving about 6 000 sole parents on social assistance in the provinces of New Brunswick and British Columbia who had been on social assistance for at least a year but often longer (Michalopoulos *et al.*, 2002); the SSP Plus study, involving 600 sole parents in New Brunswick (Lei and Michalopoulos, 2001); and, the "Applicant study" concerning 3 300 sole-parent claimants of social assistance in the province of British Columbia who had not been in receipt of social assistance six months prior to their most recent claim (Ford *et al.*, 2003). In all three studies half of the selected sole parents were randomly assigned to a programme group and the other half to a control group, with those in the programme group becoming eligible for generous earnings supplements for up to 36 months provided they did not claim social assistance and worked full time (on average at least 30 hours per week during the reference month). The SSP findings included:

- Financial incentive structures affect the speed with which sole parents leave welfare rolls: sole parents who were long-term social assistance claimants (the "recipient study") left welfare rolls for full-time employment much faster if they had access to generous earnings supplements, with the biggest effect immediately after the close of the one-year period limit for finding full-time employment. However, the effect was *temporary*: six years after random assignment, employment rates (full-time) among clients with and without access to earnings supplements were close to 30%.

- Financial incentives had the largest effect on clients with recent employment experience: 45% of the clients in the "applicants study" who were eligible for the earnings supplement were in full-time employment six years upon random assignment (compared to 30% for the "recipient group" while this was 41% for those without earnings supplements. A design feature of this "applicant study" was that clients had to wait for 12 months before becoming eligible for the earnings supplement. This delayed exits for those still on social assistance after three months of benefit receipt; with the largest employment effect on those with earnings supplement just two years following the random assignment.

Making work pay policies can thus limit benefit dependency and reduce the poverty risk for sole parents and their children. The cost to public budgets of introducing such policies is limited when targeted at clients with relatively recent work history: increased tax revenue and lower transfer payments covers about 90% of the total cost, whereas only one-third of programme costs are covered when clients have a longer history of social assistance receipt.

refundable tax credit is one option to increase after-tax income of low-income families and reduce child poverty, and as in Denmark, Ireland, France and Spain, the introduction of such a policy would create an aggregate welfare gain (Immervoll et al., 2005, in a study on EU15 countries found that efficiency losses of introducing in-work benefits would also be very small in Austria, Greece, Luxembourg, the Netherlands and the United Kingdom).

In the four English-speaking countries where sole-parent employment rates are traditionally low, and poverty rates have been high, policy reform over the last decade has substantially increased financial support for low-income families. In Ireland, the value of universal child benefit trebled between 1997 and 2003, while income-tested cash/tax family support in Australia increased substantially in the period 1999-2003. In New Zealand, the "Working For Families" package was introduced in 2004 to address poverty concerns and strengthen work incentives (Box 4.3).

There is an extensive body of research in the United Kingdom, which shows the effect policy changes since 1997 have had on employment and poverty outcomes (Bennett and Millar, 2005). Reforms have increased the redistribution of resources among households without children to families and among families themselves: the incomes of the poorest fifth of families have increased by more than 20% (Brewer and Shephard, 2004). Reduced joblessness and increased child benefit and employment-conditional tax credits (Sutherland et al., 2003) have reduced child poverty, especially among sole-parent families: 57% of low-paid sole mothers working 16 hours or more avoid poverty through benefit receipts, including in-work benefits and such tax credits lift 40% of these sole-parent families above the poverty line (Millar and Gardiner, 2004).

The economies of Australia, Ireland, New Zealand and the United Kingdom have all experienced strong economic growth since the late 1990s and this has led to an increase in sole-parent employment (Table 4.8). The increase in employment among sole parents in Ireland has, however, come to a halt in the new millennium, despite strong ongoing growth of the Irish economy, as reducing the expectation of long-term benefit-recipiency of "One Parent Family Payment" in Ireland has proven to be difficult. By contrast, sole parents in Australia, New Zealand and the United Kingdom have been able to strengthen their position on the labour market. Economic growth has been important in increasing sole-parent employment rates, but policy reform may also have played a role although econometric evidence on the importance of policy reform is not (yet) available for Australia and New Zealand (see Box 4.3 for New Zealand; for Australia, see below). OECD (2005a) shows that the body of evidence finds that policy reform since 1997 in the United Kingdom has contributed to the employment incidence among sole parents rising from 45% in 1997 to 57% in 2006 (NS, 2006). Employment growth was concentrated

Box 4.3. **Policy reform in New Zealand**

From October 2004 to April 2007, the New Zealand government rolled out the Working For Families (WFF) assistance package, which by the time of its full implementation in 2007 costs about NZD 1.1 billion per annum (or USD 0.8 billion). Apart from simplifying the benefit system and achieving more consistency between tax and benefit authorities, the package essentially has four components. First, maximum *Family Tax Credit* rates (the main payment per child, which used to be known as "Family Support") increased by around 75% until 2007 and will have become available to more families (partly because the abatement threshold was increased from NZD 20 000 to NZD 27 500). Second, working parents get an *In-Work Family Tax Credit* (which is paid per family) that replaced and pays more than the previous Child Tax Credit (which was paid per child). Third, *accommodation supplement* is available to more working people, and many people are entitled to more assistance. Fourth, *childcare subsidy* and *out-of-school-hours care subsidy* payment rates increased in 2005, 2006 and 2007), and by raising eligibility thresholds they are potentially available to 70% of families with dependent children.

The increase in Family Tax Credit and the new In-Work Family Tax Credit, is estimated to add up to NZD 1 billion by 2007, which is roughly 90% of the costs of the entire "Working for Families" package, whereas the costs of the childcare subsidy component are estimated at NZD 35 million or 3% of the package. One consequence of the reform is that as of 2007 for a family with two children, family benefits will cut out at around 150% of average earnings compared to roughly 100% prior to reform. Childcare subsidies are granted up to about 140% of average earnings compared to 93% in 2003.

It is estimated that the introduction of the Working for Families package may reduce child poverty by as much as 70% when measured against a 50% of median equivalised household income threshold (Perry, 2004). Estimates of effects on the financial incentive structure (and employment rates) are more ambiguous. The introduction of the WFF package has improved the financial incentive structure for sole parents, and had a small but positive effect on labour supply; about 2% of sole parents currently on income support; Fitzgerald and Maloney (2007) also find that reform had a positive effect on employment among sole mothers. The introduction of Working For Families may have discouraged labour supply among secondary earners in couple families (Dwyer, 2005; and OECD, 2005c). However, in a preliminary assessment, Fitzgerald and Maloney (2007) suggest that reform probably had a small positive effect on employment among partnered mothers.

among sole mothers with children of pre-school age, while reform had essentially no effect on employment among sole mothers with multiple older children (Francesconi and van der Klaauw, 2007). However, it is much more

Table 4.8. **Over the last ten years employment among sole parents has grown in Australia, Ireland, New Zealand and the United Kingdom from a low base**

Sole-parent employment rates

	1997	2001	2006
Australia	. .	44.2	52.3
Ireland	35.1	45.1	45.8
New Zealand	39.7	49.9	55.2
United Kingdom	45.0	51.3	56.5

Note and source: Australia, annualised monthly data from Australian Bureau of Statistics, series 6224.0.55.001; Central Statistics Office Ireland, annualised quarterly data from the quarterly national household survey, except for quarter four 1997; New Zealand, annualised quarterly data from Statistics New Zealand, Household labour Force Survey, and the United Kingdom: 1997 data from OECD (2005a) and quarterly data from Office of National Statistics (2006), "Work and Worklessness among Households", 28 July.

difficult to find a positive impact of in-work benefits on employment in couple families; if there is an upward effect on employment in couple families, it concerns fathers rather than mothers (Brewer *et al.*, 2003).

Mutual obligations

Improving financial incentives to work are one tool in the kit towards reduced long-term benefit dependency and poverty among sole parents and their children. Another one is work-focussed benefit delivery, through intensive case-management, training programmes, work-experience placements, job-search assistance and childcare support. As said above, a comprehensive system of childcare and employment in Nordic countries facilitate policy approach towards sole parents that expects them to go back to work at a relatively early stage of the child's life, just as other parents on income support (Table 4.7). In other countries, like Australia, Ireland, New Zealand and the United Kingdom, this is not so. Policy makers in these four countries are at different stages of reform towards strengthening reciprocity in benefit receipt for sole parents with young children as a tool of reducing expectations on long-term benefit receipt and enhancing early labour market re-integration.

In Ireland, where recent economic growth has been stronger than anywhere else in the OECD area, this has not led to an equivalent reduction of benefit dependency on "One Parent Family Payment". A government discussion paper (Government of Ireland, 2006) has raised the possibility of a job-search requirement for all those whose youngest child is at least five years of age, and cessation of entitlements to a new parental allowance after the youngest child reaches a specific age (*e.g.* 7 or 12, rather than 18 or 22; Table 4.7). In addition, there are plans to move towards more systemic engagement of benefit clients, providing them with greater access to employment, training and childcare supports (Government of Ireland, 2006). Such a comprehensive and integrated approach is currently absent, and without it, introducing work-testing and reducing duration of benefit entitlements are much less likely to be effective.

In New Zealand work-test requirements for sole parents on "Domestic Purposes Benefit" were abolished in 2003, only four years after they were introduced. Benefit reform in 1999 had introduced work-testing, a full-time requirement for sole parents with a child aged 14 and over, and a part-time work test for those with a child aged 6-13, as well as measures strengthening incentives to work, and increased funding for employment support. However, while the new work tests (successfully) pushed sole parents off benefit, the simultaneous increase in policy support (for example, extending generosity of the Childcare Subsidy, introduction of OSCAR-services) was not enough to address barriers to childcare participation and lack of labour market skills on a comprehensive basis.

Since 2002, the New Zealand government has taken various initiatives "to fulfil its side of the bargain", and expanded employment supports (*e.g.* the Jobs Jolt initiative), childcare and other service support for sole parents on benefit. With benefit delivery focused on *work expectations*, each client has a *Personal Development and Employment Plan* (PDEP), the nature of which often changes with the age of clients and children (plans for clients with young children tend to focus on education and training, while plans for clients with older children focus more on employment). Case management is also more intensive than before. Since October 2002, caseloads have been reduced from around 250 clients per counsellor to 183 in 2006. However, this is still relatively high: for employment counselling to be effective on a comprehensive scale and evidence gathered by the OECD secretariat suggests caseloads should be reduced to around one staff member to 100 to 125 clients. In addition, work underway on the restructuring of the benefit system, will further increase the focus on work expectations, provide more support for helping parents to find care solutions (care-matching), assist those who wish to take up small hours of work while on benefit, and help case managers focus on achieving outcomes rather than determining complex benefit entitlements. With increased financial, childcare and employment supports, and facilitated by a strong economic environment, a re-introduction of the work-test has become an option to further strengthen employment incentives and promote self-sufficiency among sole-parents with children in primary school.

Apart from tax credits to make work attractive, the UK version of a comprehensive strategy promoting autonomy among sole parents includes mandatory *Work-Focussed Interviews, the New Deal for Lone Parents* (based on voluntary participation and includes job-search and childcare assistance) and fully integrated benefit and employment support services through Jobcentre Plus, the public employment service provider. In pilot areas, there are *Work-Related Activity Premiums* for sole parents whose youngest child is 11 or over, but as the Department for Work and Pension explicitly states on its website, "any activity to prepare for work remains voluntary". As a potential 11 years outside the labour force does not enhance individual employment chances and profiles, there is a case for introducing compulsory intervention at an earlier stage (Freud, 2007). Policy reform proposals include introducing a work-test for parents on income support when their youngest child is twelve in October 2008 and then seven from October 2010 onwards when sufficient childcare support should be available.

In contrast to experiences in Ireland, New Zealand and the United Kingdom, the Australian government has moved to reduce benefit dependency and the duration of benefit-recipiency by introducing a work-test for parents whose children attend primary school in July 2006 (Box 4.4). Policy reform, announced in July 2005 is intended to make returning to work the "norm" for sole parents, and the message has not missed its effect on (potential) clients. It is difficult to disentangle reform effects from cyclical effects (unemployment in Australia is now at its lowest level in more than 30 years, with projections remaining upbeat); but in any case the sole-parent employment rate increased to on average an annual average by about 6 percentage points from July 2005 to 54.2 in July 2007 (ABS, 2007).

Box 4.4. **Reforming parenting payment in Australia, 2006**

Since 1 July 2006, the Australian government has made significant changes to the income support rules to encourage and support people on Parenting Payment in finding a job:

- Parents on Parenting Payment *before* 1 July 2006 continue to receive their payment until their youngest child turns 16. From 1 July 2007 or when their youngest child turns seven, whichever is later, they will be required to meet part-time participation requirements.

- Principal carers who have gone on to Parenting Payment (partnered) *since* 1 July 2006 receive the payment until their youngest child turns six; this is eight years for a sole parent on Parenting Payment. After that, they will need to apply for another income support payment (typically Newstart Allowance, the unemployment benefit). Both recipients of partnered and single Parenting Payment will be required to meet part-time participation requirements, once their youngest child turns six.

Part-time participation requirements include: looking for a part-time job of at least 15 hours a week, or participate in employment services. There are exemptions in special circumstances, and these include having a large family (four or more children aged under 16). Parents are not expected to take a job offer if there is no suitable childcare, or if they have to travel more than sixty minutes to get to work.

BABIES AND BOSSES: RECONCILING WORK AND FAMILY LIFE – ISBN 978-92-64-03244-6 – © OECD 2007

Box 4.4. **Reforming parenting payment in Australia, 2006** (*cont.*)

Parents are eligible for the full range of Job Network (employment) services, including a new Employment Preparation service. Job Network members (employment service providers) take account of parents' cultural backgrounds, their individual needs, and the available job opportunities. Parents with no recent workforce experience, and those with recent work-experience who are still unemployed after three months have access to Employment Preparation. Parents who are not directly employable will get immediate access to Intensive Support customised assistance.

A principal carer parent does not have to accept or continue in a job if no appropriate care and supervision is available for their child/ren (including the time taken to travel to and from work); travel time to or from the person's home to the place of work, via the place of childcare, exceeds 60 minutes; the cost of travel to and from work exceeds 10% of the gross wage; they are not at least USD 20 per week better off after the costs of employment are taken into account, compared to not working. Penalties do not apply to people who cannot access an employment service because they live in a remote area.

As part of the 2006-07 budget, the Australian government lifted a previously imposed cap on out-of-school-hours and family day-care places. This allows existing and new childcare providers to expand childcare places to meet demand. The Australian government has also provided additional funding for Jobs, Education and Training (JET) childcare, which provides extra help with the cost of approved childcare for eligible parents undertaking activities such as job search, work, study or rehabilitation to help them enter or re-enter the workforce. Parents receiving this assistance make a small co-payment of 10 cents per child per hour towards the cost of their childcare.

The number of sole-parent clients of Parenting Payment in Australia has been trending down since mid-2005. Overall, the number of recipients has gone down from around 460 000 in early 2005, to just over 405 000 in March 2007. There have been declines in beneficiary numbers in the past, but a decline of more than 10% of the stock is unprecedented in recent history.

As Chart 3.7 showed, the increasing sole-parent employment rates in Australia, New Zealand and the United Kingdom are now comparable to levels in the Netherlands where since the mid-1990s sole parents on means-tested income support are required to engage in job-search when their youngest child is five years of age. However, local welfare authorities often grant job-search dispensations and in 2001 only 19% of all sole parents on income-support had a job-search requirement. In addition to the exemption for sole parents with very young children, many others had obtained exemptions granted by local authorities, or *de facto* exemptions for clients facing medical or psychological issues (Algemene Rekenkamer, 2003). Social assistance reform in 2004 aimed to limit these exemptions from job-search, increase support for labour market re-integration (subsidised childcare for all clients) and stimulate outflows of clients (Algemene Rekenkamer, 2005). From January 2006 to February 2007, the number of social assistance recipients declined by 10% to just below 300 000 recipients (CBS, 2007), but it is unclear to what extend the decline is related to fewer job-search exemptions being awarded by municipal authorities, successful labour market integration of sole parents on income support, and/or the result of the economic upswing.

The Dutch experience shows that changes in the obligations placed on benefit recipients to look for work (as introduced in the mid-1990s and strengthened in 2004) have to be backed up by ample labour market and childcare support, as well as effective policing of job-search requirements. In other words, reform needs to increase obligations on *both* the public authorities to provide help *and* the individual to take advantage of that help. As so many clients were exempted from job-search requirements, the employment outcomes for sole parents in the Netherlands have become comparable with outcomes in Australia, New Zealand and the United Kingdom.

4.4. Conclusions

There are marked differences in the size of public welfare states across the OECD. Some countries pursue a universal comprehensive approach in social protection, and the Nordic countries in particular are successful at providing a continuum of supports for working families throughout childhood. Policy in all these countries, and Hungary, has been to provide a consistent and logical system of supports, but whereas Denmark and Sweden invest more in care and early education services for very young children, Finland, Norway and Hungary focus public resources on supporting parents, usually mothers, providing home care for very young children. This risks weakening the labour market position of women relative to men, and barriers to labour market fulfilment contribute to downward pressure on birth rates.

Rather than building a universal system of supports, most countries try to restrict spending (and the burden of taxation) by focusing public support more on some areas of social policy than others and/or by targeting resources at low-income families more generally. Such income-tested benefit systems have to be designed carefully, as there is always a risk that when (additional) earnings are made, real income increases little as simultaneously benefit income is withdrawn at an (almost) equivalent rate.

Financial incentives to work matter. Differences in tax/benefit systems affect parental labour market decisions, and, if they decide to work, whether they do so on a part-time or full-time basis. The majority of OECD countries now have individualised tax systems, but nearly all OECD countries either have some form of tax relief for non-employed spouses or some form of family assistance that aggregates incomes of spouses to determine levels of assistance. These arrangements potentially produce weak financial incentives to work (more) for (potential) second earners, as the effective marginal tax rate of the second earner is close to that of the primary earner.

Important as it may be, the financial incentive structure is not the only driver of individual labour market participation decisions. The general policy approach towards parents on income support crucially determines to what extent such families, among which are many sole-parent families, rely on benefit support.

It is in the long-term interest of all families, including sole-parent families, to engage in paid work, as this is the most effective way of reducing the risk of family poverty, enhancing child development, and generally giving children the best possible start in life. Therefore, the policy approach towards sole parents on income support in Nordic countries is the same as for any other parent: parents who are no longer entitled to paid parental leave (or home-care payments) are work-tested for benefit receipt. This requires active and early interventions towards labour market re-integration of (sole) parents on income support, involving investment in childcare, in-work benefits to make work pay, and employment supports (e.g. intensive case-management and counselling, training programmes, and work-experience placements).

Generally, OECD countries require sole parents on income support to look for work when children are of pre-school or primary school age, but in a few countries, Australia, Ireland, New Zealand and the United Kingdom, there is no work-test until the youngest child is 12, 16 or even older. This is supposed to "protect" sole parents from having to work when they "should" be looking after their children. However, the effect has been that sole-parent employment rates in Australia, Ireland, New Zealand and the United Kingdom are relatively low, at 45 to 55% compared to around 70 to 80% in the Nordic countries. The result is poverty, which damages the future life-chances of children.

In Ireland, sole parenthood is becoming an increasingly common cause of poverty, but policy reform to reverse this trend seems hard to implement. In Australia, New Zealand and the UK policy has undertaken steps towards greater labour force attachment of parents on income support. Since 1997, the United Kingdom has successively increased both the generosity of child payments and in-work benefits and childcare supports, and evidence suggests that policy reform since 1997 has increased the employment incidence among sole parents by about 4 to 7 percentage points. The introduction of Working for Families in New Zealand may also have had a small upward effect on sole parent employment rates. Australia has recently moved towards the introduction of a part-time work-test for new clients of "Parenting Payment", while simultaneously extending out-of-school-hours care support, so as to give sole parents realistic work options. This reform reflects a move towards Nordic policy practices, providing employment and care support, and requiring all benefit recipients, including sole parents to take advantage of the opportunities open to them. A system of mutual obligations should be embraced and enforced including the threat of moderate benefit sanctions if benefit recipients do not take active steps to find work or improve their employability.

Notes

1. OECD (2003b) contains an overview of standard tax reliefs related to marital status and dependent children; OECD (2007f) includes an overview of family benefits and their characteristics.

2. In most OECD countries, the combination of tax reductions and cash benefits reduces the direct tax burden on couple families with two children at average earnings by between 10 and 20% (OECD, 2007f), although there are notable outliers such as Japan (5%) and Luxembourg (25%).

3. In the Canadian province of Québec which models its policy on Scandinavian countries (Roy and Bernier, 2007), there remain gaps in the otherwise by North-American standards very extensive public childcare and out-of-school-hours care policies (OECD, 2005a).

4. In general, the proportion of financial support to families will decline as earnings increase. However, as in-work benefits are phased in, and income-support payments are not reduced at the same rate as net earnings increase, the proportion of family assistance can actually increase with earnings over parts of the (lower end) of the earnings distribution in some countries (Table 4.2).

5. Chapter 6 discusses the effect of childcare costs on the financial incentives structure. Information on work-related costs (*e.g.* travel, clothing), or the loss of household production because of participation in paid employment is not available on a cross-national basis and these items are therefore not reflected in the calculations.

6. Countries differ substantially in the safety nets they provide for workless households (OECD, 2007e). For example, the income situation of couples with two children on social assistance support in Greece, Italy, Hungary, Portugal, Spain and the United States (with data not being available for Korea, Mexico and Turkey) shows that minimum income benefits in these countries are not sufficient to lift family incomes to close to 40% of median household incomes (a low-level poverty threshold).

7. The indicators presented in this chapter are calculated using the OECD tax-benefit models and are based on assumptions and, thus, limitations (OECD, 2007e). All calculations relate to current income and therefore do not take into account any effects of the current employment status on future earnings or benefit levels. All incomes are before housing costs, childcare costs, or work-related outlays, such as clothing and travel expenditure. Indicators are computed for a particular set of individuals whose characteristics and circumstances, include ages (4 and 6 years for children and 40 years for adults), previous employment record (22 years), or housing costs (20% of average earnings).

8. Average effective tax rates for parents in couple families on unemployment benefit are frequently lower than their counterparts on social assistance benefit, as unemployment benefit programmes are more likely to include earnings disregards, whereas social assistance payments are more likely to be withdrawn on a "dollar for dollar" or "euro for euro" basis.

9. For the calculations on the tax/benefit position of families in Norway and Switzerland, use is made of the tax parameters of the unified Norwegian system and the tax system that applies to the city of Zürich (where tax is also paid to the canton of Zürich and the confederal authorities). Norwegian social assistance payment rates reflect the guidelines as applicable in the city of Oslo (in reality, caseworkers award payment rates on the merits of each individual case, OECD, 1999b), while social assistance payments in Zürich are set by the municipal authorities (OECD, 1999c).

10. Joint tax systems could incorporate measures that reduce the disincentives for second earners, as for example, via special "second-earner" allowances or exemptions. In recognition of second earners' fixed costs of work would contribute to a more equal tax treatment of families with different patterns of work at home and in the labour market.

11. Comprehensive information for recent years is not available, but around 2000 in Australia, New Zealand and Ireland more than two-thirds of sole-parent families were receiving income support benefits and more than half had transfers as their main source of income. In the United Kingdom, just over half the sole-parent population receive income support (and many others receive in-work benefits). Between 30 and 40% of sole parents receive income support benefits in Canada, Denmark, France, Hungary, the Netherlands, Norway and Sweden. Even in countries where sole parents have relatively high employment rates, they constitute a significant share of the population receiving social assistance, as for example, in Austria, Belgium, Japan, and Portugal (Bradshaw and Finch, 2002; Eydoux and Letablier, 2007; Kapsalis and Tourigny, 2002; and Puide, 2001).

12. Diverging trends in provincial social assistance receipt among different household types can also be related to differences in trends in payment rates to different client categories (Roy, 2004).

ISBN 978-92-64-03244-6
Babies and Bosses: Reconciling Work and Family Life
A Synthesis of Findings for OECD Countries
© OECD 2007

Chapter 5

Parental Leave to Care for Children

This chapter discusses child-related leave provision in OECD countries. It starts with a summary of different child-related leave programmes, and then considers their effects in view of public policy goals such as enhanced child development, greater labour supply and gender equity.

Some parents will want to care for their young children themselves regardless of other childcare options. Other parents will prefer to work, perhaps only part-time, or would prefer to do so if better labour market and childcare opportunities were available. Parental leave schemes give working parents an opportunity to care for their children themselves during the first period after childbirth, and thus co-determine parental labour market behaviour as well as the demand for (and also the supply of) childcare services for very young children (Chapter 6).

Most OECD countries provide for paid maternity leave around childbirth, and in most countries parental leave is subsequently available. However, in terms of eligibility criteria, duration and payment rates, there are marked differences in leave provisions across the OECD.

5.1. Parental leave policies are very different from one country to another

Across the OECD area, there are different types of child-related leave, which generally offer employment protection during absence from work to care for children, including maternity, pregnancy, paternity, birth and adoption leave, leave to care for children when they are ill, and, parental leave which is generally of longest duration. In addition, some countries have "home-care", or "childrearing" leaves and associated financial support, which are not necessarily tied to employment protection entitlements (Box 5.1). Sometimes workers may have access to term-time leave (leave of absence during school holidays), specific provisions such as leave for the child's first day of school, or may be able to save leave for later years. Portugal is the only country that provides grandparents living with their grandchildren access to financial support for 30 days under certain conditions. The Netherlands has developed its family leave framework to include unpaid leave (of six times weekly hours of work per annum) to provide palliative care for a parent, partner or child; and provides fiscal support for saving for income support during unpaid leave as taken over the life-cycle (SZW, 2006). Across the OECD, when leave is paid, benefits are usually included in taxable income.

In almost all OECD countries (except for Australia, and the United States)[1] there is statutory paid maternity leave, which is frequently remunerated at 100% of previous earnings or close to this level (for full details see Annex 5.A1; also see Moss and O'Brien, 2006, for a recent overview). In some states of the

Box 5.1. **Child-related leaves in OECD countries**

The five most common forms of child-related leave are:

Maternity leave (or pregnancy leave): Employment-protected leave of absence for employed women at around the time of childbirth, or adoption in some countries. The ILO convention on maternity leave stipulates the period of leave to be at least 14 weeks. In most countries beneficiaries may combine pre- with post-birth leave; in some countries a short period of pre-birth leave is compulsory as is a six- to ten-week leave period following birth. Almost all OECD countries provide for specific public income support payments that are tied to the maternity leave period.

Paternity leave: Employment-protected leave of absence for employed fathers at the time of childbirth. Paternity leave is not stipulated by an ILO convention. Periods of paternity leave are much shorter than for maternity leave, and are three weeks at maximum. Because of the short period of absence, workers on paternity leave often continue to receive full wage payments.

Parental leave: Employment-protected leave of absence for employed parents, which is often supplementary to specific maternity- and paternity-leave periods (as above), and usually, but not in all countries, follows the period of maternity leave (If there is no specified maternity leave, as in Australia, OECD, 2002a, a portion of parental leave is reserved for women, to ensure a period of physical convalescence and recovery after childbirth). Entitlement to the parental leave period is individual, while entitlement to public income support is often family-based, so that only one parent claims such support at any one time.

Home-care leaves: Leaves to care for children until they are about three years old. These leaves can be a variation of parental leaves, and payments are not restricted to parents with a prior work attachment. In Norway and Finland relevant income support payments are contingent on not using public day-care facilities. In general, payments are intended to supplement family income while one parent is at home or to purchase private care (see Box 5.3).

Short-term leave to care for sick children: Being able to care for a sick child is important to any working parent. In some countries there are legal entitlements, for example, in Norway and Sweden there is a statutory right to take off work to mind sick children, often, however, such provisions are covered in collective agreements. Arrangements are most generous in Sweden where parents are entitled to take 60 days per annum to care for sick children; the system is used excessively (about 20% of sick class taken) as for sick children under 12 no doctor's certificate is required (Engström *et al.*, 2007). In Denmark, parents are entitled to take one day off work; thereafter it is assumed that parents will be able to make other arrangements. Stipulations in collective agreements can take different forms, including allowing parents to take more days than the legal entitlement, top up income support to full wages, allowing the use of worker's sick-days to care for sick children. Often, however, arrangements are made on *ad hoc* and informal basis, so that the overall importance of short-term leave to mind sick children is unknown, but it seems difficult to overestimate its value to working families.

United States, mothers may have access to income support through Temporary Disability Insurance (and the State of California is included in Table 5.A1.1 to illustrate this). In Australia, there are maternity allowances (Table 5.A1.2) and income-tested family payments when a parent is not in paid employment as well as a substantial one-off payment at childbirth. In both countries, employers often provide paid leave; "top ups" of public leave payments are often provided by employers in other countries, and while practices differ across firms, sectors and countries, in many OECD countries these payments can be considerable.

Entitlement to maternity leave is often conditional on previous work experience on a continuous and full-time basis as an employee over a certain period (often for a year, see Table 5.A1.1). Exceptions include the Scandinavian countries (covering all mothers), the Netherlands (where some temporary and almost all part-time workers are covered) and Germany (where mothers in education and unemployment are covered).

While maternity leave with employment protection has been widespread in OECD countries for many years, paternity leave and parental leave are more recent developments. Legal entitlements to paternity leave exist in just over half the OECD countries, and while payment rates are at 100% in all but four of the OECD countries, duration is short (Chart 5.1, Panel B and Table 5.A1.3). Abstracting from periods of leave within general parental leave arrangements that are exclusively reserved for fathers, entitlements to paternity leave vary from three days or less in Austria, Greece, Ireland, Luxembourg, the Netherlands and Spain to ten days or more in Belgium, France, Poland (in a limited number of cases), the United Kingdom and the Nordic countries.

Parental leave is given in addition to maternity/paternity leave to allow parents to take care of an infant or young child. The entitlements depicted in Chart 5.1, Panel C (and the annex to this chapter) are not reserved for either the mother or father. For example, for Sweden the entitlement is for a one-year period, with the 60-day periods reserved for fathers and mothers within the parental leave legislation being reflected in Panels A and B, respectively. About three-quarters of OECD countries give parents the option to take leave of absence to care for children for at least half a year (and many others for up to one year (Chart 5.1, Panel C), so that in combination with maternity leave, mothers can provide personal care on a full-time basis for close to one year. By contrast, in the Czech Republic, France, Germany, Hungary, Poland, the Slovak Republic, and Spain, employment-protected leave to care for children can last up to three years. However, compared to maternity and paternity leaves, parental leave is often paid at low rates, if public income support is available at all (see below).

As parental leave is generally not granted for reasons of medical repose after childbirth, and as entitlements are often of relatively long duration, the design of arrangements often involves a degree of flexibility, enabling it to be

Chart 5.1. **Compared to maternity leave, income support during parental leave is limited**

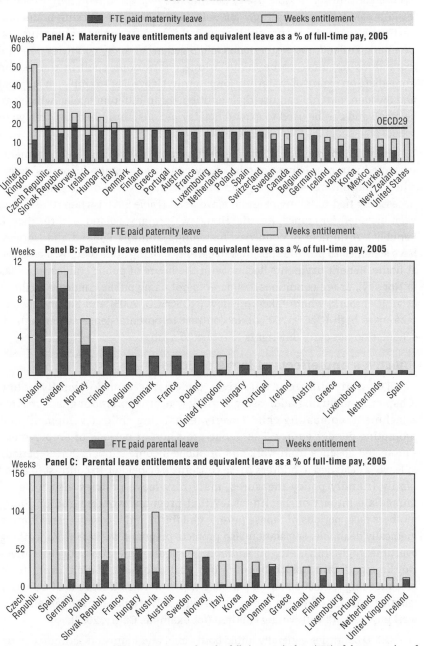

Note: The entitlement to paid leave is presented as the full-time equivalent (FTE) of the proportion of the duration of leave if it were paid at 100% of last earnings: FTE = Duration of leave in weeks * payment (as a percentage of average earnings) received by the claimant. Information in the chart and annex to this chapter refers to entitlements, benefits and payment rates applicable as of 1 January 2006.

Source: OECD Family database, *www.oecd.org/els/social/family*.

used in the way most beneficial to the family, and least intrusive to employers (whose consent for flexible use of parental leave is often required). Parental-leave programmes increasingly allow for adjustment of working hours and part-time use for parents with young children in for example, Austria, Denmark, Finland, the Netherlands and Sweden. In many countries parental leave does not have to be taken in one continuous spell in the period immediate on expiry of maternity (or paternity) leave. For example, in Portugal and Sweden, parents can use their entitlement in different spells (which can be small and can be used to extend holiday periods) until their children go to school (age six in Portugal; age seven in Sweden).

In addition (see Box 5.2 in the next section) to prolonged employment-protected parental leave periods, many countries provide income support when children are very young (up to about three years of age) that is not necessarily tied to taking parental leave itself (Table 5.A1.1 where these have been included for France, Austria, Hungary, Germany, Poland, and the Slovak Republic). A number of countries, including Denmark, Finland and Norway, have schemes to provide subsidies to parents looking after their own children at home. Benefit payments decline with the hours of public childcare use (as in Norway), or are conditional on parents not using public childcare facilities at all [Denmark, where take-up is low (NOSOSCO, 2005) and Finland, where take-up is high (OECD, 2005a)]. In contrast to parental-leave systems these schemes do not carry any rights to return to a job.

5.2. Objectives and effects of leave policies

There are different objectives underlying family-friendly policy (Chapter 1), including addressing fertility concerns, promoting labour force attachment, combating child poverty, enhancing child development and promoting gender equity. The public provision of periods of employment – protected absence from work and/or public income support during periods of leave is designed to address these concerns (see below). In contrast to other family-friendly policy measures, maternity-leave policies also have an immediate impact on health issues that pregnant workers and/or young mothers face: periods of repose prior to childbirth and recovery thereafter are medically desirable. Legislation also protects pregnant workers from working overtime, nightshifts, etc.[2] In addition, biomedical literature suggests there can be significant health benefits (for both mothers and children) from breastfeeding for a substantial period (e.g. six months). If leave is of a shorter length than this, there is a need to facilitate workplace arrangements for working mothers with young children (for example, Galtry, 2003).

OECD countries generally forbid both direct and indirect discrimination on the basis of family status, which encompasses parental-care responsibilities, protection for working mothers with children and legislation against discrimination of pregnant workers. Throughout the *Babies and Bosses* country reviews the issue of discrimination against pregnant workers was raised, but it proved impossible to be specific on the extent of such discrimination. In part this is a reporting problem: pregnant workers who feel harassed may have little desire to seek legal redress (because of costs, limited faith in the process or to avoid further deterioration of the employment relationship).

5.2.1. Child development

One of the key issues in the debate about parental leave (and formal childcare policy for that matter) is how to strike the right balance between parental employment and the provision of personal care for young children. Both parental employment and personal care are good for children. Parental employment reduces the risk of poverty and it thus reduces the likelihood of poverty and deprivation damaging child development. Personal parental care enhances child development, but when children start to learn from interaction with their peers, good-quality care provided by professional carers can also enhance child development. Thus, while maternal employment during infancy may have negative effects on children's cognitive development (*e.g.* Baum, 2003; and Ruhm, 2004), it is less clear as to what age of the child this may be so. These effects are likely to differ from one child to another, and maternal employment is not a uniform phenomenon either: from a child development perspective, regular work schedules are better than non-regular and/or very long working hours (Kamerman *et al.*, 2003).

Taking stock of the evidence (Box 5.2), it seems that child development is negatively affected when an infant does not receive full-time personal care (breast-feeding issues aside, this is not necessarily synonymous with maternal care) for at least the first 6 to 12 months of his/her life. Cognitive development of a child benefits from participation in good quality formal care

---

Box 5.2. **Parents at work and child development**

Child poverty rates are more than three times as high for jobless sole-parent families as they are for employed sole-parent families, and children in couple families where one parent is in work are almost three times more likely to be poor than children in couples where both parents work (Förster and Mira d'Ercole, 2005). Parental employment is key to reducing the risk of children growing up in poverty which has a significant negative effect on child development (Kamerman *et al.*, 2003). Policy faces particularly urgent challenges when, as for example in Portugal, there are concerns about young children who might sometimes be left unattended by parents who need to work to secure minimum levels of family income (Torres *et al.*, 2000).

Box 5.2. **Parents at work and child development** (cont.)

The evidence is ambiguous about as from what age onwards maternal employment has no negative effect on child development. For example, Ruhm (2004) finds for the United States that maternal employment when children are not yet two-three years old may negatively affect child development, but these findings may not be independent of the low level of quality of widely used low-cost (informal) care solutions. Baker et al. (2005), find that increased access to childcare in the Canadian province of Quebec and increased maternal employment may have contributed to worsened child outcomes and more parental stress, but the study does not measure the impact of increased family income on child development. Aughinbaugh and Gittleman (2003) find no evidence that maternal employment in the first three years of a child's life has a lasting effect on child development; it also does not affect the likelihood of young adolescents engaging in risky behaviour, as for example, alcohol abuse or using marijuana and/or other drugs.

For older children, access to pre-school/kindergarten is generally regarded as beneficial to child development, which underlies, for example, the provision of free pre-school on a part-time basis in the province of Québec and the United Kingdom (Ermish and Francesconi, 2001; and Lefebvre and Merrigan, 2002). Gregg and Washbrook (2003) estimated for Avon in England that full-time maternal employment in the first 18 months of the child's life may have a small negative effect on children's cognitive development, but only if care arrangements exclusively concern unpaid care by a friend, relative or neighbour on a long-term basis. Dex and Ward (2007) find no evidence of maternal employment influencing the extent of developmental problems in three-year-old children, except to the extent that not working, especially never working (as associated with factors such as low educational attainment, teenage motherhood, and living in low-income families) was associated with difficulties. Support offered to low-income families and single parents to combine work and family commitments has a positive effect on child development. Currie (2004) and Morris and Michalopoulos (2000) found that the Canadian Self-sufficiency Project (Chapter 4) which helped sole parents to leave social assistance registers for full-time jobs, had beneficial effects on cognitive outcomes and schooling achievement of their children.

Relatively little attention is paid to the role of fathers in the child development literature. However, rising maternal employment rates have generated some interest in the extent to which paternal interactions might compensate for fewer maternal interactions with their children. Gregg and Washbrook (2003) find that in households where mothers return to work when their children are still young, fathers are substantially more engaged in parenting. For the United States, the NICHD early childcare research network (2005),

---

Box 5.2. **Parents at work and child development** (cont.)

finds that maternal employment patterns did not affect paternal childrearing beliefs or caregiving activities, but that in households where mothers worked full-time, fathers were involved in caregiving activities regardless of their beliefs. Dex and Ward (2007) suggest that children were more likely to have developmental problems if their father had not used flexible working options, had left all home-based childcare to their spouse rather than sharing, taking no paternity leave around childbirth rather than a mixture of paternity and annual leave to spend some time with their child. However, these factors are likely to be also associated with education and earnings' levels of fathers, so a direct causal link between taking a few days of paternity leave on child development may be hard to prove. Positive effects of flexible working practices and spending more time with children over a sustained period intuitively seem to be a more important factor in the paternal enhancement of child development.

The policy choices in the Scandinavian welfare models of comprehensive parental leave and childcare support are based on the notion that, as long as formal childcare services are of good quality, its use is beneficial to the child. In Finland, the right of each child (regardless of age) to access childcare suggests childcare is considered beneficial at all ages, whereas the Swedish extension of access to subsidised care for those on parental leave suggests that entry into formal care can benefit children prior to the first birthday. In practical terms, however, Scandinavian models have a rather different perspective on the age of the child as from which mothers are encouraged to be at work. In Finland and Norway, the system of paid parental leave and homecare allowances financially encourages (one of the) parents to provide full-time parental care until the child turns three (see below), while in Sweden children often start to participate in childcare and early education services as from around 18 months of age; in Denmark, this is around the child's first birthday. In a recent study for Denmark, Deding *et al.* (2007) do not find any support for the notion that maternal employment negatively affects children at a later age, or that maternal employment is more detrimental in the first years of a child's life. In fact, the effect found was positive and stronger for boys than for girls.

(and interaction with peers) from approximately age 2-3. This generalisation of the evidence stands or falls with the quality of formal childcare, but as formal care and education is supplementary to parental care, also with the intensity and quality of interactions at home: the positive effects of formal care are biggest for children in disadvantaged families (see, for example, Lanfranchi *et al.*, 2003).

5.2.2. Staying in employment or at home

The withdrawal of (skilled) workers from the labour market can contribute to labour supply concerns, which are exacerbated by demographic trends. This can lead governments to intervene to make labour force participation more attractive for (potential) mothers.

Apart from the medical and child developmental reasons for granting employment-protected leave, labour supply objectives may also play a role. Paying income support during leave can further strengthen labour force attachment, while it obviously also reduces family poverty risks. Appropriate maternity and parental-leave policies with employment protection can be expected to raise mother's employment rates; the main reason why employers offer to extend periods of leave or continue (partial) wage payments during the leave of absence is to increase retention rates of mothers, thereby avoiding recruitment and training costs. If leave periods are too short, parents (usually mothers) are more likely to withdraw from the labour force for a considerable period. The evidence for the United States, where employment-protected child-related leave is relatively new, suggests that the provision of such leave (even when unpaid), increases the chance that women return to the same employer and take leave for shorter periods. In the absence of employment-protected leave, they would take off more time and are more likely to work for another employer (Hofferth and Curtin, 2003).

There is a danger that long periods of maternity, parental and/or home-care leave lead to detachment from the labour market, resulting in lower employment rates and thus affecting career prospects and earnings for mothers in the longer term. Ruhm (1998), in an analysis of 16 OECD countries, concludes that short spells of maternity leave (three months) are associated with higher female employment rates and finds that longer periods of leave (over nine months) reduce future earnings capacity. In another cross-national study, Jaumotte (2003) finds that, considered from a narrow labour supply perspective, the optimal full-time equivalent[3] period of maternity leave is about five months (measured in full-time equivalents). Similarly, (often large) enterprises that were interviewed in the course of the *Babies and Bosses* reviews offered at least four to five months paid leave, as otherwise many mothers would not return to work for the company.

The extent to which parents return to work, and at what time, depends on their individual preferences, the family situation and opportunity costs. Reflecting a more general pattern, parents in low-income families are most likely to provide parental care on a full-time basis, with mothers with high earnings are least likely to leave employment after childbirth, given the high opportunity cost of not being in work (Chapter 3). By making income support available for prolonged periods of time or not, public policy reduces the cost of not being in work, and influences the return to work decision by parents. Financial incentives to return to work after taking leave exist in Korea and Japan; in Japan, a payment equivalent to 30% of previous earnings is paid during the leave period, together with a bonus worth 10% (reform in October 2007 will increase this to 20%) of previous earnings when the leave-taker actually returns to work (OECD, 2003a).

In Finland, parents with a child not yet three years old have a choice: they can either exercise their right to affordable municipal day care or receive a payment for not using this service, and, generally, provide parental care on a full-time basis. In all, parents with a very young child in Helsinki who do not use municipal day care will receive transfers which, including non-payment of parental childcare fees, are worth about one-third of net average family income (Box 5.3). As a result, about two-thirds of mothers with very young children stay at home for a prolonged period; maternal employment rates of mothers with young children are relatively low. Employers, including public employers, are not to keen to hire women of childbearing age, as they may take off for up to three years, so the incidence of temporary employment contracts for young Finnish women is relatively high (OECD, 20005a). The Finnish Home Care Allowance payments are at odds with the avowed policy objective to raise female employment rates to 70% by 2010.

Box 5.3. **Some municipalities in Finland pay parents not to use formal childcare services**

In Finland, parents with young children are entitled to a subsidised childcare place, but can opt to receive, a home care allowance, if they do not use the municipal childcare system. In addition to the nationwide home care allowance, some (often larger) municipalities offer locally financed home care allowances, and about a quarter of all home care allowance recipients also receive a municipal home care payment (OECD, 2005a).

From a municipal budgetary perspective, it makes sense to pay parents to stay at home and care for toddlers rather than provide more expensive centre-based childcare for children below the age of three. With central government covering 30% of spending on both the national Home Care Allowance and a municipal childcare place, and the former costing less than half of the latter, municipalities have a very strong incentive to discourage parents with young children from using childcare. This explains why most of the larger municipalities (including Helsinki) provide additional incentives to parents not to use childcare by paying an additional municipal "home care payment"; in Helsinki this was worth about EUR 2 600 per annum in 2003.

Similarly, the 2002 parental-leave reform in Austria was introduced to give parents greater choice, by extending payments but also by extending coverage of health and pension insurance to parents who were not entitled to parental-leave benefit, and by extending work options for those currently on employment-protected parental leave.[4] As in Finland, the childcare benefit together with other child benefits (family allowance, child tax credits), are worth about 30% of average earnings and with supplements for sole parents and low income couples, this cab rise to almost 40% of average earnings (OECD, 2003a).

Transfers of such a magnitude lead to a strong financial disincentive to work. Experience with parental-leave reform during the 1990s in Austria suggests that the longer period of benefit payment will increase the average length of time that mothers are not in work after childbirth. Initial evidence on the 2002 parental leave reform (Lutz, 2003) suggested that Austrian mothers are likely to stay at home for at least 30 months (the period for which childcare benefit is paid), thereby losing their entitlement to return to their previous employer (since the duration of employment-protected leave is 24 months). Riesenfelder et al. (2006) corroborate these findings. Although the overall likelihood of labour market return (and return to the previous employer) has changed little, employment rates for parents with children aged 18 to 30 months have dropped by some 20 percentage points: many parents with very young children receive the childcare benefit payment for the full 30 months. At the same time, there is a very small increase (2 percentage points) in employment rates three to 18 months after childbirth, which is related to increased earnings disregards which facilitates part-time (small hours) employment without losing entitlement to childcare benefit.

Recent French policy reform also intends to give more choice to parents through home-care payments. In 1994, eligibility for the prolonged parental leave payment (APE) was extended to families with two children (prior to that only families with three children had access). This reform led to a significant reduction in the employment rate of mothers in the age group 20-49 with two children: from 70% in 1994 to 55% in 1997. Over the same period, employment rates for mothers with one or three children did not change (DREES, 2005). Prior to 1 January 2004, the *Allocation parentale d'éducation* (APE) provided income-tested income support for parents who themselves cared on a full-time basis for their child not yet three years of age. Almost 37% of children not yet three years of age were cared for by a parent on a full-time basis, of whom two-thirds of parents were in receipt of APE (Thibault et al., 2004). Since then, the *Prestation d'accueil pour jeune enfant* (PAJE) scheme has superseded various supports for families with very young children. PAJE consists of a birth grant, an income-tested allowance that covers about 90% of families with children under three, and a "free choice" (*Complément de libre* choix d'activité, CLCA) supplement that can be received when using registered childminders, home-care services or when parents care for their child on a full-time basis (the CLCA is only available to parents of first-born children for six months). Over the 2004-06 period; the CLCA replaced the APE, and in 2005 these two programmes covered about 25% of all children in France (Berger et al., 2006).

On 1 January 2007, Germany replaced its means-tested long-leave programme by a year-long earnings-related parental-leave scheme, a roughly revenue-neutral reform. Initial estimates suggest that during the second year of a child's life maternal working hours will increase by 12% and the maternal participation rate will rise three percentage points to 39%. Research has suggested that the likely effect of leave reform will be relatively large compared to alternative policies, such as increased individualisation of the tax system or the reduction of childcare fees (Spiess and Wrohlich, 2006).

5.2.3. Gender equity objectives

Employment patterns of fathers are hardly affected by the presence of children in households. If anything, fathers increase hours of work when they have children. In most couple families, earnings of the father exceed those of the (often younger) mother, so if the objective of a family is to minimise the financial consequences of having a child, it makes more sense when the mother rather than the father takes time off to provide personal care for children.

This divergence in parental employment patterns results in gender inequality. In many countries, policy makers are hesitant to interfere too obviously in household decisions about the distribution of labour supply in couple families. However, parental-leave policies provide policy makers with an option to pursue gender equity objectives, although in most countries policy shies away from trying to break firmly embedded gender-specific patterns of care provision. At issue are not just gender-equity objectives per se, but also a growing realisation in countries with low fertility rates and emerging labour supply concerns, that mothers need support with caring tasks from their partners in order to be able to both participate in the labour market and have children.

In general, maternity and paternity leaves are individual entitlements. Other than in Portugal (OECD, 2004) and Poland (but with limited coverage, Table 5.A1.3), maternity-leave entitlements cannot be transferred to fathers even partially, and of course the few days of paternity leave that most countries offer cannot be transferred to mothers. The entitlement to parental leave is individually based, but the entitlement to paid leave often is not: fathers and mothers cannot take leave at the same time and both receive income support. The different reasons why fathers do not take more leave include: the wage loss resulting from taking leave (which is higher if the father takes leave than if the mother does because leave payments are less than 100% of previous earnings and, as noted above, men generally earn more than their female partners); concerns about career patterns and earnings profiles (employers are reported to regard fathers taking parental leave as signalling a lack of commitment to their jobs); no desire to provide personal care on short- or long-term basis; and, gendered views on appropriate roles in providing care.

The majority of men in the EU are aware that they have a right to parental leave but they do not take it up (EFILWC, 2004). Of the 2 819 current or prospective fathers polled across the EU15 in 2003, 75%, or 2 108 respondents, knew of this entitlement. However, 84% of those 2 108 said they had not taken parental leave or were not intending to do so. The main factors deterring fathers from staying at home to look after a new baby or a small child are financial, lack of information and concerns about their careers. Eighteen per cent of respondents said they had not or would not take parental leave because they could not afford to, and another 42% said insufficient financial compensation was the main factor that discouraged them from taking parental leave. Thirty-one per cent said they felt their careers would be affected and just over 20% of respondents said they did not want to interrupt their careers. Although the EU directive on parental leave was passed in 1996, 34% said they did not have enough information about parental leave, and almost 20% regarded parental leave as being more for women. One in ten of the respondents said they would not take up leave as they feared that they "they would be stuck at home and have less social life".

Factors that would encourage men to take up the right to parental leave include more financial compensation (38%), better guarantees in respect of their job or career during or after the period of parental leave (30%) and better information (27%). A more open mind towards parental leave from superiors and colleagues would also help (23%), as would the possibility of splitting the leave or taking leave on a part-time basis (18%). The average figures for the EU15 conceal wide variations between member states and between socio-demographic groups. Thirty-four per cent of Swedes, 10% of Danes and 9% of Finns said they had taken or were considering taking parental leave for all or several of their children, compared to 1% or less in Luxembourg, Germany, Spain, Ireland, Austria and Portugal. Concerns about financial compensation rose in line with educational attainment: Thirty-eight per cent of those who left school at 15 or younger cited this reason compared to almost half of those who had studied up to the age of 20 or older.

In order to stimulate more fathers to take leave policy reforms in Nordic countries and Portugal have introduced measures that reserve parts of the paid leave entitlement for the *exclusive* use of the father. These so-called "father quotas" are available on a "use-it-or-lose-it" basis and cannot be transferred to the mother.[5] Fathers in Portugal, for example, can now take leave for 20 days while legal provisions also allow transferral of paid maternity-leave entitlements six weeks after childbirth. The emphasis in Portuguese policy on gender equity appears to have had some effect. The paid father quota in leave entitlement was introduced in 2000 and about 30 to 40% of eligible fathers used it in 2003.

Paternity leave take-up rates have reached 58% in Denmark (100% in the public sector where the scheme is fully paid), 64% in Sweden and 80% in Norway. In addition, in some of the Nordic countries, substantial proportions of fathers are now taking up at least part of the parental leave that is reserved for them. Recent take-up rates of childcare leave by fathers were almost 80% for Norway and 36% for Sweden (EFILWC, 2004). However, the amount of leave taken is relatively limited, in 2003 the fathers' share of total parental leave days was 17% (up from 11% in 1994). It seems that while the introduction of "father quota" in paid-leave schemes has increased take-up of parental leave among fathers, this does not reflect a fundamental behavioural change, as mothers almost exclusively take long periods of leave; fathers generally take a few weeks around summer and Christmas holidays.

Paternal behaviour is not the only issue. Mothers' attitudes are important too, and they may be lukewarm about sharing their leave entitlement with their partner. For example, in New Zealand, only 1% of eligible mothers transferred their parental leave entitlement to the father of the child at some point during leave. Available evidence for the Netherlands and Sweden suggests there is a positive correlation between sharing of leave or taking leave on a part-time basis by both partners, and levels of educational attainment and employment in the public sector.

A more equal distribution of care (and work) commitments among partners in couples families during the early months of a child's life could be generated by a fully individualised leave system which equally shares leave entitlements among partners. Such a system does not yet exist in the OECD area, but Iceland's system goes furthest entitling each parent to three months paid leave, and a further three months to be shared among parents (Box 5.4). As a result, fathers now use about one-third of the available parental leave days; much higher than elsewhere in the OECD.

> ### Box 5.4. **Promoting gender equity and a more equal sharing of parental leave in Iceland**
>
> In OECD countries entitlements to unpaid employment-protected leave are individual, whereas entitlements to paid leave (which strongly influences the effective duration of leave) are family-based, and often it is the mother who uses large chunks, if not the whole of the paid-leave entitlement. Since reform introduced on 1 January 2001 each parent has the right to a non-transferable three-month leave period and a shared three-month period until the child turns 18 months old. Eligible working parents in Iceland receive uncapped leave related benefits equivalent to 80% of average earnings and non-working parents receive a guaranteed minimum payment ranging from 18% to 40% of average earnings. Public spending on leave benefits was estimated to be around 0.75% of GDP in 2003 (OECD, 2003b).
>
> In 2000, the share of parental leave days in Iceland was only 3.3%, the lowest among Nordic countries (Valdimarsdóttir, 2006), but reform has increased uptake dramatically. In 2001, fathers took fathers take an average of 39 days leave or 17% of the total leave days used, while in 2004 fathers used 96 days leave on average or 35% of all leave days used (Einarsdóttir and Pétursdóttir, 2004; Gíslason, 2007; and *www.faedingarorlof.is*).

5.3. Conclusions

There is a wide array of parental leave arrangements across the OECD area. If there is something like a common trend, it is that in many countries the combined duration of maternity and parental leave is about one year, while policy in about a quarter of OECD countries provides supports for a three-year full-time parental care.

The different policy objectives that underlie public leave policies often reinforce each other, but there can also be some tension between them. Parental leave can promote labour supply, but if it is too short or too long, parents, in practice mothers, are less likely to return to work for their previous employer. From a narrow labour market perspective, the optimal period of leave seems to be around four to six months. In terms of child development, the available evidence seems to suggest that child development is negatively affected when an infant does not receive full-time personal parental care for the first six months of a child's life. Cognitive development of a child benefits from participation in good-quality formal care (and interaction with its peers) from approximately age two, with the evidence being ambiguous regarding the intermediary period. If both parents were to take their individual leave entitlements consecutively (or take their leaves simultaneously on a part-time basis, as, for example, is allowed in the Netherlands), this would go some way

118

towards covering this period. However, while entitlement to employment-protected leave is individual, entitlements to paid leave (which strongly influences the effective duration of leave) are family-based, and, frequently mothers, rather than fathers, use the paid leave entitlement.

The use of long leaves by mothers, however, can permanently damage their ability to achieve their labour market potential, affect personal well-being, increase the financial consequences of relationship instability, and limits future earnings and family income. In order to reduce the penalty on women for taking leave, policies in different OECD countries (for example, Austria, Portugal and Scandinavia) try to get more fathers to take parental leave for longer by reserving some (more or less generously) paid weeks of leave exclusively for their use. These policies have had some limited success in increasing take-up of leave by fathers, but this does not reflect a fundamental behavioural change, as mothers almost exclusively take long periods of leave. Paternal attitudes are not the only issue, as mothers frequently seem reluctant to give up leave to their partner's benefit. One way forward would be to increase the importance of individual entitlements to paid leave. A fully individualised paid parental-leave system does not yet exist in OECD countries, but Icelandic arrangements are closest with three months each for fathers and mothers, with an additional three-month entitlement to be shared among parents in line with their choice. In all other OECD countries, the policy debate about a more equal sharing of the care burden during the early months has yet to start in earnest.

Finally, maternity, paternity and parental leaves (and in some countries home-care benefits) are most valuable to parents as part of an *overall* policy support system supporting the reconciliation of work and family life. All too often, however, policy does not provide a continuum of supports (see previous chapter), in which case decisions concerning a few months early in a child's life, though very important, do not change much the overall work and family balance that parents face throughout the child-raising years. For example, recent reform of parental leave in Germany may affect the timing of labour supply decisions, and earnings profiles. However, as parental leave policy is not integrated with formal childcare policy, it is unlikely that parental leave reform on its own will address concerns about the reconciliation of work and family life and fertility rates in Germany.

Notes

1. New Zealand introduced paid parental leave was in 2002 in New Zealand and Switzerland introduced paid maternity leave in 2005.

2. Health and safety measures generally protect pregnant workers from working long and/or non-standard hours, or allow them to take time off for pregnancy-

related reasons. For example, in Portugal pregnant workers and mothers with infants are exempted from working at night for 112 days, and can attend medical appointments during pregnancy when necessary. In New Zealand, legislation provides for ten days of special leave for pregnant workers to attend medical appointments, pregnancy classes, etc.

3. In other words, ten months of leave paid at 50% of previous earnings are considered equivalent to five months leave paid at 100%.

4. In 2002, the Austrian system of paid parental leave was reformed into two separate schemes: i) a largely unchanged employment-protected parental leave covering employees with a sufficient work record; and, ii) a childcare benefit covering all parents who are entitled to family allowance and whose annual (individual) income is below a specified amount (around two-thirds of average earnings).

5. It is sometimes suggested that increases in public income support during parental leave may also increase paternal leave take-up. However, this would be a very expensive way of trying to achieve gender equity objectives which may well prove to be counterproductive, as increased income support may well lead to a further increase of the effective duration of leave taken by mothers via an income effect.

ANNEX 5.A1

Key Characteristics of Parental Leave Support

This annex present summary information on maternity or pregnancy leave (Table 5.A1.1), maternity allowances or grants (Table 5.A1.2), paternity leave (Table 5.A1.3), and parental leave (Table 5.A1.4). Information included in one table is not included again in another table. For example, leave recorded as paternity leave is not included again in the Table on parental leave.

In general, leave benefits and other income support for families with very young children, as arranged by local governments (for example, in the Canadian province of Québec (Roy and Bernier, 2007), certain *Länder* in Germany (Adema *et al.*, 2003), or some municipalities in Finland (OECD, 2005a) are not included in this annex (except for payments in the State of California in Table 5.A1.1).

Information on employer-provided top-up payments (over and above the statutory minimum) for those on maternity, paternity or parental leave is also not included in this annex.

Table 5.A1.4 includes income payments for families with young children (30 months) in Austria as these payments used to be tied to the period of employment-protected leave. Home-care payments in Norway and Finland (usually also paid to parents with children up to 26 months of age) and which are related to the use of public childcare facilities are not included in Table 5.A1.4.

Table 5.A1.1. Employment-protected statutory maternity leave arrangements,[1] 2005-06

Country	Maximum duration (weeks)	Eligibility criteria for payments	Paid	Payment	Financing
Austria	16 (can be 20 for medical reasons)	No qualifying conditions	Yes	100%	State/SI
Belgium	15 (17 multiple births)	All insured women	Yes	30 days: 82% after: 75%	SI
Canada	15 (varies across provinces)	600 contributable hours in the year pre-leave period	Yes	55% of average insured earnings with a maximum of CAD 413 per week	SI
Czech Republic	28 (37 multiple births)	All women residents	Yes	69% (up to EUR 25 daily)	
Denmark	18	Six weeks of residence	Yes	100% up to (DKR 3 115 p/w)	Employer
Finland	105 days = around 17.5 weeks	All parents are eligible	Yes	100-60% (four) Decreases with earnings; daily minimum EUR 11.45	SI
France	1st/2nd child: 16; 3rd: 26 (+3 multiple births)	Ten months insurance contributions	Yes	100% up to maximum (EUR 2 432 p/m)	SI
Germany	14 (18 multiple births)	All insured women	Yes	100%	SI (< ERU 13) + employer
Greece	17	200 days work in last two years	Yes	100% (max. EUR 42 p/d)	SI/employer
Hungary	24	All insured women	Yes	Pre-natal (min. 4 weeks): 70%, next: allowance	SI
Iceland	13	> 6 months in workforce	Yes	80%	SI
Ireland	26	39 ins. contributions paid in the 12 months pre-leave	18 weeks	70% with minimum and maximum	State
Italy	21 (5 months)	All women residents	Yes	80%	SI
Japan	14 (22 for multiple births)	Currently in covered employment	Yes	60% (66% as of April 2007)	Health insurance
Korea	13 (90 days)	All employed women	Yes	100%	
Luxembourg	16 (20 if multiple birth)	All insured women	Yes	100% (with minimum and maximum payments)	SI
Netherlands	16	All insured women	Yes	100% up to maximum	SI
Mexico	12	Currently in covered employment	Yes	100%	SI
New Zealand	12	Currently in covered employment	Yes	50%	State
Norway	9 weeks (embedded in parental leave, see below)	6 out of preceding 10 months in work (either parent)	Yes	Varies if period is 42 weeks: pay is 100%; for 52 weeks pay is 80%, max EUR 590	State
Poland	First child: 16; second child or more: 18; multiple births: 24	No qualifying conditions	Yes	100%	SI/employer
Portugal	17	6 months insurance contributions	Yes	100% with a minimum	State
Slovak Republic	28 (37 if multiple birth)	All women residents	Yes	55% net wage up to a low maximum (SKK 350 p/d – SKK 7 500 p/m)	SI
Spain	16 (18 if three or more)	180 days ins contributions paid in last five years	Yes	100%	State
Sweden	Seven weeks pregnancy leave + 60 days allocation of parental leave	All parents are eligible	Yes	80% (min. EUR 19 p/d)	State
Switzerland	16	Currently in covered employment	Yes	100%	Employer
Turkey	12	All insured women	Yes	66%	
United Kingdom	52	Employment for a continuous period of 26 weeks ending 15 weeks before the expected week of childbirth	26 weeks	First 6 weeks: 90% then final 20 weeks: EUR 154 p/w or 90% average weekly earnings if lower + 26 weeks unpaid	Employer (refunded for at least 92%)
United States, California	12 weeks	In employment for 12 months and at least 1 250 hours	No	See family leave provision in Table 5.A1.4	
	6 weeks	Covered by Temporary Disability Insurance	Yes	60% (max USD 728 p/w)	State

SI: social, health or unemployment insurance. SSC: A certain amount of social security contributions must have been paid for the claimant; WT: working time has to be over a lower limit.
1. Private sector employees. In many countries, civil servants have access to more generous entitlements. Self-employed often have less favourable statutory schemes.
Source: OECD Family database, December 2006 (*www.oecd.org/els/social/family*).

Table 5.A1.2. **Maternity allowance[1] and maternity grants[2] in place of, or in supplement to, statutory maternity pay, 2005-06**

	Allowance[1]			Grant[2]		
	Allowance	Eligibility	Details	Grant	Eligibility	Details
Australia	No			No	Birth grant	USD 3 040 (conditions apply re. vaccinations)
Austria	Yes	Women not covered by statutory maternity 1) Self-employed in agriculture, trade and industry 2) Others (part-time, contract workers)	1) EUR 23 p/d for 16 weeks leave in order to hire a substitute 2) EUR 6.91 p/d for 16 weeks			
Belgium	Yes	Self-employed maternity leave	EUR 889 p/m for three months	Yes	Birth grant	EUR 945 for first child EUR 711 for subsequent children
Finland	No	–	–	Yes	All residents (pregnancy over 154 days)	Choice between a generous maternity pack or lump sum payment (EUR 140)
France	Yes, No in 2004	Means-tested (around 80% of families are eligible)	During nine months from the 5th month of pregnancy; EUR 168 p/m	No, Yes in 2004	New scheme in 2004, means-tested, such as to include 90% of families	EUR 840 once at birth
Germany	Yes	To women not entitled to statutory maternity allowance	EUR 210 p/m	Yes	"Entbindungsgeld" for mothers in statutory maternity leave	
Greece	Yes	Not entitled to social insurance Means-tested state aid	EUR 500 in two parts (half for a period of 42 days before birth, half for the 42 days after birth)	Yes	Insured mothers having worked at least 50 days in the year before birth	30 days minimum wage (but amounts vary highly in other social security regimes)
Hungary	No			Yes	To unemployed and atypical workers not entitled to statutory maternity leave (also to a certain extent to those entitled)	EUR 1 747 per child, paid by health insurance
Italy	Yes	No employment records and not entitled to statutory maternity leave, means-tested at household level	EUR 283 p/m during 5 months for each child born or adopted (EUR 1 419 in total); paid by state through municipality	Yes	Mother and child have medical examination	EUR 1 740 divided into three: EUR 512 lump sums: prenatal, birth and postnatal (child's 2nd birthday)
Luxembourg	Yes	Not entitled to insured maternity benefit	Allowance paid for 16 weeks, non-cumulative with similar benefits (EUR 185 p/w)	Yes		
Norway	No	–	Four first months of child's life, minimum: PLN 50 p/m	Yes	Woman not entitled to statutory parental leave[3]	NOK 33 584 (around EUR 4 077)
Poland	Yes	Social assistance recipients		Yes	Social assistance recipients (in the past: all mothers)	EUR 129 (one time childbirth benefit)
Slovakia	Yes	Women not entitled to paid statutory maternity leave	Paid leave (lower amount)	Yes	For each child born	Lump sum EUR 118
Spain	No	–	–	Yes	Birth of third or more children and multiple births. Income-related child benefit EUR 450	
Sweden	Yes	Pregnancy leave	80% pay up to maximum (see tables on maternity and parental leave)	No	–	–
United Kingdom	Yes	Employed or self-employed for a certain period and not entitled to statutory maternity pay or under min. earnings requirements	26 weeks: 90% of average weekly earnings up to a max. of GBP 100 p/w	Yes	Either partner getting income support, income based jobseeker's allowance, Child Tax Credit, Working Tax Credit	Lump sum payment: EUR 728: can claim from 30th week of pregnancy until 3 months after

1. Maternity allowance: amount of money paid at interval for a certain period after a child is born.
2. Maternity grant: lump sump amount paid once at or around the childbirth.
3. In this situation parental leave for father is reduced to 29 weeks fully paid or to 39 weeks paid 80%.
Source: OECD Family database, December 2006 (www.oecd.org/els/social/family).

Table 5.A1.3. **Statutory paternity leave arrangements,** [1] **2005-06**

	Statutory	Criteria[2]	No of days	Paid for whole period	Level of payment	Job guarantee
Austria	No statutory paternity arrangements (but collective agreements generally providing for one or two days)					
Belgium	Statutory	EMP	Ten days to be taken with 30 days after birth (or adoption)	Yes	Three days: 100% (employer); next: 82% up to max. (health insurance)	Yes
Denmark	Statutory	EMP	Two weeks to be taken within 14 weeks after birth	Yes	90% up to maximum	Yes
Finland	Statutory	EMP	18 week days; extended up to 1-12 days conditional on taking as many days parental leave	Yes	100-60% (same rules as maternity leave); may be fragmented (day)	Yes
France	Statutory	EMP	Two weeks (three weeks if multiple births)	Yes	Three first days: 100% (up to maximum afterwards)	Yes
Greece	Statutory	EMP	Three days	Yes	100%	Yes
Hungary	Statutory	EMP	Five days	Yes	100%	Yes
Ireland	No statutory paternity arrangements (but three paid days leave are used to be granted by employers at birth)					
Italy	Limited cases	EMP + only if lone father or if mother ill. Income related	Total leave or the part which mother is ill for	Yes	80% by health insurance; also in case of adoption	Yes
Luxembourg	Statutory	EMP	Two days at child's birth	Yes	100% (employer)	Yes
Netherlands	Statutory	EMP	Two days (within a month after birth)	Yes	100%	Yes
Norway	No specific paternity leave. Statutory parental leave provision	EMP/QP for both parents. Four week father's quota depends on mother's employment prior to birth. No father's quota if mother has worked less than 50% full-time	Minimum: four weeks father's quota reserved to father (out of 52 weeks parental leave) (+ two weeks unpaid leave after birth). Maximum paid leave = 43 weeks[3] (33 weeks 100% pay).[4] If the mother not in employment, the father is allowed only 38 weeks (28 weeks 100% pay)	Yes	– 100% if both parents take up to 42 weeks (up to maximum NOK 341 000) (28 weeks if mother not employed) – 80% if 52 weeks (38 if mother not employed) – reduced compensation of father quota if mother between 50 and 75% FT-work	Yes
Poland	Limited cases	EMP: part of maternity leave over 14 weeks may be used by father	First child: two weeks maximum (16-14). Two and more: four weeks maximum (18-14)	Yes	100%	Yes
Portugal	Statutory	EMP	Five days in first month after birth	Yes	100%	Yes
Spain	Statutory	EMP	Two days (+ two days if another town) (ten weeks maternity leave may be transferred to the father if both parents fulfil conditions)	Yes	100% (employer)	Yes
Sweden	Statutory	EMP	Ten days after the child's birth to be used during the first 60 days and simultaneously with the mother	Yes	80% up to maximum	Yes
United Kingdom	Statutory	EMP/QP (26 weeks)	Two weeks to be taken by blocks of one week within eight weeks of birth	Yes	GBP 100 p/w or 90% of earnings if this is less	Yes

1. Details on paternity leave provision are for private sector employees. Self-employed are often excluded from paternity leave provision.
2. EMP: has to be working/employed to be eligible. QP: qualifying period: employed have to be in work for a certain amount of time within a certain reference period to be eligible.
3. 52 weeks parental leave of which nine reserved to the mother (four are reserved to the mother and the rest may be shared).
4. 42 weeks parental 100% paid leave of which nine reserved to the mother.
Source: OECD Family database, December 2006 (www.oecd.org/els/social/family).

Table 5.A1.4. Statutory parental leave arrangements, 2005-06

	Statutory type	Duration	Age limit	Payment	Other	Paid father quota
Australia	Parental leave	52 weeks		—		
Austria	Parental leave	Two years taken each by parents by periods of 3 months (except 1 month taken together). Two years also if simultaneous part-time. Four years if lone parent PT or both parents work part-time alternatively	Two years, can postpone 3 months up to 7 years old	Separate benefit of EUR 14.53 p/d for a period > than the parental leave: 30 months (36 if parents take leave alternatively) Earnings disregard of EUR 14 600 p/y	Part-time work possible; independent right for father to a minimum of 3 continuous months. Priority to the mother for the remaining rights; 6 months leave for adoptive parents (child's age limit is 30 months if adopted between 18 and 24 months, 7 years if adopted after 2)	
Belgium	Parental leave	Three months per parent per child (6 months if half time work) (15 months if 80% part-time work)	Four; eight if child is disabled	Separate flat rate leave benefit not specific to parental leave: EUR 537 p/m (FT leave); EUR 268 p/t	FT leave may be taken in three blocks of one month; 80% part-time work may be split in blocks of at least 3 months	
Canada	Parental	35 weeks		55% of APW (max CAD 330 p/w)		
Czech Republic	Parental	156 weeks	Three	10% of APW (or EUR 121 p/m)		
Denmark	Parental leave	32 weeks per child to be shared (in continuation of maternity, paternity or even other's parent parental leave) + individual right of eight unpaid weeks (can spread 32 weeks payment over total 40 weeks leave)	Nine	Total of 32 weeks 90 % up to maximum (DKR 3 115 p/w) to be shared	Possibility to work part-time with reduced payment accordingly	
Finland	1. Parental leave	1. 158 days (approx 26 weeks) after mat. Leave, shared among parents	1. Under 1	1. Around 60% (same rules as maternity allowance)	1. Extended in case of multiple births by 60 days per additional child; part-time possible for both parents; also for adoptive parents	
	2. Homecare leave (child not in municipal childcare)	2. Up to 3rd birthday of younger child; taken after paid parental leave	2. 3 years old	2. Basic allowance: EUR 252.3 p/m for first child + subsequent EUR 84.1 p/m (if under 3 years) or EUR 50.5 p/m (if over 3 years); possible supplements		
	3. part-time	3. Right to PT work to care for child > second school year	3. 8 years	3. Allowance of EUR 70 p/m	3. Salary is reduced proportionally	
France	1. Parental leave	1. 3 years per parent per child (1 year renewable twice); 1 year if adoption	1. Three	1. Separate benefit per household: if two+ children, and worked certain numbers of years	1. EUR 521 p/m	
	2. Part-time	2. Right to part-time	2. None		2. Cannot be refused by employer unless strong reasons	
Germany	Parental leave	3 years per parent per child; the 2 first years of the child, and the 3rd year before the child is 8. Couple parents working part-time (15-30 hours) can take leave simultaneously	Three	Separate benefit during first 2 years (means tested and income related) Max: EUR 300 per child and month during first 24 months or EUR 450 during 12 first months	Lone parent working up to of 30 hours maximum is entitled parental leave Also for adoptive parents	
Greece	Parental leave	3.5 months per parent	3.5	Unpaid	Part-time only upon employer's approval.; also for adoptive parents	
Hungary	Parental leave (GYED)	Up to a child's 2nd birthday	Two	70% of previous salary (up to a ceiling of 70% of double the minimum wage)		
Iceland	Parental	13 weeks per parent, non transferable		80%		13 weeks
Ireland	Parental leave	14 weeks per parent (in one block unless employer's agreement)	Five	Unpaid	Also in case of adoption. No part-time	

Source: OECD Family database, December 2006 (*www.oecd.org/els/social/family*).

Table 5.A1.4. **Statutory parental leave arrangements, 2005-06** (cont.)

	Statutory type	Duration	Age limit	Payment	Other	Paid father quota
Italy	Parental leave	11 months per child to be shared: 6 months max. for the mother and 6 for the father; extended to 7 if the father claims at least 3 months; 10 months for lone parent	Eight (six if adoption)	Child under 3: 30% for 6 months maximum; 30% over 6 months only if incomes below a maximum; child aged 3-8: unpaid	Also for adoption. Duration of paid leave up to 3 year for severely handicapped child. Also 3 months 30% paid leave for self-employed during first child year	
Korea	Parental leave	Nine months	Five	Flat rate of USD 500 p/m		
Luxembourg	Parental leave	Six months per parent per child (12 months if work under 50% full-time), to be taken after mat. leave, and before 5th child's birthday for the other parent	After maternity leave	EUR 1 840 per month during 6 months if full-time; EUR 920 p/m during 12 months if part-time	To be taken in 1 block. Part-time only on employer's approval. 2 supplementary full-time months if multiple birth	
Netherlands	1. Parental leave 2. PT work	1. Three months per parent per child (6 months if half part-time work); 1 parent at a time (mother has priority). 2. Right to change working time	1. Eight 2. No	1. Unpaid, except civil servant (75%) or favourable collective agreements 2. Wage reduced accordingly	1. Flexibility: leave to be taken in blocks of at least 1 month; also 4 months adoption unpaid leave (for child up to 12). 2. Also right to increase working time	
Norway (see also maternity and paternity leaves)	1. Paid parental leave 2. Additional unpaid leave 3. Part-time	1. 42 or 52 paid weeks per child can be shared (9: mother; 4: father). 2. One year per parent per child to be taken after paid leave (2 years for lone parent or parent if not in employment). 3. Cash benefit if day care is not used	1. Three 2. Two 3. One-three	1. 42 weeks 100% or 52 weeks at 80% (max. limit is annual income of NOK 341 000). 2. Unpaid. 3. NOK 3 657 p/m	The sharable period (39 or 29 weeks) may be taken simultaneously by parents working part-time	Four weeks, if the mother works at least 50% of FT week
Poland	Parental leave	Three years per parent	Four (18 if Disability)	EUR 103 p/m; means-tested benefit at household level for 3 years at maximum	To be taken in no more than four blocks	
Portugal	1. Parental leave 2. Special leave 3. Part-time	1. Three months per parent (six months if part-time). 2. Two years (three years for three+ children, four years if handicapped child). 3. One more child under 12	1. Six 2. Six; 12 if PT 3. 12	1. Unpaid. 2. Unpaid	1. part-time possible. 2. Possibility to work part-time. 3. Also right to flexible hours	15 days
Slovak Republic	Parental leave	Up to child's 3rd birthday; Individual right to be taken after maternity leave	Three	SKK 3 790 p/m; (SKK 1 200 if the parent is working or on sick-pay)	22 weeks leave for adoptive parents	
Spain	Parental; part-time	Three years per parent per child; reduction daily work time of 30-50%	Three (6 if PT)	Unpaid; no		
Sweden	Parental leave 60 days for fathers	(480 days to be shared between the parents, 60 days reserved each parent)	Eight	First 390 days: 80% (> max SEK 294 750 p/m. Next 90 days: SEK 60 p/d	Parental leave is fully flexible: may be divided in full days, half, 1/4, 1/8 (1 hour); same leave for adoptive parents	60 days for fathers
United Kingdom	Parental leave	13 weeks per child (18 if disabled and both working parents); max. 4 weeks per year by blocks of at least 1 week	Five	Unpaid	Adoptive parents have right to paid statutory maternity leave and unpaid parental leave	
United States	Family leave	12 weeks unpaid for each parent			Covers maternity, adoption, care for spouse, child, parents with serious health condition	

Source: OECD Family database, December 2006 (*www.oecd.org/els/social/family*).

BABIES AND BOSSES: RECONCILING WORK AND FAMILY LIFE – ISBN 978-92-64-03244-6 – © OECD 2007

ISBN 978-92-64-03244-6
Babies and Bosses: Reconciling Work and Family Life
A Synthesis of Findings for OECD Countries
© OECD 2007

Chapter 6

Formal Child
and Out-of-School-Hours Care Support

This chapter discusses public childcare and early education services as well as out-of-school-hours care. It describes past policy trends and current drivers of public investment in childcare. The chapter then provides an overview of formal public childcare and early education supports, including funding mechanisms, and discusses provision of early years' services across OECD countries, before different aspects of quality and out-of-school-hours care services are considered. Before concluding, the chapter examines parental childcare fees and whether work pays after taking into account the cost of childcare.

6.1. Past policy trends and current policy objectives

Increased female labour market participation has generally preceded the development of childcare services. In turn, the development of formal childcare has allowed female employment to expand further, both in terms of the number of female workers and the hours they engage in paid employment. The Danish and Swedish experiences, countries which have been frontrunners in the development of formal childcare and early education systems, illustrate these patterns. In the late 1960s/early 1970s, employment rates for prime-aged female workers were around 60-65%, while enrolment in childcare for two-year olds was about 20% (OECD, 2002a and 2005a). Since the early 1970s, formal childcare expanded rapidly, and by the mid-1990s, the proportion for two-year olds participation in childcare has been in excess of 60% in both Denmark and Sweden, and prime-age female employment rates have risen to around 75-80%, most of which is full time (OECD, 2002a and 2005a).

In terms of female employment rates (Chapter 3) the current situation in many OECD countries is not all that different from what it was in Denmark and Sweden in the late 1960s/early 1970s. In many other countries female employment has grown in recent years, is often of a part-time nature (*e.g.* Australia, Switzerland and the United Kingdom) and/or has been accomplished on the back of parents using a mix of formal and informal care solutions provided by grandmothers and sisters (*e.g.* Ireland and the Netherlands). However, with increased mobility, and as mothers and sisters are increasingly in work themselves, this source of informal care is drying up, which increases pressure for future investment in child- and out-of-school-hours care.

Childcare systems differ greatly between countries, but a reasonable summary is that in many OECD countries the proportion of three-to-six year-old children using some type of non-parental childcare is high, while it is relatively low for children under age three. This chapter considers policy concerns in view of some immediate targets of childcare policy to increase childcare capacity; equity (in access to public support) among parents; user choice in service and provider; and quality of service. Realising these intermediate goals would contribute to achieving the broader objectives of childcare policy: to improve child welfare; to promote child development, to raise gender equity and female labour supply; and, as part of a broader work/

family reconciliation strategy which gives parents more realistic options to combine work and care commitments, to sustain birth rates.

In many OECD countries public investment in childcare and early education systems is increasing, with the highest expenditures in Denmark and Sweden at around 1.5% of GDP. Moreover, many policy makers consider this level as too high for an increase of female employment rates by 15 percentage points (and gains would be smaller when measured in full-time equivalents). Then again, labour supply concerns and gender equity objectives are not the only reasons for increasing public childcare support.

Indeed, changing female labour market behaviour may have triggered the development of formal childcare system, but child development and education concerns have become an integral part of policy formulation in, for example, Nordic countries and New Zealand, where policy increasingly stresses the pedagogic role of pre-school care. Participation in good-quality childcare (from 12-18 months) onwards is seen as beneficial to the child, and in some countries, e.g. Sweden, pre-school education (as childcare is known in that country) is an integral part of the education system with its own curriculum and is expressly considered as the first step in the life-long learning process. In other countries, day-care services for younger children are supervised by ministries responsible for social policy. That is not to say that there is always a clear dichotomy between care and education: "care" for young children involves "education" and "education" for young children involves "providing care", although the balance between the two may alter with age.[1]

As with parental leave arrangements discussed in the previous chapter, in Nordic countries (and policy in the Canadian province of Québec has similar aspirations, see for example, Roy and Bernier, 2007) childcare systems are seen as an integral part of a universal welfare policy with comprehensive support so that individuals can both pursue labour market aspirations and be a parent and have as many children as they desire (Batljan, 2001).

In the United Kingdom, the high political priority given to reducing child poverty since 1997 has triggered the development of a more extensive childcare policy. Substantial childcare subsidies to reduce barriers to paid work are the complements to a more extensive use of income-tested child benefits (Chapter 4). Child development concerns led to the development of a free part-time (2.5 hours per day) early education offer for three- and four-year-olds; the "free early education offer" reduces the overall cost of childcare to parents (which nevertheless remains relatively high in the United Kingdom, see below). To support working parents, UK policy is also developing an access guarantee for child- and out-of-school hours care from 8 a.m. to 6 p.m. for parents who wish to use it.

6.1.1. Beyond childcare and early education

UK policy development also illustrates another general trend across OECD countries – the development of services aiming to promote child development in disadvantaged areas or among disadvantaged groups. Such policies are beyond the scope of this report, but as most such policies have a childcare element, their broad outlines are summarised here.

The *Sure Start Children's Centre* programme has involved the development of integrated family support services, initially targeted at the most disadvantaged areas (Box 6.1). New Zealand has also started to pilot various initiatives providing "early intervention support" to vulnerable and disadvantaged families. The initiatives include intensive home-based family service delivery (Family Start),

---

Box 6.1. A more holistic approach to family support – Sure Start and Children's Centres in England

A centrepiece of UK anti-poverty policy is the Sure Start policy which through its Children's Centres programme offers integrated day care and early learning, health, family and parenting support, initially in the most disadvantaged areas. The aim is to establish 3 500 Children's Centres across England by 2010 (Scotland has a different set-up of support programmes overseen by the Scottish Executive). The policy objectives underlying Sure Start are threefold: i) increase the availability and sustainability of affordable childcare places for children, especially those who are disadvantaged, ii) provide integrated services for health, education and emotional development of young children; and iii) provide services to parents to support them as parents and to help them become job-ready. To co-ordinate all early childhood-related policies and programmes in England a Sure Start Unit has been created in central government which is accountable to both the Department for Education and Skills and the Department for Work and Pensions.

Sure Start local programmes were set up in 1998 with the initial objective being 250 local (community-level) programmes in disadvantaged areas, but in 2003 there were 524 programmes in the most disadvantaged communities across England delivering services to families to about 400 000 children and their families (i.e. about 16% of all children under four in England and one-third of all children living in poverty). In October 2006, the 1 000th Children's Centre was opened extending coverage to about 800 000 children in England. There are projected to be 2 500 such centres by 2008, to be increased to 3 500 by 2010. By 2007-08 public spending on the Sure Starts Children's Centre initiative will be close to USD 3.5 billion, up from USD 600 million in 2003-04.

Box 6.1. **A more holistic approach to family support –
Sure Start and Children's Centres in England** (cont.)

Local Sure Start programmes and Children's Centres deliver holistic family support services for children and families from pregnancy through to starting school. Programmes can involve a wide range of services, including day-care services, but also, for example, ante-natal support, advice to parents-to-be and general parenting and family support. In deprived areas, family workers often have to deal with debt-related issues, depression, stress and abuse issues. Family workers have to deal with a generation of children who were not stimulated at school and whose parents do not provide a role model of work and/or strong work ethos. Through early intervention, the Sure Start and Children's Centre initiative aims to build up confidence among children and parents, stimulate people to make their own decisions, break the pattern of intergenerational welfare dependency, and help prevent disadvantage later in life. In a preliminary evaluation of Sure Start Local Programmes (SSLP), Belsky *et al.* (2006), evidence on a positive effect on child well-being was mixed, and it was found that while more families benefited than not, programmes seemed to benefit relatively less socially deprived parents, but seemed to have an adverse effect on the most disadvantaged children. (The study suffers from sample-selection bias as it compares results for children in Sure Start areas (which were selected because of their disadvantage) with areas that were better off). This finding underlies the importance of getting the most disadvantaged (including teenage mothers) to participate in programmes. Indeed, Belsky *et al.* (2006), also find that programmes led by health services (with an existing network of health visitors) are more effective in serving the most disadvantaged that programmes led by other agencies.

---

free care and education services for 20 hours per week for about 1 750 children enrolled, and a pilot parenting support provided through early childhood education centres.

Over the years US policy has developed a range of investment programmes targeted to reduce child poverty and disadvantage. Among programmes targeted at young children, the most important is *Head Start*, a pre-school programme for disadvantaged children that serves over 800 000 children in predominantly part-day programmes, at a budgetary cost of over USD 5 billion. Currie (2001) found that "[...] the short- and medium-term benefits (*e.g.* improving health and nutrition, preventing special education and grade repetition) could easily offset 40 to 60% of the costs of large-scale, publicly funded early intervention programmes such as *Head Start*", and that "even relatively small long-term benefits (*e.g.* improving schooling and wages, reducing crime and teen pregnancy) of such programmes may be sufficient to offset the costs of public investment". Ludwig and Phillips (2007) also suggest that *Head Start* generates long-term benefits and passes a cost-benefit test.

6.2. Diversity in childcare and early years services

Across the OECD, there is a wide variety in the type of childcare services provided, especially those provided to very young children (Table 6.1). For very young children up to the age of three, there is a multitude of childcare services. Such services can range from centre-based day-care services, to centre-based playgroups or other part-time services (for examples "haltes gardaries" in France), to family day-care services in the home environment of the provider or by childminders at the home of the child. For example, in France in 2002, 17% of children aged zero to three use family-day care arrangements, 9% attend *crèches* and 1% of children are regularly cared for by carer in their own home (Blanpain, 2005).

In most countries kindergarten or similar pre-school services exist for children age three and older, and in some countries such services are part of the primary education system (for example, Ireland and the Netherlands). However, this type of pre-school education involves attendance for about three to five hours per day for five days per week, so that in the absence of comprehensive out-of-school-hours care services in many countries, participation in these early education services does not in itself enable parents to hold down a full-time job. It is difficult to generalise from the surveys on the use of different childcare sources reported by parents, but as the different *Babies and Bosses* reviews have shown, parents often have to juggle use of subsidised kindergarten, formal and informal care services to find a mix (and duration) of services that best suits their needs.[2]

Given its very nature, comprehensive information on the use of informal care is not available, but some national surveys may serve to illustrate its importance. In 2005, in the Netherlands, for about 20% of households with children under four years of age unpaid childminding by relatives, neighbours and friends was the most important form of childcare, while for about 30% of households with children formal care arrangements were the most important source of childcare (Riele, 2006). In Ireland in 2005, one-tenth of families used day-care centres while almost 12% of families with pre-school children relied on unpaid relatives to provide childcare (CSO, 2006).

Because the cost of domestic services (including childminding services) is relatively low in the United States, many US parents make use of the low-paid (largely informal) childcare sector. More generally, the low cost of all domestic

Table 6.1. **Typology of childcare**

	Centre-based care				Pre-school		Compulsory school	
	Family day care							
Public[1]								
Private[2]								
Age	0	1	2	3	4	5	6	7
Australia	Approved long day care, family day care and occasional care (Child Care Benefit is available for either 24 hours or 50 hours care depending on the work status of the parents)				Reception/pre-school classes (usually 15 h per week), with primary school (full time, frequently with out-of-school-hours care)		Compulsory schooling	
Austria	*Tagesmutter* (FDC) and *Krippen* (centre-based); part-time (25 h)				*Kindergarten* (part-time, 25 h); out of school care provision under development		Compulsory schooling	
Belgium	*Kinderdagverbliif* (centre-based crèches) and FDC; *crèche* (centre-based) and *gardiennes encadrées* (FDC)				*Kleuterschool*, part-time or full time, with out-of-school-hours care; *école maternelle*, part-time or full time, with out-of-school-hours care		Compulsory schooling	
Canada	Centre-based and family day care				Junior kindergarten Ontario	Kindergarten/ maternelles in Québec	Compulsory schooling	
Czech Rep.	*Crèche* (centre-based care), FT		*Materska skola* (state kindergarten)				Compulsory schooling	
Denmark	*Dagpleje* (FDC) and *Vuggestuer* (crèche) full time (> 32 h)		*Bornehaver* (kindergarten) full time (> 32 h)					Compulsory schooling
	Adlersintegrer (age-integrated facility) full time (> 32 h)						*Bornehaver* (> 32 h)	
Finland	*Perhepaivahoito* (FDC) and *Paivakoti* (municipal early development centres), full time (< 50 h)						*Esiopetus* pre-school	Compulsory schooling
France	*Crèche* (centre-based care) and *Assistant maternelles* (FDC), FT		*École maternelle* (pre-school) with out-of-school-hours care				Compulsory schooling	
Germany	*Krippen* (centre-based crèche)		*Kindergarten* (pre-school)				Compulsory schooling	
Greece	*Vrefonipiaki stahmi* (crèche for children < 2.5 and nursery school for > 2.5)						Compulsory schooling	
			Nipiagogeia (kindergarten)					
Hungary	*Bolcsode* (crèches), full time (40 h)		*Ovoda* (kindergarten)		Compulsory schooling			
Iceland	Day-care centres and "day mothers"(FDC)		Pre-school				Compulsory schooling	
Ireland	Regulated FDC and nurseries (centre-based)				Early Start and Infant school (pre-school), with primary school		Compulsory schooling	
			Pre-school playgroups					
Italy	*Asili nidi* (crèches) part-time (20 h) and full time (< 50 h)		*Scuola dell'infanzia* (pre-school)				Compulsory schooling	
Japan	Centre-based care						Compulsory schooling	
	Family day care		Kindergartens					
Korea	Childcare centres						Compulsory schooling	
			Kindergartens					
			Hakwon (pre-school)					
Luxembourg	*Crèche* (centre-based care) and *Tagesmutter* (FDC)		*Enseignement pré-scolaire* (pre-school)				Compulsory schooling	
Mexico	*Educación inicial* (centre-based crèche)				Compulsory educación prescolar (pre-school)	Compulsory schooling		
Netherlands	*Gastouderopvang* (FDC), *Kinderopvang* (childcare centres) and playgroups				Group 1, with primary school	Compulsory schooling (Group 2 onwards)		

1. Provision is largely publicly funded and managed (more than 50% of enrolments are in publicly operated facilities).
2. Provision is largely managed by private stakeholders (both for-profit and not-for-profit providers) and is publicly and privately financed.

Source: OECD Family database (*www.oecd.org/els/social/family*)

Table 6.1. **Typology of childcare** (cont.)

	Centre-based care			Family day care		Pre-school		Compulsory school
Public[1]								
Private[2]								
Age	0	1	2	3	4	5	6	7
New Zealand	Childcare centres, family-day care, playcentres and *Te Kohanga Reo*					Compulsory schooling		
				Community-based kindergarten (mainly 3- and 4-year-old children)				
Norway	*Barnehage*, including rural *familiebarnhager*, full time (40 h)						Compulsory schooling	
Poland	Nurseries			Pre-school/nursery schools				Compulsory schooling
Portugal	*Creche familiare* (FDC) and centre-based crèches			*Jardims de infancia* (pre-school)			Compulsory schooling	
Slovakia	Nursery schools			Kindergarten			Compulsory schooling	
Spain	*Educación pre-scolar* (centre-based)			*Educatión infantile* (pre-school), with primary school			Compulsory schooling	
Sweden	*Forskola* (pre-school) full time, 30 h, some *Familiedaghem* (FDC) particularly in rural areas						*Forskole-klass* (pre-school, PT)	Compulsory schooling
Switzerland	*Crèche, Krippen*, varies across cantons (centre-based)			Pre-school, mandatory in some cantons			Compulsory schooling	
Turkey	Crèche			*Ana Okullari* (kindergartens)			Compulsory schooling	
United Kingdom	Nurseries, child minders and playgroups			Playgroups and nurseries, PT	Reception class, with primary school	Compulsory schooling		
United States	Childcare centres and FDC			Educational programmes, incl. private kindergartens, Head Start (State kindergartens)			Compulsory schooling	

1. Provision is largely publicly funded and managed (more than 50% of enrolments are in publicly operated facilities).
2. Provision is largely managed by private stakeholders (both for-profit and not-for-profit providers) and is publicly and privately financed.

Source: OECD Family database (*www.oecd.org/els/social/family*)

services helps to explain the high proportion of female US workers engaged in paid work for over 40 hours per week (Chapter 7).

6.3. Public spending and participation in childcare and pre-primary education

Public spending on childcare, including early education services, is highest in Nordic countries and France, at around 1.4% of GDP (Chart 6.1). Within the group of Nordic countries there is variation as income support during home-care leave in Finland and Norway is available until the youngest child is three years of age (Chapter 5), which obviously reduces overall public outlays on formal childcare. Compared to spending on day-care services for very young children, there is less variation across countries in spending on early education services such as kindergarten (OECD, 2006e). Although there are differences, many countries across the OECD have a pre-primary education service of two years duration, while public support for day-care services varies from substantive (Nordic countries), to limited in Hungary, Ireland, Korea, Mexico and Poland.

Chart 6.1. **Public spending on childcare is highest in the Nordic countries and in France**

Public spending on childcare including pre-primary education, 2003

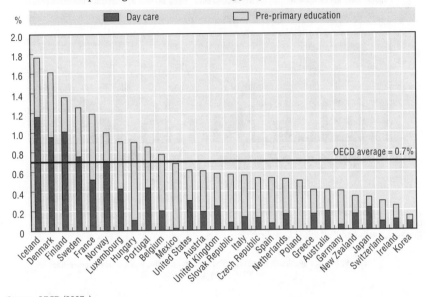

Source: OECD (2007a).

As a result of the system of comprehensive public financial support for childcare, enrolment rates for very young children under three years of age are around 40% or above in Finland[3], Norway and Sweden. Enrolment rates are even higher in Denmark and Iceland, the countries with relatively short periods of paid leave. Participation in formal childcare in the United States for young children is also high at around 40% (OECD, 2007g), of whom about 15% are in means-tested assistance programmes (Gornick and Meyers, 2003); the large majority of children are in private centres. On average across the OECD countries for which data are available, 23% of zero- to three-year-olds use formal childcare; in Austria, the Czech Republic, Italy, Greece, Germany, Mexico and Poland, it was less than 10% in 2004 (Chart 6.2, Panel A).

With an average enrolment rate of 74% of three-six-years-olds, coverage of kindergarten and other pre-primary early years services for three-six-year-olds is generally high (Chart 6.2, Panel B). In about half of the OECD countries more than 80% of three-six years participate in such early years services, reaching almost 100% in Belgium, France, Italy and Spain. In Europe, the concept of universal access for three-six-year-olds is broadly accepted, and most countries offer all children at least two years of free, publicly funded provision before they begin primary schooling; often access is a statutory entitlement from age three onwards. In Mexico, states are legally obliged to

Chart 6.2. **For children aged three and over childcare participation rates are generally high**

Panel A: Average enrolment rate of children aged under three years of age in formal childcare (2004)

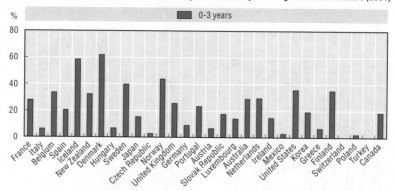

Data for Canada, Germany and Poland concern 2001; data for France reflects 2002; data for Greece, Iceland, Luxembourg, Mexico, Norway and the Slovak Republic concerns 2003; and data for Australia, Denmark, Korea and the United States concerns 2005.

Panel B: Average enrolment rate of children aged three to five years of age in pre-school educational programmes (2004)

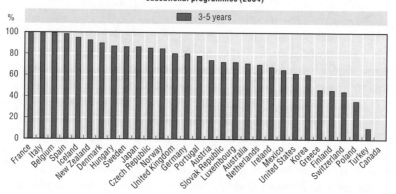

Countries are ranked in descending order of three to five year old enrolment rates.
Source: OECD Family database and OECD Education database.

provide pre-primary school/kindergarten services for children over three years. Entitlements to half-day kindergarten exist for children from the age of five years onwards in most states in the United States.

The cross-national differences in childcare participation rates do not, however, fully reflect differences in the intensity of use across countries. Comprehensive data on the number of hours children participate in childcare and other early years services is not available, but information on "typical practices" can be used to illustrate the significant cross-national differences.

In Nordic countries, use of formal childcare often is on a full-time weekly basis. For Sweden, for example, this means that children attend childcare (pre-school) centres for about six hours per day. Early years centres in Nordic countries are often open from about 7 a.m. to 5 p.m – long enough to permit full-time work by the parents (weekly working hours in Nordic countries being considerably shorter than in, for example, Japan (Chapter 7).

From age three, children in France generally participate in *maternelles* which provide morning and afternoon sessions of education supervised by certified teachers (with support from assistant teachers). Municipalities cater for children at lunch-time, and they frequently run before and after-school-hours services to help parents work full time. In all, *maternelles* provide care and education for children of working parents (children in families with a non-employed parent often do not have access to lunch-time services) on a full-day full-week basis. The organisation of the services around the hours of education are the (financial) responsibility of municipalities, and not all municipalities provide this services (which is generally not used by children living in families where one parent is not in paid work on a full-time basis). Ruault and Daniel (2003) found that 21% of children attend out-of-school-hour services in 2002.

Practice is rather different in most other OECD countries, where most kindergarten are run on the basis of a limited number of hours per day (for example, in Austria, Germany or New Zealand) or involve lunch breaks of 90 to 120 minutes (for example, Luxembourg and Switzerland). This is understandable from a narrow child development perspective which considers that cognitive development and peer interaction is beneficial to children from age 2-3 (looking at the design of pre-school systems, see below, many countries put the starting age at three in practice) for a few hours per day.

6.3.1. Priority groups

There are no clearcut rules across OECD countries on the definition and treatment of priority groups regarding placements, waiting lists, and waiving of fees. Many countries provide childcare places for child welfare purposes when there are specific care, neglect or abuse concerns, and in these situations childcare costs are frequently covered by the public if that is considered appropriate.[4] Otherwise, many childcare centres serve their clients on a "first-come, first-serve" basis, and give priority to whichever family has been waiting longest for childcare, irrespective of employment status or family composition. In some cases, for example, recent migrants but also occasionally parents who need access to care if they are to be able to take up employment, specific families may be placed at the head of the waiting list.

Children of working mothers may have priority access to nurseries in the city of Zürich, while municipalities in Japan would typically grant priority access to dual-earner couples and the longer the working hours of both parents, the higher they are on the priority list. Dual-earner couples frequently have priority access to all-day supervision services in pre-schools and schools as they do in, for example, France and the Austrian capital Vienna.

In Japan, each local government determines the criteria and priority listing for admission to licensed centres and children from sole-parent families are always given priority. In other countries, including for example, Australia, the Netherlands and Portugal, public childcare supports are made available to (sole) parents on income support who enter work or a training programme while on benefit.

6.3.2. Financing issues

Public spending on childcare is high in Nordic countries because the quality of care is good, because it is provided on a full-time basis and because coverage of the population is high.[5]

The *Babies and Bosses* reviews found little reason for the Nordic countries to depart from this strategy. However, other countries may not be prepared to tolerate Nordic public spending and tax levels, nor do they have a strong tradition of good-quality local public service delivery or considerable taxing powers for local government (Chapter 4). The Nordic model is therefore not directly exportable to other OECD countries which are in the process of building up childcare capacity and quality. Furthermore, notwithstanding a growing awareness that participation in childcare serves a child-development purpose, many countries still consider formal childcare as a labour supply incentive for which working parents and employers (see below and Chapter 7) should largely pay themselves.

When childcare capacity is not comprehensive, countries face equity issues in access to subsidised childcare and the coverage of public funding.[6] This issue was one of the key drivers for the 1997 childcare financing reform in Australia. At that time, direct operational funding to providers was largely withdrawn, and the emphasis moved to funding parents to help pay the cost of childcare fees.

In Australia, childcare funding now follows parental choices. Earmarked public support (or vouchers) is made available to eligible parents in order to improve efficiency through competition and choice in terms of providers and types of care, including out-of-school-hours care. Further, in order for a voucher system to contribute to quality care and early years provision, vouchers should be linked to *licensed* providers only (see below). Through income-testing and (partial) linkage of entitlements to working hours, employment objectives can be pursued while scarce resources are targeted at those most in need (Box 6.2).

Box 6.2. **Child Care Benefit in Australia**

The number of children using Australian government-supported childcare services more than doubled between 1991 and 2004, from 262 200 to 646 800 (AIHW, 2006). Over this period, the number of children attending long-day-care centres almost tripled, to 383 000, while the number attending outside-school-hours (OSH) care more than tripled to 160 800. Paralleling this trend, the use of vacation care services has also increased markedly. Of the children who used formal childcare during 2004, 59% attended long-day-care centres; 14% family day care. Children who attended OSH-care (18%) are likely to overlap with those who attended vacation care (16%).

For children who are using approved care, the Australian government funds the Child Care Benefit (CCB), which is a payment made to families to help with the cost of care. The rate of CCB varies depending on family income, the number of children in care and the type of care used. Families using approved services who are on the lowest incomes receive the highest rate of CCB. (FaCSIA, 2006). In 2007, for families with incomes of USD 28 100 or less, the maximum rate of CCB (USD 121 per week) is applied. This rate is for one child who is not at school, and who is in care for 50 hours per week. The rate under these conditions is equivalent to USD 2.42 per hour. If families earn more than USD 28 100, the CCB tapers down to a minimum rate of USD 20.35 per child for 50 hours of care per week – or USD 0.41 per hour. If a family has an income greater than USD 80 568, they are eligible for only the minimum rate. The rate of CCB for children at school is 85% of that payable for children not at school.

In addition, since 2005 there has been the Child Care Tax Rebate, which covers 30% of out-of-pocket childcare expenses for approved childcare for working parents, with a rebate of up to USD 3 277 (indexed) per child per year. Out-of-pocket expenses are the total fees paid for childcare expenses for approved care, less the amount of Child Care Benefit (CCB) received.

The accessibility of childcare services is a concern for both parents and governments. Unmet demand is an important indicator of accessibility. One direct measure of unmet demand comes from the 2002 ABS Child Care Survey, which asked parents whether they wanted to use either some formal childcare or additional formal care, but did not do so. In these terms, about 6% of children aged under 12 years needed additional formal care, well below the level of 16% in 1993. Unmet demand decreased the most for pre-school services (83%) and occasional care (80%) Even so, this amounted to 174 500 children requiring additional formal care in 2002. Of this group, 27% required after-school-hours care, 27% required long day care and 22% occasional care. Unmet need was higher among children aged 0-4 years (9%) than those aged 5-11 years (4%).

Box 6.2. **Child Care Benefit in Australia** *(cont.)*

Quality is another key issue, and the Australian quality assurance system is an innovative way of monitoring quality and supporting a large involvement by the private sector in providing care services. Child Care Benefit receipt is contingent on adhering to quality standards which facilitates the provision of approved childcare that is of a high standard. The National Childcare Accreditation Council in Australia was established to administer the Quality Improvement and Accreditation System (QIAS) for long day care centres, Family Day Care Quality Assurance (FDCQA), and Out-of-School-Hours Care Quality Assurance (OSHCQA). The three systems follow a five-step process which service providers must go through in order to become and remain accredited: *i)* Registration; *ii)* self-study and submitting a continuing improvement plan to the NCAC every 2.5 years; *iii)* validation – through visits by NCAC professional validators; *iv)* moderation to ensure consistency of assessments on a national basis; and *v)* accreditation decision. There are appeal procedures and centres that fail are required to submit another self-study report six months from the date of the NCAC decision.

State and territorial governments in Australia legislate minimum standards for childcare services, and a move to an integrated quality assurance system was announced in May 2006 along with a number of other measures. The integrated system will enable other service types to come under the system of accreditation over time, thereby linking government-funding approval directly to the quality of care. It will also address concerns about the administrative complexity of the current systems and reduce any overlap and duplication with state and territory licensing regulations.

Central to the integrated quality assurance system will be a set of core quality standards against which assessments across all service types will be made. Supporting these core standards will be a number of age and service specific indicators to cater for the unique characteristics of children and service types. Service providers will provide information on how they are meeting the standard in their service and their claims will then be assessed against the agreed standards and indicators through a validation and moderation process. Services that meet all the quality standards will be rated as accredited.

Indeed, the Australian Child Care Benefit (CCB)[7] experience shows that if sufficient voucher and subsidy money is made available, independent family day carers and commercial providers will respond to the business opportunity and quickly expand provision, while tying benefit receipt to quality standards ensures quality early childhood services.

In the United Kingdom, public resources for childcare initially were used as seed funding to encourage community-based initiatives and business start-ups. However, funding mechanisms are now more conventional. A large part of the public sector subsidy comes through local authorities who, on the basis of grants (and a specific subsidy towards the "free educational offer") finance Sure Start Children's Centres, and Neighbourhood Nurseries, while low-income families can claim support towards the parental costs of childcare through the childcare elements in Working Tax Credit (OECD, 2005a). Similarly, the Netherlands and New Zealand have income-tested childcare payments (which can also be used towards out-of-school-hours care) for parents, to which Dutch employers have recently been obliged to contribute about one-third of the costs (Chapter 7). This reflects the dominance of the labour supply objective in the childcare debate in the Netherlands, and childcare policy is based on the notion that the public, employers and working parents should share the costs.

One problem that has arisen in several countries which use public funds to stimulate supply of childcare places is that private sector childcare is a low-margin business with many providers struggling to maintain capacity at a high enough level for operations to be financially viable (NAO, 2004). This contributes to patchy geographic coverage, with relatively few providers in deprived and/or scarcely populated areas, or the lack of provision of services to children with special needs. Therefore, Australian, British, Dutch, New Zealand and other OECD governments are trying to find the optimal mixture between demand-side funding and subsidies to providers who work in particular areas or cater for clients with special needs.

6.3.3. Quality

The quality of childcare and early-years services is important. Not only does poor quality restrict take up of early-years services, but it is also crucial for child development, an increasingly important driver of public investment in the area (Box 6.3). The objectives set and the means used to monitor and promote the adoption of high standards of quality of childcare and early education services differ across countries. Quality is not a narrowly defined concept, and it has many aspects such as standards of hygiene and safety, staff-to-child ratios and the size of groups, parent involvement and compliance with certain educational policies, sometimes laid down in a curriculum, which are key factors for regulating quality, qualifications, training and remuneration of childcare staff.

Box 6.3. **The quality of care and child development**

There is consensus that the first years of life are critical for cognitive, physical, social and emotional development. Some research suggests that young people who participate in quality early childhood education and care are likely to develop better reasoning and problem-solving skills; to be more co-operative and to develop greater self-esteem, even though some of the direct gains such as in IQ rating appear to fade over time. Child development is influenced by the type of care children are exposed to – at home and outside of the home. Child development is also promoted by quality care and education services, if not by a parent, then by professional carers, educators and "pedagogs" (OECD, 2006e). There is no evidence which *prima facie* favours full-time over part-time care, which contributes, for example, the provision of free pre-school services on a part-time basis in the United Kingdom, or half-time participation of three years olds in the French "maternelle" system.

Brooks-Gunn (2003) finds positive effects from quality early interventions on performance later in childhood, notably: i) high-quality centre-based programmes enhance the school-related achievement and behaviour of young children; ii) these effects are strongest for poor children and for children whose parents have low levels of educational attainment; iii) positive but smaller effects continue into late elementary school and high school years, and iv) programmes that are continued into primary school and that offer intensive early intervention have the most sustained long-term effects. On basis of a longitudinal survey in the United Kingdom, Sylva *et al.* (2004) concluded that: i) pre-school experience, compared to none, had a significant positive effect on child development; ii) an earlier start (before age three) is better for intellectual development at age six and improved independence, concentration and sociability at that age; and iii) part-time attendance was no better or worse than full-time attendance. Evangelou *et al.* (2005) also find that children who are at risk of low educational achievement benefit from early interventions in a cluster of skill related to literacy access, including vocabulary, understanding of books, print and writing. Vulnerable or disadvantaged children benefit most from good-quality pre-school experiences (*e.g.*, Oreopoulos, 2003), especially if the children in the group are of different social backgrounds. Recent findings of the New Zealand competent learners study also illustrate the importance of investment in early-years care and education (New Zealand Ministry of Education, 2006).

Belsky (2005) finds that participating in childcare through the first two or even 4.5 years of one's life may increase problem behaviour (aggression, disobedience), but also notes that childcare effects as more problem behaviour or greater cognitive-linguistic competence are not particularly sizeable in magnitude and are often dwarfed by the effects of external factors such as, for example, family, maternal sensitivity or the paternal presence. Similarly, NICHD

> Box 6.3. **The quality of care and child development** (*cont.*)
>
> early childcare research network (2005) also suggests that in both the cognitive and socio-emotional domains, quality and type of childcare have a clear impact on child outcomes, even after controlling for family factors. However, family influences are consistently better predictors of children's outcomes than early childcare experiences alone, and maternal education would be a stronger predictor of maternal sensitivity and mother-child relations than either formal childcare hours or quality of care. Sylva *et al.* (2004) also find that for all children's language and pre-literacy skills the quality of home learning environment is even more important than parental occupation, education, and income: "what parents do is more important than who parents are".

Helping children to move from childcare, pre-primary and other early-years services into primary-school systems is another quality aspect of early childhood support systems, as more than in the past, primary schools are expected to provide a flexible and supportive child-friendly setting to children entering school for the first time (OECD, 2006e). This transition is arguably easiest in Nordic countries with more or less integrated systems for zero-seven-year-olds, with a pre-school-class for six-year-olds facilitating the transition to primary school which starts at age seven. In other countries the transitions from childcare into pre-schools or pre-schools into primary schools is not as smooth. The prolongation of kindergarten learning approaches into the first years of the primary school may be one way of improving this. Alternatively, better co-ordination between pre-primary and primary institutions and carers/educators/teachers is indispensable. For example, in the Netherlands, the pre-primary and primary schools have been integrated into one system, but there is little co-operation between childcare centres and these schools. More common elements in professional development courses for early childhood and primary school teachers could also help.

Child-to-staff ratios

Measuring the quality of formal childcare and early education services is fraught with difficulty and there is no single indicator which adequately reflects the quality of service environment and the quality of interaction between staff and children. Although restricted to a single aspect of quality, child-to-staff ratios give a quantitative indication of the frequency of contacts between carers/educators and children. Most countries have regulations specifying child-to-staff ratios which typically increase with the age of children (Chart 6.3, Panels A and B, and Annex Tables 6.A1.1 and 6.A1.2 for more detail).

Chart 6.3. **Denmark has low child-to-staff ratios in childcare and pre-primary education**

Panel A: Child-to-staff ratios in formal day-care services, average for 0-3 year olds

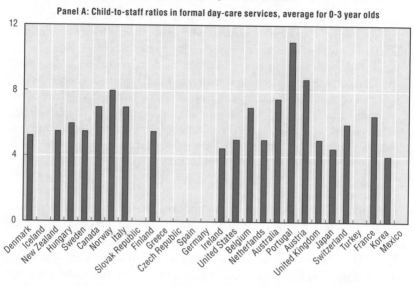

Panel B: Child-to-staff ratios in kindergarten and other pre-primary education services, average for 3-6 year olds

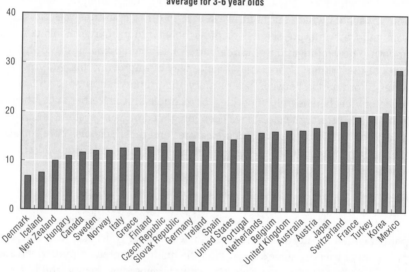

Source: For 0-3 year olds, OECD, *Babies and Bosses* (various issues) and OECD (2006), *Starting Strong II*; for 3-6 year olds, OECD (2007), *Education at a Glance*.

Chart 6.3, Panel A shows the average child-to-staff ratio for children aged 0-3 who attend licensed day-care facilities; in most OECD countries there are about five to seven children per childcare worker. This ratio is considerably higher for three- to six-year-olds in pre-primary programmes (Chart 6.3, Panel B); on average about 14 to 15 children per contact staff (where information is available, the ratio of contact staff, teachers and classroom and teacher assistants, is also shown in Annex Table 6.A1.2). The relatively low intensity of personnel in pre-primary facilities contributes to its low cost compared to operating childcare services for very young children. This helps explain why there is greater access to pre-primary facilities than to childcare services for the very young, and why in some countries policies financially support parental care for very young children (see previous chapter).

Staff qualifications and curricula

By and large, the dichotomy which exists between the care and education sectors in many countries is a false one. However, qualifications of childcare workers vary greatly across countries and types of childcare service. Lead childcare workers frequently have a vocational-level diploma, generally at children's nurse level, or staff with secondary schooling and a one- to two-year vocational diploma. Similarly, support staff qualifications vary hugely: from no qualifications to a few years of vocational training in Nordic countries.

Pre-primary teachers are frequently trained at the same level and in the same training institution as primary school teachers. This profile is found in for example, Australia, Austria, Canada, France, Ireland, the Netherlands, the United Kingdom and the United States (in some of these countries, e.g. France, Ireland, and the Netherlands, the pre-primary teacher is trained both for the pre-school and primary sector). In federal countries, variation exists across different states or provinces, but the predominant type of training is in primary-school-oriented pedagogy, which is understandable as readiness-for-school is an important goal of pre-primary education (OECD, 2006e).

In Nordic and central European countries, teachers/pedagogues in pre-schools/kindergarten often have completed upper-secondary or tertiary education, with a focus on early childhood services rather than primary teaching. The social pedagogy tradition approach to children encompasses care, upbringing and education, with the focus placed on supporting children in their current developmental tasks and interests, not the achievement of a pre-set level of knowledge, as in primary school curricula. For example, pre-schools in Sweden establish individual plans with targets for individual children. National pre-school curricula, should they exist, often establish a set of pedagogical orientations and guidelines, with interpretation up to local policy makers and professionals.

Annex Tables 6.A1.1 and 6.A1.2 provide information on qualifications and the work environment of certified staff in day-care and pre-school services, respectively. This information gives some indication on the quality of staff, although information on the proportion of certified staff in facilities is not available. Even if this were available, such information would not give a complete picture of staff-quality, as the latter is crucially affected by other factors, for example, personal aptitude and work-experience.

In general, childcare workers have less formal qualifications that pre-primary staff and childcare workers generally earn less than their colleagues in pre-primary education, especially when employed in the private sector on more or less precarious employment conditions (Tougas, 2002). Low-pay makes staff turnover more likely, which is not beneficial to children. High turnover rates also diminish employer-provided training opportunities. Especially in rapidly developing childcare sectors (e.g. Ireland and the United Kingdom), investment has not kept pace with the need for childcare workers, and investment in this area is therefore of particularly pressing concern in these countries (OECD, 2005a).

Control over the curriculum is one way through which governments can exercise some quality control. Unlike the centrally imposed primary school curricula, childcare and pre-primary curricula frequently are relatively short, allow for local interpretation (e.g. in Nordic countries where decentralized responsibility is part and parcel of childcare, education and health service delivery and policy development), provide guidance to professionals, promote parent-staff communication, identify general quality goals and indicate how they may be attained. The Nordic countries have "guideline-curricula" for all early-years services, while national curricula for services to 3-6-year-olds apply in Belgium (both Flemish and French-speaking communities), France, Germany, Ireland, Italy, New Zealand, Portugal, Korea, Mexico and large parts of the United Kingdom (OECD, 2004a and 2006e).

Broadly speaking, there are two approaches to existing curricula (see OECD, 2006e, for a detailed overview). The early education approach (fostering school readiness) involves a more centralising and academic approach to *curriculum* content, with structured programming and attention to basic language skills, including attention to preparing for primary school. Curricula in the pedagogic tradition of Nordic and some central European countries but also New Zealand (OECD, 2004a) are more child-centred, and build on the natural learning strategies of the child such as curiosity, creativity, play with or without peers rather than a focus on pre-set standards.

The role of parents

Formal care and early education services supplement parental care and education services. Given the primary role of parents in child development, it is somewhat of a anomaly that they traditionally play such a limited role in early years policy development and the supervision of services. Early education institutes struggle more in getting parents involved than do childcare centres (or pre-schools in Nordic countries). In some countries, policy increasingly tries to involve parents in kindergarten programmes (OECD, 2006e). In the United States, seventeen States stipulate the implementation of parental involvement policies; and another seventeen States awards grants to school boards and districts to involve parents in education programmes. Many States also encourage or direct employers to enable parents to attend school activities, such as parent-teacher meetings and conferences.

Among the countries which participated in the OECD *Babies and Bosses* reviews, Denmark has arguably the strongest emphasis on the parental input to and oversight of improving quality. Since 1993, childcare has been overseen by parent boards (as well as by municipal authorities). The parent boards are elected and have some decision-making powers related to setting principles for activities in the centre and for budget management. They also have recommendatory powers related to staffing issues. The boards play a major part in setting the annual plans for the childcare services, which are the main mechanism for ensuring quality, and are submitted to the local authority funding the service. Municipal pedagogical advisers guide staff and parents in developing plans and in determining their own quality monitoring processes, and without any external benchmarking, local professionals are in a very powerful position, relative to parents.

6.3.4. Out-of-school-hours care: an emerging priority

School schedules are often not compatible with work hours. On average across the OECD, scheduled primary school teaching hours are about 700 per annum (OECD, 2006b), while *de facto* school hours are sometimes considerably shorter. Even this understates the problem faced by parents: parents in the Netherlands face a big headache in reconciling work and school hours, because the latter are unpredictable. Schools find it difficult to provide the scheduled number of hours due to the lack of replacement teachers to cover for teachers who have taken additional holidays on short notice or who are absent because of illness. As a result classes (most frequently for the youngest children) are not given and parents are informed about this at short notice,[8] leaving them to juggle for quick solutions to care for their children. According to a survey of the school year 2000-01, 35% of the schools (and more than 50% of the inner-city schools) had to send their children home on occasion because of teacher shortages (van Langen and Hulsen, 2001), and there is no reason to believe the situation has improved significantly since then.

Working parents in France face another issue. Traditionally, schools are not open on Wednesday, but are open on Saturday morning instead. This means that working parents have to look for alternative childcare solutions on Wednesdays.

With parents increasingly in paid work, there is growing demand for all-day supervisory services in order to make school schedules more compatible with full-time employment. Out-of-school-hours care services (OSH) provided at school facilities or elsewhere are important in helping parents combine their family and work commitments when children get older. These services are relatively cheap, if only because child-to-staff ratios are relatively high, for example, costs per child amount to one-third of the cost in day care in Sweden. Nevertheless, these services are underdeveloped in most OECD countries, which contributes to the existence of so-called "latch-key kids"; many US-based evidence reports behavioural problems for children who are in "self care" after school hours (e.g., Blau and Currie, 2004).

There are a few countries and jurisdictions where OSH-care is available on a more or less comprehensive basis, and Box 6.4 reports on relevant practices in Denmark, Sweden, and the Canadian province of Québec (OECD, 2006e, also reports considerable coverage of OSH-care in eastern Länder in Germany). As discussed above, many municipalities in France provide full-day services, and primary schools may provide a similar service.

In many other countries coverage is low, but in some at least, this is recognized as a policy problem. As part of the 2006-07 budget, the Australian government lifted the existing cap on OSH-care places to allow existing and new OSH providers to expand childcare places to meet demand. New Zealand has small scale support for out-of-school hours care (Adema, 2006a), and in the Netherlands from the 2007-08 school year onwards schools are "obliged to facilitate" out-of-school-hours care services, usually by private providers. However, there is no entitlement to a place and demand is likely to exceed supply in the near future. For a comprehensive OSH-care system to be developed (as in Denmark and Sweden) at a relatively low price it is important to make better use of existing school-buildings paid for by taxpayers. In the Netherlands, and in other countries policy has yet to convince independent school boards to overcome their traditional reluctance to make school premises available of out-of-school hours care services.

British policy has moved towards expanding OSH-care capacity (DfES, 2004). OSH-care capacity in 2001 was estimated to cover about 7% of children in the age group three to five, and 19% of the 6- to 12-year-olds. In the 2002-03 school year, the Department for Education and Skills (DfES) sponsored twenty five local education authorities (LEAs) to develop extended schools pathfinder projects (Cummings et al., 2004). Initiatives differed in focus, but generally involved delivery of community and family services, often in areas of deprivation. In addition to their "core business of teaching", extended schools offer services to pupils and their families, before and after school hours, at weekends and during school holidays. From September 2005, about 1 300 schools (on 23 000 in all) had started to roll out extended services.

Box 6.4. **Out-of-school-hours (OSH) care services in Denmark, Sweden and the Canadian province of Québec**

A comparison of working hours and school schedules implies that many (pre-)school children require additional care arrangements covering the time before school starts, during lunchtime and after school (and sometimes from early afternoon onwards). This demand is increasingly met through the use of out-of-school-care services (OSH), which are most developed in Denmark, Sweden and the Canadian province of Québec.

Around 2000, four out of five children of school-age in Denmark participated in OSH care (up from three out of five in the mid-1990s). No OECD country has OSH-care services that are integrated with the (pre-)school education curriculum, but in the countries where OSH-care is provided on a large scale programmes are often run in conjunction with pre-schools and primary schools. Frequently, leisure time facilities as OSH-services are known in Denmark, are located at schools and come under the management of the school principal (with a supervisory role for a parental board). They are funded through municipal education and culture budgets. Parental contributions are expected, however, and unlike for childcare, there is no maximum contribution. Even so, on average parents cover only about 30 to 40% of the costs.

In Sweden, OSH-care services are generally provided in leisure time centres whose number has increased significantly during the 1990s. OSH-services are available to children from age 6 onwards until age 12. In general, OSH-services are provided from 2 p.m. onwards when school finishes, until around 5 p.m. depending on parental working hours. Eighty per cent of all six, seven and eight-year-olds use an OSH service, but from age nine onwards the desire to use OSH-services diminishes rapidly (about 40% of all 6- to 12-year-olds make use of OSH care). For OSH-care the maximum fee for the first child is 2% of gross family income (with a maximum of about EUR 100 per month), and half that for second and third children, other children are not charged fees. The management of leisure time centres is integrated with primary school management to a large extent and both institutions are supervised by the National Agency of Education.

In the province of Québec, family policy reform in 1997 initiated a rapid growth of OSH-care provision at subsidised fees, but at CAD 7 for three hours of care, OSH-care is relatively expensive to parents (in comparison to ten hours of childcare in a day-care place for the same fee). In 2003, there were 1 579 registered out-of-school care services in Québec (some of them covering several of the 2000 primary schools in the province) which catered for 174 548 regular users (and 57 667 non-regular users), or about 38% of children aged 5 to 12. In 2001, this was considered somewhat below demand for OSH-care which was estimated at around 50% of all children in that age group.

Box 6.4. **Out-of-school-hours (OSH) care services in Denmark, Sweden and the Canadian province of Québec** (cont.)

Most of these services that involve leisure time activities but also facilitate preparing homework are provided within the school system; OSH services are carried out under supervision of the Ministry of Education. Municipalities are obliged to provide OSH places when there are at least 15 children in the area who require the service. Care is delivered for at least 2h30 per day, and about 80% of these services are available from 6.30 or 7 a.m., while school days generally start at 8 or 8.30 a.m. OSH services are also available for 90 minutes at lunchtime (when attendance is at maximum), and at the end of the school day from about 4 p.m. to 6-6.30 p.m. The majority of children use OSH-places regularly, *i.e.* for than three days per week and/or over 2h30 per day). During the summer school holiday, which lasts nine weeks, municipalities often organise leisure activities (or financially support the organising NGO), for which parents can claim tax relief. Such services are often not provided until the end of summer as the students who supervise leisure activities start their academic year before the primary school year commences.

Extended schools and Children's Centres are central planks in the government strategy to enhance child development, strengthen families and communities (Cummings *et al.*, 2006), and help parents in England to reconcile their work and care commitment. By 2010, all parents of children aged 3-11 who wish to use formal care services should have access to affordable care facilities from 8 a.m. to 6 p.m. on weekdays all year round (HM Treasury, 2004).

6.3.5. *Fees and the net cost of childcare to parents*

Any comparison of the cost of childcare across countries is inevitably based on assumptions. These assumptions concern the age of children, family status, different earnings' levels and the fee paid by parents for their child's participation in early-years care and education services, and the intensity of its use. This section is based on one such set of assumptions. One important fact to be borne in mind in interpreting these numbers is that in practice, fees vary not only by country but also by the type of care provided and, frequently, by region and/or characteristics of the children or parents. The calculations in this section assume that fees are paid for full-time care, whereas in reality, there is considerable difference across countries and parents as to the mix of parental and non-parental care. For example, childcare use in Sweden is typically for 30 hours per week, whereas in the Netherlands childcare participation is often on a part-time basis; for example, two days per week in formal care, one day of informal care by relatives and neighbours, and two days of full-time parental care is not an uncommon "childcare package" in the

Netherlands. These differences should be kept in mind when interpreting the comparison of childcare costs as below.

Together with the financial support provided to parents, the affordability of purchased childcare services is determined by the fee charged by providers. Chart 6.4 shows that on average across OECD countries, the average "typical" parental fee paid for a two-year old in full-time care is just over 16% of average earnings, with wide variation across countries form a low around 5% to a high of 33% in Luxembourg and Switzerland. Across countries fees differ because of different market structures and government subsidies to childcare providers.

Chart 6.4. **Childcare fees range from 5% of average earnings in central and eastern European countries and Sweden to one-third in Luxembourg and Switzerland**

Childcare fee per two-year old attending accredited early-years care and education services, 2004

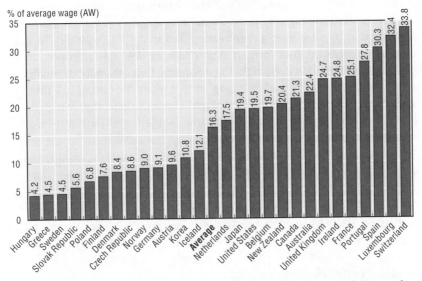

Note: The "average wage" reflects the earnings of an average worker (OECD, 2007e). Fees are those payable for a two-year old, for one month of full-time care not accounting for periods where childcare may not be available or required (e.g. vacation). Where fee information is provided per hour of care, full-time care is assumed to cover 40 hours per week. Fees are the gross amounts charged to parents, i.e. after any subsidies paid to the provider but before any childcare-related cash benefits, tax advantages available to parents or childcare refunds/rebates that are akin to benefits. Where prices depend on income or family characteristics, the maximum applicable fee is shown. Unless fees are rule-based or uniform across institutions, averages or "typical" fees are shown.

Source: OECD (2007f).

Childcare fees are often reduced for families in specific circumstances, such as low-income households and/or sole-parent families, families with multiple children participating in childcare, and fees can also decrease with the child's age. Such measures aim at addressing equity concerns, ensuring accessibility of childcare service for families with limited means or demographic objectives (reducing the cost of children for larger families). They may also be designed to encourage the use of non-parental care in quite specific cases, and examples include fee reductions for lone parents to enable them to stay in employment or look for and take up a new job, or students, to allow them to complete their studies. Governments and, to some extent, semi-private not-for-profit childcare providers use differentiated fee schedules in order to target childcare subsidies or otherwise redistribute between different types of childcare users.

In certain cases, a non-differentiation (or limited differentiation) of parental fees can be used to the same effect. For example, providers, including some commercial providers, as for example in New Zealand, maintain the same or similar fees for very young children and older children, even though the cost of care (due to relatively low children-to-staff ratios) for very young children is relatively high. By cross-subsidising among age groups, barriers to participation by very young children are reduced (OECD, 2004a). In many childcare centres the fees for part-time childcare are largely proportional to full-time care fees. However, in Portugal parental fees generally do not decline with part-time use of formal childcare, so that while the cost of full-time care is relatively low in Portugal, the cost of part-time care is relatively high (OECD, 2004a), which may contribute to the low incidence of part-time work in Portugal (Chapter 3).

In addition, countries that do not subsidise providers on a comprehensive basis as in, for example the Nordic countries, provide a range of cash and fiscal benefits aimed at helping parents reduce the net cost of purchased childcare. For example, spending on the Australian Child Care Benefit amounted to about USD 1 billion in 2003, while the Canadian Childcare Expense (tax) Deduction was worth about USD 850 million in 2003 (OECD, 2007a).

Childcare costs related to earnings

A comparison of costs in relation to average gross wages can be misleading since taxes and cash benefits, and therefore the net budgets available to families for purchasing items such as childcare, vary considerably across countries. In practice, parents need to take into account the costs of childcare relative to the net gain from employment. This is illustrated in the charts below.

In countries without comprehensive government support for childcare *providers*, the net cost of childcare to parents can be substantially lower as parental fees, because of fiscal support and childcare support payments to *parents*. Nevertheless, after accounting for tax reductions and childcare benefits, overall costs remain substantial in many countries. Considering dual-earner couples with earnings at 167% of the average worker's earnings, the average out-of-pocket expenses for two children in full-time care are about one sixth of average earnings (Chart 6.5, Panel A).

Net childcare costs are low in countries where fees are relatively low and in Belgium and Portugal, where there is considerable fee support (Chart 6.5). In these mostly eastern and northern European countries, net childcare costs for families with two children at moderately high earnings are close to or below 10% of overall family net incomes. Participating in formal childcare services is most expensive for working couples in the Canadian province of Ontario (as in Chart 6.5; the situation in the Canadian province of Québec is rather different, and is more comparable to the situation in Finland and Sweden, see OECD, 2005a), New Zealand, Switzerland (city of Zürich). At 45% of average earnings, the out-of-pocket expenses of working couples with earnings of 167% of the average are highest in Ireland and the United Kingdom, and can amount to around one-third of family net income (as shown at the bottom of the Chart). Calculations, not presented here, for dual-earner families with household earnings equivalent to 133 and 200% of the average wage, generate results similar to those in Chart 6.5 (OECD, 2007e).

Cost considerations loom larger for sole parents who, in the absence of a supporting partner, are likely to need formal childcare support to meet work commitments. For a sole parent with earnings at two/thirds of the average wage, out-of-pocket expenses are substantially lower than for dual-earner families in absolute terms (Chart 6.5, Panels A and B). Compared to dual-earner families, childcare fees for sole parents are significantly lower Belgium, while in other countries, in particular, Australia, New Zealand, the United Kingdom and the United States (Michigan), net cost reductions are achieved through targeted childcare benefits and rebates. Nevertheless, despite fee support in the United Kingdom, out-of-pocket costs for sole parents amount to 21% of the average wage in the United Kingdom rising to 35% in the Canadian province of Ontario (in the province of Québec it was about 10%), and 45% in Ireland.

At 8% of average wages, the net cost of childcare is around half that faced by two-parent households, but childcare spending still consumes about on average 12% of a sole-parent family budget, and more than half the family budget in Ireland. Obviously this has implications for incentives to work (below), and thus for the risk of suffering from poverty. Moreover, OECD (2004b) showed that sole parents with earnings in the 67% to 100% of average earnings range have at best net incomes only slightly above (and sometimes clearly below) commonly used poverty thresholds. Even relatively low levels of childcare expenses can many sole-parent families at a high risk of poverty.

Chart 6.5. **Net childcare costs are highest in Ireland**

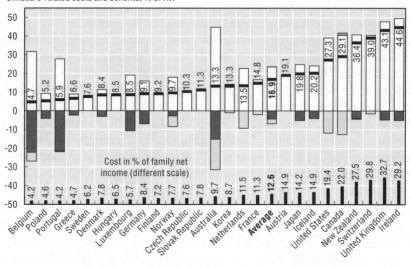

Panel A: Net childcare costs for a dual-earner family with full-time earnings of 167% of the average wage, 2004

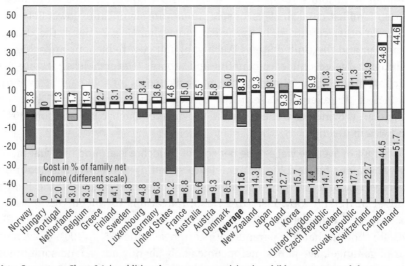

Panel B: Net childcare costs for a sole-parent family with full-time earnings of 67% of the average wage, 2004

Note: See note to Chart 6.4; in addition there are two participating children age two and three.
Source: OECD (2007f).

Targeting childcare subsidies on particular family types or income groups is more common in countries which rely on demand-side subsidies such as rebates and cash transfers. In some such countries, childcare costs are cut by about half for lower income groups (for example, Australia and the United Kingdom) while they are reduced to low levels from high (Japan) or very high levels (United States) for sole parents. Norwegian sole parents in low-wage employment can actually benefit financially from using childcare services: Panel B of Chart 6.5 shows that the combined effect of tax reductions and cash benefits more than compensates childcare fees.

Because low-income sole parents have limited tax liabilities, granting tax relief is not an effective tool for ensuring that childcare support gets to those who need it most. If tax relief is the main or only support available, and when it is "wastable" or "non-refundable", then the value to low-income parents is limited. In contrast to the province of Québec (OECD, 2005a), low-earning sole parent families in Ontario, Canada, receive very little support with their childcare costs (Chart 6.5, Panel B).

6.3.6. Financial incentives to work after childcare costs

Chart 6.6 shows by how much income taxes, employees' social security contributions and cash benefits change following a transition from labour market inactivity to employment, after subtracting childcare costs. Changes are shown relative to gross employment incomes in the new job for a parent taking up low-wage employment (defined as paying 67% of the average wage). The horizontal markers indicate the fraction of in-work earnings that is effectively "taxed away" for the parent entering work. As discussed in Chapter 4, the "Average Effective Tax Rate" (AETR) is the sum of tax increases and benefit losses that result from taking up employment.

Compared to sole parents, AETRs in the two-parent scenario are almost entirely driven by the tax and contribution burden; withdrawals of income-related transfers are generally negligible (Chart 6.6, Panel A). In most countries, even if one parent is inactive, entitlements, if any, are low due to the earnings of the working parent. Yet in some cases, full-time employment stops entitlements to – sometimes generous – home-care and child-raising allowances that would be available to stay-at-home parents, as in Australia, Austria, the Czech Republic, Finland, France, Hungary and the Slovak Republic (Chapter 5).[9]

Chart 6.6, Panel B, shows the importance of childcare costs in eroding the net gains from work in dual-earner families. Childcare fees are a key factor in reducing gains from work, though other factors are even more important in some countries – tax burdens (Denmark and Iceland), for example, and benefit withdrawals (childrearing payments in Austria, Finland, France, Hungary and the Slovak Republic). Averaged across OECD countries, childcare fees use up

Chart 6.6. **Net income gains from work for dual-earner families using childcare are smallest in Ireland and the United Kingdom**

Change of taxes and benefits relative to earnings in the new job, 2004

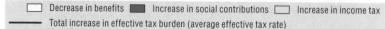

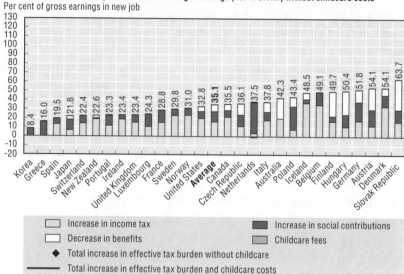

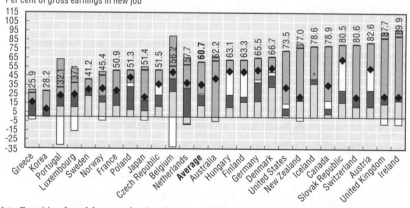

Note: Transition from labour-market inactivity to a full-time low-wage job (67% of AW) for the second earner in a couple family with two children (age two and three); the primary earner has an average wage (AW). All tax and benefit changes relate to the household as a whole. The Average Effective Tax Rate is the fraction of earnings that does not produce a net income gain as it is offset by higher taxes and lower benefits. "Benefits" include minimum-income/social assistance benefits, housing benefits, employment-conditional ("in-work") benefits and family benefits (including special lone-parent benefits and childcare related benefits that do not depend on the use of purchased childcare, such as homecare or child-raising allowances and the *Allocation parentale d'éducation* in France). Other childcare benefits and childcare costs are not included in Panel A, but they are accounted for in the calculations underlying Panel B.

Source: OECD (2007f).

nearly 40% of the gross earnings of a low-wage second earner – more than taxes, social contributions and benefit losses combined. Only one-third of gross earnings are at the disposal of the family for consumption. In more than half of the countries, AETRs are even higher, and only about 20% of additional earnings are left for consumption by the family.

Chart 6.7 confirms the important role of benefit withdrawals in employment decisions of sole parents. On average, sole parents starting a low-wage job lose almost half of their gross earnings to reduced transfer payments and almost 20% due to taxes and contributions they are liable to pay as employees. This leaves about one-third of gross earnings as an addition to household income, which is not enough to cover childcare costs, let alone other work-related expenses, in the Canadian province of Ontario, Ireland, France, and the city of Zürich in Switzerland. Much more than for second earners, childcare fees are crucial to short-term net returns to work for sole-parent families. Policy in many countries has responded by granting significant childcare support payments to sole parents, but despite these measures AETRs for sole parents at moderate earnings exceed those of second earners in all countries, except for Greece, Hungary and the United States (compare Panels B, Charts 6.6 and 6.7).

Comparing the results in Panels B of Charts 6.6 and 6.7 with Tables 4.4 and 4.7, shows that financial incentives to work change with the age of children. When children are very young (below three years of age), moving into employment is not immediately rewarding because of the loss of childrearing payments in Austria, Finland, France, Hungary and the Slovak Republic, and the increase in childcare costs, in many OECD countries. Parents in eastern and northern European countries are in the lucky position of having stronger incentives to work. Generally, work pays more, the older children get. The absence of services, rather than the cost of out-of-school-hours care, contributes to many mothers considering part-time employment opportunities on a long-term basis.

Chart 6.7. **There are no short-term net income gains from work for sole parents with moderate earnings using childcare in France, Canada (Ontario), Switzerland (Zürich) and Ireland**

Change of taxes and benefits relative to earnings in the new job, 2004

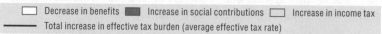

Panel A: Sole parent with two-thirds of average earnings without childcare costs

Per cent of gross earnings in new job

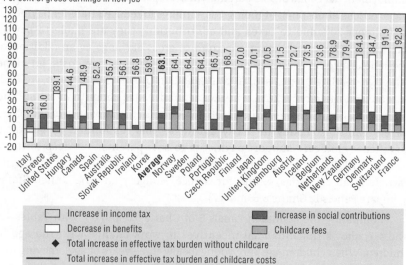

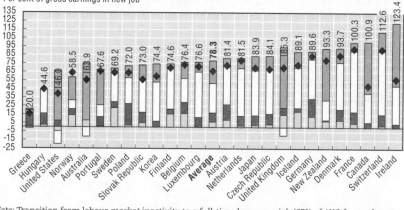

Panel B: Sole parent with two-thirds of average earnings and accounting for childcare costs

Per cent of gross earnings in new job

Note: Transition from labour-market inactivity to a full-time low-wage job (67% of AW) for a sole parent with two children (aged two and three). All tax and benefit changes relate to the household as a whole. The Average Effective Tax Rate is the fraction of earnings that does not produce a net income gain as it is offset by higher taxes and lower benefits. "Benefits" include minimum-income/social assistance benefits, housing benefits, employment-conditional ("in-work") benefits and family benefits (incl. special lone-parent benefits and childcare-related benefits that do not depend on the use of purchased childcare, such as homecare or child-raising allowances and the *Allocation parentale d'éducation* in France). Other childcare benefits and childcare costs are not included in Panel A, but they are in accounted for in the calculations underlying Panel B.

Source: OECD (2007f).

6.4. Conclusions

In many OECD countries there are parents who wish to engage in paid work, but cannot do so, because childcare capacity is constrained and/or prohibitively expensive, and/or not available at the hours it is required. Often, parental labour force participation depends on having access to cheap informal care by relatives and neighbours. However, this source of care is drying up: with the rise in female employment rates, mothers, sisters and neighbours of working mothers are increasingly in work themselves. Therefore, policy makers across the OECD area are increasingly interested in public early years care and education policies, from formal home-based care to centre-based facilities integrated in the education system.

Nordic countries were the first to start developing formal childcare systems and they remain in the lead of childcare policy development, in terms of participation, equity in access and quality. Systems are comprehensive and with out-of-school-hours-care support the policy model ensures that combining work and family responsibilities is a realistic life choice. In other countries coverage is less widespread and is low among 0-3-year-olds. Many 3-6-year-olds participate in pre-school programmes, but not necessarily on a full-time basis.

There is a more-or-less general trend across the OECD towards more investment in childcare capacity and quality. Budgetary costs are controlled through income testing and targeting of public supports on families which need it most.

Both demand and supply-side funding can be effective in achieving policy goals, as long as support is made available only to good-quality care. Quality standards should not merely cover health and safety aspects, but could also include child development goals. Parents are key stakeholders in the development of a childcare system, and some countries have had success in involving them in supervision of childcare centres.

The few countries across the OECD area that have a comprehensive out-of-school-hours care service or leisure-time system (*e.g.* Denmark and Sweden) use existing public infrastructure, often school buildings, for the purpose of delivering such services. This practice avoids unnecessarily public outlays, and saves children (and parents) the costly hassle of transport between service providers. Policy makers in many OECD countries should be more vigorous in overcoming the reluctance among school authorities to allow such services to be provided on school premises. More intensive use of existing school buildings and high child-to-staff ratios make the development and provision of out-of-school-hours care services a relatively cheap policy option. The development of out-of-school-hours services deserves a higher priority than it currently gets in many OECD countries.

Generally, work pays for parents, even after accounting for childcare costs. In Nordic countries, subsidies to parents using quality childcare centres are generally so high (see above), that one is almost "a thief of one's own wallet" if one does not use public childcare facilities and engage in paid work. In other countries, the story is rather different. Parental fees are often high, and formal childcare support may not be universally accessible for (working) parents. After accounting for income-tested childcare support, out-of-pocket costs often remain substantial, and they exceed 20% of net income of a dual earner family with full-time earnings of 167% of the average wage in Canada (except for the province of Québec), Ireland, New Zealand, Switzerland and the United Kingdom. Childcare costs are above 40% of a family budget of a sole parent with two-thirds of average earnings in Canada (Ontario) and Ireland. In Ireland and the United Kingdom, the costs of childcare can be so high, that in the short-term work does not pay for many second earners in couple families and this applies to sole-parent families in the Canadian province of Ontario, Ireland, France, and the city of Zürich in Switzerland.

Notes

1. Without taking anything away from the pedagogic and/or educational value of early years' services, the OECD *Babies and Bosses* reviews used the term "childcare" to capture the wide variety of formal care, pedagogy and education services that is available during the early years, until children enter school.

2. For example, see Robertson (2007) on considerations by parents using multiple childcare services in New Zealand.

3. Even though Finland is the only OECD country with a legal entitlement to childcare for all children not yet of schooling age, the home-care payments effectively discourage the use of childcare facilities (see previous chapter).

4. One of the most effective aspects of the Danish system is its social role. The system of health visitors for all children, high coverage of municipal care facilities, and short lines of communication with municipal social workers, facilitates early identification and intervention in favour of children with specific care needs and/or in neglect situations.

5. Cleveland and Krashinsky (2003) argue that early care and education services are a public good as they deliver externalities beyond the benefit of immediate, personal consumption, including a significant contribution to the health, development and learning of children, the development of social capital and reduced outlays regarding negative outcomes later in life.

6. For example, in the, by Canadian standards, very extensive childcare support network in the province of Québec, low-income parents cannot always access the CAD 7 per day childcare places. Extension of childcare capacity is underway: it should be a policy priority to ensure access to childcare facilities for all low-income families who wish to use them (OECD, 2005a).

7. Child Care Benefit (CCB) in Australia is available for two different types of childcare: registered childcare and approved childcare. Parents using registered childcare are

entitled to the minimum rate of CCB provided both parents, or the sole parent, in the family satisfy the "work, training, study test". Registered care may be provided by grandparents, relatives and friends, as well as some pre-schools, kindergartens, out-of-school-hours care services and occasional care centres, as long as the carers have been registered through the Family Assistance Office (FAO). Families using approved care can be eligible for up to the maximum level of CCB and can choose to have their CCB paid to the childcare service (i.e. directly reduce the fees that they pay) or can receive it in the form of a lump sum from the FAO at the end of the financial year. Families using registered care can claim CCB from the FAO during the year by submitting the childcare receipts within 12 months of having the care provided. In January 2005, a Grandparent Child Care Benefit was introduced which pays the full cost of childcare for grandparents who are the primary carers of their grandchildren and are on income support payments. The work, training, study test was waived for all grandparent carers so they can receive CCB for up to 50 hours a week, regardless of whether or not they are working or studying. In addition to CCB, the Australian government has introduced the childcare Tax Rebate (CCTR) which covers 30% of a family's out-of-pocket expenses for approved childcare (the amount of the fee less the CCB entitlement) where the parents meet the work, training, study test. The maximum CCTR payable for expenses incurred in 2006-07 is USD 3 701 per child.

8. During the 1980s, the Netherlands had an excess supply of teachers, and teachers were given extra holidays (the so-called ADV-dagen or "labour-duration-shortening" in Dutch). At present, there is a shortage of teachers in the Netherlands, but the 14.5 ADV days still exist on top of the 55 scheduled holidays for primary-school teachers in the Netherlands.

9. Even when not accounting for childcare costs, the AETRs in Chapter 6 are slightly different from those presented in Chapter 4 due to the different ages of children which are assumed for the calculations (four and six in Chapter 4, and two and three in Chapter 6). Because of the lower ages in Chapter 6, AETRs in countries with prolonged childrearing or home-care benefits (Chapter 5) are significantly higher.

ANNEX 6.A1

Qualifications of Childcare and Pre-school Staff

Tables 6.A1.1 and 6.A1.2 provide information on the qualifications and work-environment of certified staff in day-care and pre-school services, respectively. This information gives some indication on the quality of staff, although information on the proportion of certified staff in facilities is not available. Even if this were available, such information would not give a complete picture of staff-quality, as the latter is crucially affected by other factors, as, for example, personal aptitude and work experience, and attention for the child rather than a pre-set standards, whether or not included in a *curriculum*. The tables also include information on child-to-staff ratios for specific ages. Where available, information is presented on "in-work" or "continuous training".

Any classification of staff in the childcare and early-education sector is fraught with difficulties related to the osmosis of care and education: "Care is education, and education is care" to a large extent. Nevertheless, some broad groups of carers and educators in the day-care and pre-school service sectors can be identified:

Childcare workers. The qualifications of childcare workers differ greatly from country to country and from service to service. In most countries, lead childcare workers have a vocational-level diploma, generally at children's nurse level (upper secondary, vocational level), although many countries will also have specialist staff trained to secondary-level graduation, plus a one- to two-year tertiary level vocational diploma.

Auxiliary staff. There are many types of auxiliary staff working in centres who are trained to different levels. On one end of the scale is auxiliary staff with no formal qualification in the area, while auxiliaries in the pre-school service sector in Nordic countries often have undergone a couple of years of upper-secondary vocational training.

BABIES AND BOSSES: RECONCILING WORK AND FAMILY LIFE – ISBN 978-92-64-03244-6 – © OECD 2007

The pre-primary/primary teacher (or kindergarten/pre-school teachers in Australia, Canada and the United States): Pre-primary teachers are generally trained at the same level and in the same training institution as primary school teachers. The profile is found in Australia, Canada, France, Ireland, the Netherlands, the United Kingdom and the United States (in some of these countries, *e.g.* France, Ireland, and the Netherlands, the pre-primary teacher is trained both for the pre-school and primary sector). In federal countries, variation exists across different states or provinces, but the predominant type of training is in primary-school-oriented pedagogy (readiness-for-school is a primary aim of early education).

In Nordic and central European countries, there are many *pedagogues* who have been trained (upper-secondary or tertiary education) with a focus on early childhood services rather than primary teaching. Pedagogues may also have received training in other settings, as for example, youth work or elderly care.

Table 6.A1.1. **Qualifications of certified childcare workers and main place of work**

	Main type of staff	Initial training requirements	Age range	Main field of work	Continuous training	Child-to-staff ratio
Australia	Childcare worker	Two- to three-years or tertiary training (or four-year tertiary programme)	0-5	Kindergartens; long day care	Childcare – limited to some services	5.0 (0-2 years), 10.0 (2-3)
Austria	Erzieherinnen, Kindergartenpädagoginnen	Five-year vocational secondary	0-5	Krippen and Hort, Kindergarten	Funding by provinces; 3-5 days per year	8.7
Belgium	Kinderverzorgster/Puéricultrice	Three-year post-16 vocational secondary	0-3	Kinderdagverblijf/Crèches (or assistant in école maternelle)		7.0
Canada	Early childhood educator	Two-year ECE	0-12	Childcare, nursery school, pre-school		5.5 (0-1 year), 8.5 (2-3 years)
Czech Republic	Detska sestra	Four-year secondary nursing school	0-3	Crèche	Voluntary – offered by regional centres	
Denmark	Paedagog	Three- to five-year vocational, or tertiary education (depending on prior experience)	0-5	Educational, social care, special needs institutions (incl. day care)	Funding decentralised to municipalities	3.3 (0-2 years), 7.2 (3-5 years)
Finland	Sosionomi (social pedagogues), Lähihoitaja (practical nurses)	Three-year secondary vocational	0-6	Päiväkoti(children's day care centre), Avoin päivakoti	Municipalities have to provide 3-10 days annual training	4.0 (0-3 years), 7.0 (3+ years)
France	Puéricultrices, Éducateurs de jeunes enfants	Nurse/mid-wife + one-year specialisation 27-month post-Bac in training centre	0-3 0-6	Crèches/assistant in école maternelle		5.0 (0-2 years), 8.0 (2-3 years)
Germany	Kinderpflegerinnen	Two-year secondary vocational training	0-6	Kindergarten		
Greece						
Hungary	Gondozó (childcare worker)	Three-year post-secondary voc. training or specialist certificate	0-3	Bölcsöde (for children < three)		6.0
Iceland						
Ireland	Childcarer/child minder	Wide variation	0-6	Childcare centres		3.0 (> 1), 6.0 (2-3 years)
Italy	Educatrice	Secondary vocational diploma	0-3	Asili nido	Municipality or director/inspector decides	7
Japan	Nursery teacher	Graduation from a nursery training school	0-6	Daycare, crèche, nursery		3 (< 1), 6 (1-3 inclusive)
Korea	Childcare worker	Two-year tertiary or one-year training after high school	0-6	Childcare centre, Hakwon (private learning academy)	Offered by regional centres to all childcare and kindergarten teachers	3 (1 year), 5 (2 years), 15 (3 years)
Luxembourg						
Mexico						
Netherlands	Leidster kinder-centra	Two-year post-18 training	0-4	Kinderopvang	Funding decentralised to municipalities	4 (1 year), 5 (2 years), 6 (3 years)

Table 6.A1.1. Qualifications of certified childcare workers and main place of work (cont.)

	Main type of staff	Initial training requirements	Age range	Main field of work	Continuous training	Child-to-staff ratio
New Zealand	Early childhood teacher	Diploma of Teaching (ECE) – a three-year course – or an equivalent approved qualification				4-5 (0-2), 8-12.5 (2-3)
Norway	Assistents	Two-year post-16 apprenticeship	0-7	Barnehager/SFO		8 (> 3 years)
Poland						
Portugal	Educadora de infância	Four-year university or polytechnic	0-6	Crèches, ATL	Offered by regional teacher centres and universities to all teachers	11
Slovak Republic						
Spain						
Sweden	Barnskötare	Two-year post-16 secondary	0-7	Oppen Förskola, Fritidshem	Funding decentralised to municipalities	5.5
Switzerland	Childcare worker	Varies per canton		Crèches, nurseries		4-5 (0-2), 7-8 (2-3)
Turkey	Trained nursery teacher, Nursery nurse	Two-year post-16 secondary	3-11, 0-5	Nurseries (or pre-school assistant)	Limited for day-care workers	3 (> 2 years), 4 (2-3 years), 8 (3-5 years)
United Kingdom						
United States	Childcare teacher	One year course to four-year university	0-5	Public schools, Head Start, Childcare centre	Most States require a certain number of hours per year	Five

Source: OECD Family database, December 2006 (www.oecd.org/els/social/family).

Table 6.A1.2. Qualifications of pre-school teachers and main place of work

	Main type of staff	Initial training requirements	Age range	Main field of work	Continuous training	Ratio of child to teacher (% male teachers)
Australia	Teacher	Three- to four-year tertiary training	0-8	Pre-school/pre-primary	Teachers – several funded days/year	
Austria	Erzieherinnen, Kindergartenpädagoginnen	Five-year vocational secondary	0-5	Krippen and Hort, Kindergarten	Provincial funding: 3-5 days per year	17.0 (0.8%)
Belgium	Kleuteronderwijzer(es)/ Institutrice de maternelle	Three-year pedagogical – tertiary	2.5-6	Kleuterschool/École maternelle	Funding decentralised to schools	16.1 (1.6%)
Canada	Teacher	Four-year tertiary (not PEI)	0-5/5-10	(pre-) Kindergarten and primary school	Provided for kindergarten teachers	8 to 15 for five-year-olds, (31.9% – 2001 data)
Czech Republic	Ucitel materske skoly	Four-year secondary pedagogical or three-year tertiary	3-6	Materská skola		13.4 (0.3%)
Denmark	Paedagog	Three- to five-year vocational or tertiary education (depending on prior experience)	0-10	Educational, social care, special needs institutions (including day care)	Funding decentralised to municipalities	6.6 (16% – 2001 data)
Finland	Lastentarhanopettaja (kindergarten teachers)	3-4-5-year university or 3- to 5-year polytechnic	0-7	6-vuotiaiden esiopetus (pre-school class as well as kindergarten)	Funding decentralised to municipalities	12.5 (3.1%)
France	Professeurs d'école	Four-year university education + vocational training	2-6	École maternelle		19.3 (19%)
Germany	Erzieherinnen	Three-year secondary vocational training + one-year internship	0-6	Kindergarten		13.9 (1.7%)
Greece						12.5 (0.6%)
Hungary	Pedagogue	Three-year tertiary degree	0-7	Óvoda (kindergarten for children 3-7)		10.7 (0.2%)
Iceland						7.3 (3.2%)
Ireland	Teacher	Three-year tertiary degree	4-12	Schools		13.9 (7.7%)
Italy	Insegnante di scuola materna	Four-year tertiary degree	3-6	Scuola materna	Municipality or director/inspector decides	12.4 (0.4%)
Japan	Kindergarten teacher	Kindergarten teacher license (junior college, university or graduate school	3-6	Kindergarten		17.4 (2%)
Korea	Kindergarten teacher	Four-year tertiary degree	3-6	Kindergarten	Offered by regional centres to all childcare kindergarten teachers	20.2 (0.7%)
Luxembourg						
Mexico	Teacher	University degree – licentiatura	0-6	Educación inicial, Educación preescolar	Several funded days/year	(1.7%)
Netherlands	Leraar basisonderwijs	Three-year voc. higher education	4-12	Bassischool		28.9 (4.6%)
New Zealand	Kindergarten teacher	Diploma of Teaching (ECE) – a three-year course – or an equivalent approved qualification	3-5	Kindergarten	Funding decentralised to municipalities	9.8 (1.1%)
Norway	Pedagogiske ledere	Three-year vocational higher education	0-7	Barnehager, SFO		
Poland						

BABIES AND BOSSES: RECONCILING WORK AND FAMILY LIFE – ISBN 978-92-64-03244-6 – © OECD 2007

Table 6.A1.2. **Qualifications of pre-school teachers and main place of work** (cont.)

	Main type of staff	Initial training requirements	Age range	Main field of work	Continuous training	Ratio of child to teacher (% male teachers)
Portugal	Educadora de infância	Four-year university or polytechnic	0-6	Jardim de infância	Offered by regional teacher centres and universities to all teachers	15.4 (1.8%)
Slovak Republic						14.1 (8.7%)
Spain						11.2
Sweden	Förskollärare, Fritidspedagog	Three-year university, three-year university	0-7	Förskoleclass, Förskola	Funding decentralised to municipalities	18.3 (1.9%)
Switzerland	Kindergarten teacher	Three-year upper-secondary and tertiary degree	3-6	Kindergarten/centre de vie enfantine/infant schools		19.7 (4.8%)
Turkey						16.3 (3.1%)
United Kingdom	Qualified teacher	Four-year university	4-8 (0-8)	Nursery classes, reception class	Regular access for teachers	14.5 (8.4%)
United States	Public school teacher, Head Start teacher	Four-year university, CDA = one-year voc. tertiary	3-5		Most States require a certain number of hours per year	

Source: OECD Family database, December 2006 (www.oecd.org/els/social/family).

ISBN 978-92-64-03244-6
Babies and Bosses: Reconciling Work and Family Life
A Synthesis of Findings for OECD Countries
© OECD 2007

Chapter 7

Family-Friendly Workplace Practices

Working hours are very important to people trying to reconcile work and family life. They differ enormously across countries, but also within countries, with different types of workers having different access to different types of flexible workplace measures. The first section of this chapter illustrates cross-national differences in usual working hours, and documents national policy differences on weekly working hours, paid annual leave and the part-time employment conditions. Subsequent sections illustrate the potential business case for family-friendly workplaces, with some practices (e.g. part-time work, flexitime) being more prevalent than others (e.g. teleworking, childcare support). The chapter concludes with a discussion of different public policy approaches to extending family-friendly workplace practices, which range from encouragement of employers to expand such provisions, to ensuring that all workers have some access to family-friendly workplace support.

Many parents in OECD countries are satisfied with the number of hours they work and the level of family income this generates. Many others, however, feel that they face a poor set of choices in working time and are overwhelmed by a "time crunch", leading them to feel they do not spend enough time with their families, but are constrained by inflexible and long working hours. The number of hours parents engage in paid work depends on many factors, including their preferences, career attachment, household income, the age of children, the availability of quality childcare (Chapter 6) and the extent to which tax/benefit systems financially sustain not being in paid employment (Chapters 4 and 5). Furthermore, much depends on whether prevailing workplace practices help parents to find the time to combine paid work and parenthood. Often enough, they do not.

In theory employers might be attracted by the idea of providing workplace support for working parents, as such support might attract new employees, reduce staff-turnover and absenteeism, and generally increase workplace productivity. Alternatively, workers might value such workplace supports by more than the equivalent cash cost to employers, in which case employers could reduce costs by providing such services rather than paying higher salaries. In each case, the result would be greater profits. This possibility is what is referred to as the "business case" for family friendly work practices, which in its most naïve and optimistic form holds that all that is required to transform the labour market is for employers to understand that it is in their own best interest to introduce more supports for parents with children.

In practice, however, there are limits to the extent to which the business case alone can be relied upon to spread family-friendly workplaces more widely. The evidence that there are profit opportunities just awaiting exploitation is lacking. The evidence does suggest that some employers might find it in their interest to provide such measures to some of their staff, but not all employers and not all staff. If the provision of workplace support were left to individual and collective industrial bargaining, such support will be restricted to a few measures (reduced and flexible working hours, and some forms of leave support) and groups of workers in certain sectors.

If employers do not rush to provide family-friendly workplaces, and workers and their unions do not insist on their provision, then it looks like wishful thinking to imagine that industrial agreements will help parents more in the future. However, governments may have a case for intervening in such agreements, because society as a whole has interests in the outcome of bargains between employers and employees which go beyond the interests of those involved in the bargaining. For example, concerns about fertility rates and gender equity objectives (Chapter 1) might not be considered by those bargaining over workplace conditions, but as workplace conditions do affect these outcomes, governments may feel the need to intervene.

7.1. Time at work

Workplace practices in large part determine families' ability to balance work and family life. They are particularly important when other policies, such as public supports in the tax/benefit, parental leave and childcare areas (see previous chapters), are relatively underdeveloped. Access to and use of flexible working practices and reduced hours schedules and other workplace supports are sometimes crucial in balancing work and care commitments, but not all parents have access to such measures to the same extent, and even if they do have access to such workplace support, they do not always feel comfortable with making use of it. As a result, working schedules differ widely across occupations and sectors as well as countries.

Chart 7.1 gives a feel for the very different working-time outcomes in OECD countries. In 2005, over 50% of male workers aged 20-54 worked just over 40 hours per week in Canada, the Czech Republic, Hungary, Iceland, Italy, Luxembourg, Poland, Portugal, the Slovak Republic, Spain, Sweden, Switzerland and the United States. Greece, Iceland, Luxembourg, Poland, Portugal, the Slovak Republic and the United States are the OECD countries where at least about half of the female workers aged 20-54 work 40 to 44 hours per week. Arguably the strongest concentration of working hours around the 40-44 hour band can be found in Hungary where five out of six men and women work that many hours per week. Weekly working hours are concentrated around a shorter full-time working week of around 35-39 hours in Belgium, Denmark, France and Norway, while a similar concentration of working hours among females aged 20-54 can be found in Denmark, Finland, France and Norway. Working parents in France and Nordic countries not only have access to child and out-of-school-hours support but also have working weeks that in terms of duration are below the OECD average.

In other countries, many women work part-time,[1] 40% or more of women aged 20-54 work 34 hours per week or less in Australia, Austria, Belgium, the Czech Republic, Germany, Iceland, Ireland, the Netherlands, New Zealand, Norway, Switzerland and the United Kingdom. There is cross-country variation in the incidence of "short part-time hours" (less than 20 per week) and "long part-time hours" (20 to 30 hours per week). More than 20% of women aged 20-54 work less than 20 hours per week in Australia, the Czech Republic, Germany, the Netherlands and Switzerland. About one in five women aged 20-54 work long part-time hours in Austria, Belgium, the Czech Republic, Germany, Iceland,

Chart 7.1. **Long hours are most usual in Australia, Austria, Greece, Japan, Korea, Mexico, New Zealand, Poland, Turkey and the United Kingdom**

Incidence of actual weekly hours of work among workers aged 20-54, 2005, percentages

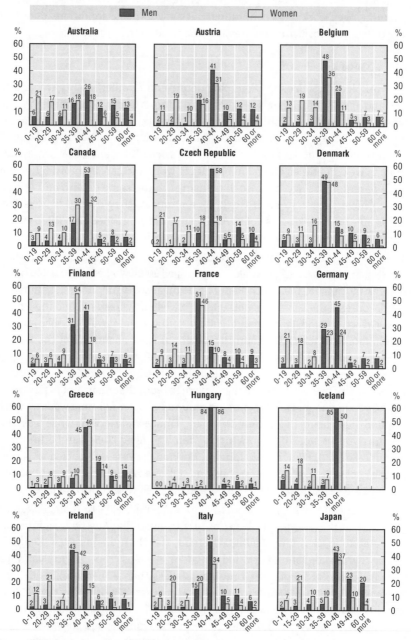

Source: OECD database on Usual Weekly Hours of Work.

BABIES AND BOSSES: RECONCILING WORK AND FAMILY LIFE – ISBN 978-92-64-03244-6 – © OECD 2007

Chart 7.1. **Long hours are most usual in Australia, Austria, Greece, Japan, Korea, Mexico, New Zealand, Poland, Turkey and the United Kingdom** *(cont.)*

Incidence of actual weekly hours of work among workers aged 20-54, 2005, percentages

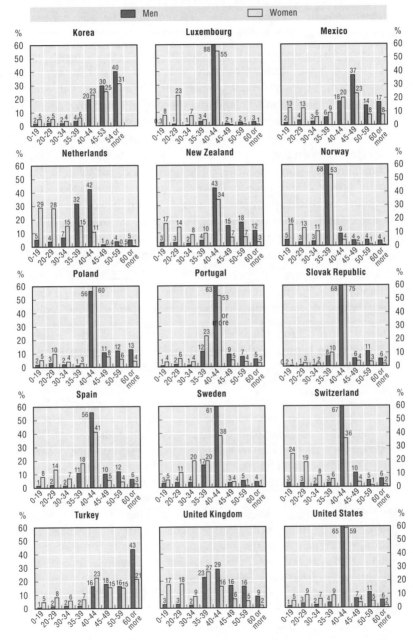

Source: OECD database on Usual Weekly Hours of Work.

Ireland, Italy, Japan, Luxembourg, the Netherlands, Switzerland and the United Kingdom. Women rather than men engage in working reduced hours; in Australia and the Netherlands, only about 15% of male workers work 35 hours per week or less (Chart 7.1). In fact, Australia and the United Kingdom (and to a lesser extent Austria, Mexico and New Zealand) have the least concentrated weekly working hours distributions in the OECD.

Chart 7.1 also shows that long hours are most common in Australia, Austria, Greece, Japan, Korea, Mexico, New Zealand, Poland, Turkey and the United Kingdom. There are more women working long hours in Australia, Austria, Greece, New Zealand, Poland and the United Kingdom than in many other OECD countries. However, the incidence of long hours among women is highest in Korea, Mexico and Turkey where more than 40% of women in the 20-54 age group work more than 45 hours per week, and this proportion is over 60% for men in these three countries.[2] The hours bands for Japan in Chart 7.1 are slightly different from those for other countries, but nevertheless illustrate the prevailing long-hours culture with over 40% of male workers and 15% of females working 50 hours per week or more. More so than in other OECD countries, the prevailing employment conditions in Japan and Korea imply that family life is heavily dependent on mothers providing personal care (Box 7.1).

Information on parental working hours is not available on a comparable cross-country basis, but the presence of children does not often lead to fathers reducing working hours. Paternal working hours seem to be similar to those for

---

Box 7.1. In Japan and Korea labour market institutions and workplace practices restrict maternal employment and contribute to low birth rates

The male-breadwinner model involved a clear allocation of responsibilities and time: women spent their time caring for children at home, while men spent their time at the workplace generating income for the family. In Japan and Korea, the male-breadwinner notion was transposed into a dichotomized labour market system of long-term employment relations (which sits well within the enterprise bargaining system, Araki, 2002) for regular workers who are covered by bargaining outcomes. Non-regular workers are not covered by collective bargaining, and their employment conditions are not as good as those of regular employees. In other OECD countries too, there exist significant discrepancies in the nature of employment conditions between regular and other sizeable groups such as casual workers in Australia (though such workers receive a higher wage in compensation), or workers employed by temporary work agencies in the Netherlands. However, the differences in employment conditions in these countries are nowhere near as large as those between regular and non-regular workers in Japan (OECD, 2003a) and Korea

---

Box 7.1. **In Japan and Korea labour market institutions and workplace practices restrict maternal employment and contribute to low birth rates** (cont.)

(for more detail, see Grubb et al., 2007), nor do they have such a significant and lasting effect on female labour market behaviour.

About 75% of the Japanese workforce and over 85% of male workers, are so-called regular employees, whereas 65% of non-regular workers are female in Japan (Statistics Bureau, 2006). Regular employees constitute about 52% of the Korean workforce; over 62% of male workers and 38% of female workers (KNSO, 2005). Non-regular workers are on renewable, daily to annual contracts, in order to carry out a particular job/task, often at relatively low pay. Regular workers are hired into a firm (not a job), and such workers have a long-term employment relationship with their employer. Regular employees are trained in-house and often receive spousal, child and/or housing allowances that reflect the traditional concern of employers for the well-being of the families of their male employees. Dismissals tend to be avoided, and compensation is strongly linked to certified skills (e.g. university degree), age and tenure, which is seen as indicating loyalty to the firm. There have been moves to increase the role of performance – related pay and diminish the role of seniority in setting wages (Morishima, 2002), but these have so far had only a limited effect.

In return, for long-term employment, regular employees accept a "flexible" adjustment of working conditions. Workers signal their commitment to their employer and career by putting in long hours, including unpaid overtime, and taking less leave than that to which they are entitled. Many regular workers believe that a failure to signal complete devotion to work is inadvisable in terms of career progression and remuneration. Regular employees in Japan often hesitate asking for payment of overtime and taking up their full leave entitlements (Section 7.2.1). Such work patterns are unattractive to mothers (and fathers, for that matter) who wish to devote part of their time to rearing children.

About half of Japanese enterprises with more than 5 000 employees have adopted a "career-track system" that employs regular employees into one of two broad career streams: the fast-track "sougou-shoku" (where workers are groomed for management, with employment conditions generally involving longer working hours and transferability whenever the employer so desires) and the more routine track of "ippan-shoku" workers. Only 3.5% of "sougou-shoku" workers are female, while in just over half of all companies only men are in this stream.

Differences in employment opportunities between men and women continue over the life course, as many employers in Japan and Korea expect women, regardless of their level of educational attainment to withdraw (at

> Box 7.1. **In Japan and Korea labour market institutions and workplace practices restrict maternal employment and contribute to low birth rates** (cont.)
>
> least temporarily) from the labour force upon marriage and/or childbirth, despite the fact that social policies are in place for women who would rather retain their career. Employers are therefore less likely to invest in female workers and their career prospects. To some extent this is a vicious circle. As female workers have limited incentives to pursue a career if they perceive the likelihood of advancement to be more limited than for men, they are more likely to leave the labour force upon childbirth.
>
> Furthermore, "mother returners" who, after having withdrawn from the labour market to care for children then return to work, often end up in (part-time) non-regular employment (as "incentivised" by the social security system in Japan; spouses who earn less than about one/third of average earnings do not have to pay social security contributions for their entitlements, Chapter 4). Once in non-regular work it is difficult to get (back) into regular employment. Sometimes this is because of age-related entry barriers into occupations. For example, to work as a regular public childcare worker in some municipalities an applicant has to be younger than 28 years of age, if not only non-regular employment contracts can be obtained. There are large wage gaps: on average, a female non-regular worker earns 33% less than her regular counterpart does. Under these conditions it is no surprise that women who wish to pursue a career frequently decide not to have children, while potential "mothers returners" will be tempted to stay at home, if family income allows it, rather than engage in jobs that are often low in job-content compared with their potential.

men in general, but in some countries fathers work longer hours than men in general. For example, in the United Kingdom, fathers on average work three more hours per week (Stevens *et al.*, 2004). As illustrated in Chapter 3, mothers with very young children are more likely to work part-time than women in general.

Workplace cultures which involve long-working hours can cause stress in the home life of their employees. Chart 7.2 shows that 20% of the workforce aged 30-44 (persons in this age group are most likely to have responsibilities for young children) in European countries experience medium or high levels of work-life conflict (EFILWC, 2007).[3] The proportion of workers with medium or high conflict levels increases to almost 40% for Greece and Turkey (which, coincidentally or not, are countries with relatively long weekly working hours). Directly comparable information is not available for the non-European OECD countries, but Duxbury and Higgins (2003) suggest for Canada that about

Chart 7.2. **The majority of workers do not face major conflicts in their work/life balance**

Degree of conflict between working hours and family and/or other social commitments, age group 30-44, 2005

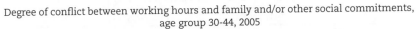
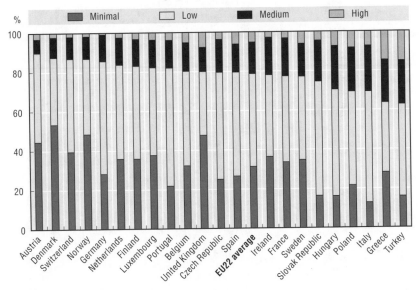

Source: EFILWC (2007).

40% of the Canadian labour force experiences at least moderate levels of conflict in balancing their professional and personal lives.

Differences in work-life conflict levels do not differ much between part-time and full-time employment, but employees who work more than 55 hours per week experience medium to high levels of work-life conflict most frequently (Annex Table 7.A1.1).

7.1.1. *Regular full-time weekly working hours and annual leave entitlements*

Most OECD countries stipulate maximum or "normal" working hours in labour legislation (there is also legislation at the European Union level) and generally also set a minimum employee entitlement to paid annual leave, thereby influencing the actual number of annual hours worked. The establishment of a normal (or standard) full-time workweek, generally refers to the threshold above which overtime becomes payable (Gornick and Meyers, 2003). Some European countries establish normal weekly hours through legislation and collective agreement, while others regulate maximum hours with collective agreements determining "normal hours" (Table 7.1). Some European countries set their maximum weekly hours at the 48 hours specified

Table 7.1. **European workers often have seven weeks of paid holidays per annum**
Statutory and collectively agreed weekly working hours and annual leave, 2005

	Weekly working hours			Days of paid annual leave		
	Statutory maximum[1]	Normal	Collectively agreed (average)	Statutory minimum[2]	Collectively agreed (average)	Public holidays[3]
Australia	48[4]	38	..	20	..	8 to 10
Austria	40	..	38.8	25	25	10
Belgium	38	38	38	20	..	8
Canada	48[5]	40[5]	..	10 to 20	..	10
Czech Republic	40	..	38	20	25	8
Denmark	48	..	37	25	30	9
Finland	40	..	37.5	20	25	10
France	48	35	35	25	25	11
Germany	48	..	37.7	20	30	9
Greece	48	..	40	20	23	10
Hungary	48	..	40	20	..	6
Ireland	48	..	39	20	..	9
Japan	..	40	39.4	10 to 20	..	15
Italy	48	40	38	20	28	10
Korea	44	..	..	8 to 20	..	14
Luxembourg	48	..	39	25	28	10
Netherlands	48	..	37	20	25.6	8
New Zealand		..		(15) 20[6]	..	11
Norway	40	..	37.5	21	25	8
Poland	40	..	40	20	..	11
Portugal	40	..	38.3	22	24.5	12
Slovak Republic	40	..	38.6	20	21.3	12
Spain	40	..	38.5	22	..	11
Sweden	40	40	38.8	25	33	9
Switzerland	45 to 50[7]	..	..	20 to 25	..	8
United Kingdom	48[8]	..	37.2	20	24.6	8
United States		40	..	0	..	10

1. In the context of working time flexibility, working hours can exceed the statutory maximum as long as they adhere to the statutory maximum on an average basis for a given reference period. For example, in Austria, weekly hours may be varied up to a maximum of 50 over a reference period, if an average 40-hour week is maintained (Carley, 2006 for a detailed overview of practice in Europe), while in Canada weekly working hours can be longer than 48 hours per week, as long as they average 48 hours over a two-week period (Federal Labour Standards Review, 2006).
2. In Canada, Japan, Korea and Switzerland, the length of minimum holiday entitlement increases with tenure.
3. For federal countries, this is subject to variation across cantons/provinces and states. Typically, these jurisdictions recognize one or two additional public holidays, but in the Canadian province of Newfoundland there are six additional public holidays.
4. Maximum workweek, subject to Australian Industrial relations Testcase decision which stipulates that an employee may refuse to work overtime because the working of such overtime would result in the employee working hours which are unreasonable having regard to i) any risk to employee health and safety; ii) the employee's personal circumstances including any family responsibilities; the needs of the workplace or enterprise; iii) the notice (if any) given by the employer of the overtime and by the employee of his or her intention to refuse it; and iv) any other relevant matter.
5. This is the Federal standard; normal and statutory maximum working hours vary across provinces.
6. 20 days from 1 April 2007 onwards (beforehand 15 days).
7. 45 hours for industrial enterprises and employees, 50 weekly working hours for all others.
8. Individual workers can opt-out of the weekly working time limits.

Source: Australian government (*www.workchoices.gov.au*); European Industrial Relations Observatory (EIRO) on line (*www.eurofound.europa.eu/eiro*); Gornick and Heron (2006); Human Resource and Skills Development Canada (*www.hrsdc.gc.ca/asp/gateway.asp?hr=en/lp/spila/clli/eslc/01Employment_Standards_Legislation_in_Canada.shtml*) and Canadian Heritage (*www.pch.gc.ca/progs/cpsc-ccsp/jfa-ha/index_e.cfm*); International Labour Organisation, National Labour Law Profiles, Republic of Korea and the Swiss Confederation (*www.ilo.org/public/english/dialogue/ifpdial/info/national/index.htm*); and New Zealand Department of Labor, Employment Relations (*www.ers.govt.nz/*).

in the EU working-time directive, but about as large a group of European countries set a limit of about 40 hours, and working time flexibility schemes allow weekly hours to vary around an average over a reference period (see notes to Table 7.1). In France, 35 hours per week is the "norm", and in many European OECD countries it ranges between 37 and 39 hours per week. Both Japan and the United States set statutory normal hours at 40 hours per week. In the United States, however, the Fair Labor Standards Act (FLSA) excludes about 27% of full-time workers from entitlement to overtime, including managers and supervisors and those over specified earnings limits (Gornick and Heron, 2006).

Policy also influences the number of days worked per annum through statutory holiday entitlements and public holidays. Most OECD countries set a statutory minimum (in many European countries that is at least 20 days per annum in line with the 1993 EU Working-Time Directive). In practice, European workers are typically entitled to around 30-35 days per year of paid vacation, when including public holidays; correspondingly full-year work amounts 45 to 46 weeks a year. In New Zealand, paid annual leave entitlements were extended to four weeks in April 2007, leading to about 30 annual days, while in Japan and Korea the relatively high number of public holidays ensures that the overall number of holidays is comparable to practice in Europe.

Workers in Japan are entitled by law to ten vacation days after six months of continuous service, increasing with length of service to a maximum of 20 days; in addition there are about 15 public holidays in Japan. The FLSA in the United States does not stipulate a minimum entitlement of paid annual leave. However, the longer tenure is, the more holidays. Most Australian, European, New Zealand and North American workers will use their holiday entitlements: in Japan, average take-up is substantially below what workers are entitled to: in 2002, paid leave entitlements amounted to an average of 18 days paid leave per worker, of which only 48% was used (OECD, 2003a).

7.1.2. Policies to strengthen the position of part-time workers

Since the 1980s part-time work has become a widely used labour market feature in many OECD countries (Chapter 3). Part-time employment opportunities may have been promoted for different reasons across countries, time and employment sectors, including: particularly during the 1980s, an emphasis on combating unemployment by spreading available work on as many people as possible; flexibility of production of services; and, pursuing a better reconciliation of work and family commitments. In France, the rationale for reducing working time to 35 hours per week included supporting a more even distribution of paid and unpaid work between men and women (Fagnani and Letablier, 2004), while in the Netherlands (Claassen, 2007) both work/life balance and gender-equity objectives are fuelling a debate on a full-time 30 hour working week (Box 7.2).

Box 7.2. **Men, women and time to care**

The total amount of time spent by men and women in paid and unpaid is about the same In the United States and many European countries, except Italy and possibly some other southern European countries (Burda *et al.*, 2007). However, women do more unpaid (domestic) work (and take leave to care for children) than men. There is some economic logic to this as in couple families the husband typically earns 33-66% (see Chapter 3) more than his spouse, so the opportunity cost to households of caring is less if women reduce their labour force activity.

In European countries, fathers on average spend less than five hours per week on caring for children, while this is closer to eight hours per week in Nordic countries, the Netherlands and Switzerland. In these countries mothers spend on average twice as much time as men on caring for children, while in general across Europe this is about 2.5 to 3 times as much (data do not include time devoted to unpaid housework, EFILWC, 2007). Among married couples in the United States in 2002, mothers spent about 3.4 hours per day caring for children, while that was 2.7 hours per day for fathers (up from 1.8 hours in 1977 (Families and Work Institute, 2004). Even among dual-earning couples, men spend far less time than their partners in both housework and childcare-giving. Often fathers' involvement in basic childcare tasks – *e.g.*, feeding, bathing, dressing children – is especially limited. The long working hours in Korea and Japan, combined with long commuting times in urban areas (and for men at least, the culture of socialising with colleagues after working hours), means there is little time for fathers to be involved in housework chores. Indeed, in 2001, Japanese men with non-employed spouses contribute about 18 minutes a day to housework and care (Ministry of Internal Affairs and Communication, 2001) compared with an average of about half an hour for Korean men (KNSO, 2005).

In response to the increased incidence of part-time work, policy makers in the majority of OECD countries have moved to introduce legislation which enshrines the equal rights of part-time workers. Such legislation includes stipulating *pro rata* pay and benefits between part-time and full-time workers, and/or enabling (groups of) workers (see above) to shift from full-time to part-time work and *vice versa* without being forced to change jobs. The effects of part-time legislation on part-time work rates and/or part-time workers' remuneration are not well known. Bardasi and Gornick (2002) suggest that such measures may also have contributed to smaller part-time/full-time wage differentials than exist in countries without such legislation.

As the incidence of part-time employment has grown, so has the incidence of non-standard work schedules, with less control and less predictability of working times for working parents. An increasing number of employers across the OECD (often in Europe, with the most prescriptive legislation in this regard, see above) are operating various "annualised hours" schemes (EFILWC, 2006), which allow for an averaging of working hours over periods of time longer than a week – and, in some cases, up to a year. Annualised hours arrangements are often favoured by employees' representatives and offered in compensation for a reduction in total work hours (Kouzis and Kretzos, 2003).

For workers with family care responsibilities, even with reduced total hours, having a non-standard, uncontrollable and/or unpredictable schedule can make reconciling work and family responsibilities difficult. Controlling for total hours worked, conflict is also significantly higher when daily hours vary, work days per week vary, starting and finishing times vary, if schedules change with little or no notice, or if workers have little control over their working hours. Working atypical hours may be necessary to square work and care commitments, but most parents would prefer to work predictable standard hours (La Valle et al., 2002; DARES, 2004). On the basis of evidence for France, Fagnani and Letablier (2004) conclude that it is not sufficient to reduce working time for there to be an improvement in the daily lives of working parents; the scheduling of hours, and the processes governing that scheduling, matter a great deal.[4] Enforceable minimum notification periods for changes in working schedules and/or time-bank agreements that divide control over scheduling between employers and workers can play an important role in ensuring that the potential advantages for parents of shorter work hours are not offset by scheduling issues.

One option to manage work/life balance for parents in dual-earner families is to organise their individual work schedules in tandem to ensure continuous parental care (shift parenting). In Canada, nearly half of all dual-earner couples with children are organised such that both parents are working in shifts. Nearly half of all British fathers work before and after school hours, while mothers who work atypical hours are more likely to be working on weekends, presumably when spouses care for children.

7.2. Flexible workplace practices

Family-friendly arrangements in firms are defined as practices facilitating the reconciliation of work and family life, which firms introduce to complement statutory requirements. Family-friendly arrangements can include:

● Changes to work arrangements for family reasons include reductions in working hours (part-time work and/or job/sharing), term-time only working contracts, teleworking,[5] working at home, and flexible working time arrangements (including working a full-time working week but at non-standard hours).

- Leave from work; includes provisions for extra-statutory maternity, paternity and parental leave support, career breaks, leave saving, leave to care for elderly relatives, and emergency leave to deal with a sick child or problems with childcare arrangements.
- Support with child and out-of-school care and elder-care costs.[6]

7.2.1. Flexible working hours

Flexibility in working time allows parents to adjust their schedules to co-ordinate with school or childcare centre hours. Comprehensive cross-national data are not available for OECD countries, but the different sources illustrate some common patterns in flexible workplace practices, of which part-time employment and "flexible hours" are the most common forms. In Australia in 2005, 41% of Australian Workplace Agreements (AWAs) included provisions for flexible use of paid annual leave, 25% for part-time work and 16% for working from home. This was higher for AWAs among working mothers: 44% had flexible hours; 35% involved part-time work, and 17% involved working from home (Australian government, 2006). In the United States many employers report they allow for career breaks for staff, while a gradual return after childbirth and flexible timing of daily working hours are the most prevalent forms of flexible workplace supports for employees at work. Compressed working weeks, *e.g.* working four days per week; job-sharing, *e.g.*, 2.5 days per week, are also fairly widespread, but teleworking is not (Table 7.2). Teleworking is also uncommon in Europe (EFILWC, 2007). In contrast to employer-provided childcare support, large enterprises (1 000+) are less likely to grant flexible worktime practices than workplaces with 50 to 100 employees. Smaller companies in Canada also appear to be more amenable than large employers to creating flexibility in working hours for their employees (Annex Table 7.A2.2).

Many Canadian and UK firms provide a host of time-related policies to help parents, with the most common option being part-time work, as offered by around 75% of employers, followed by flexible hours (see annex tables). Large employers in the United Kingdom, especially those within the public sector, are most likely to offer alternative family-friendly policies such as term-time employment (*i.e.* work-schedules in parallel with school calendars) and job-sharing. Since the late 1980s, a growing number of collective agreements covering large Canadian companies include flexible work arrangements such as job-sharing (10%) and compressed working time (20%). About a quarter of employees in Ireland, Italy and the United Kingdom are able to vary the start and end of their daily work-schedule, while across Europe the equivalent proportion is reported to be around 16%, with the larger enterprises leading the way (EFILWC, 2006).

Table 7.2. **Access to flexible workplace practices in the United States**

Percentage of employees in the United States with access to flexible workplace practices, 2005

| Types of flexible workplace practices available: | Responses from human resource directors[1] | | | |
| | Applicable to only some employees (%) | Applicable to all or most employees) (%) | Where applicable to all (or most) employees | |
			Firm size = 50-99 (%)	Firm size = 1 000+ (%)
Flexible start and end of daily work (periodical)	68	33	37	26
Flexible start and end of daily work (daily)	34	13	17	4
Job share	46	13	15	4
Compressed week	39	10	12	8
Telework (periodical)	34	3	3	2
Telework (occasional)	31	3	4	2
Career breaks for care giving/family responsibilities	73	57	53	48
Gradual return after childbirth	86	67	66	49
Childcare provided at/near workplace[2]	7	..	5	17
Childcare for school age children on vacation[2]	3	..	3	8

1. Sample: 1 092 employers with 50 or more employees (66% for-profit and 34% non-profit organisations).
2. Applicable to all employees.
Source: Bond *et al.* (2005).

7.2.2. *Employer-provided leave*

Much of the employer support in terms of parental leave depends on the nature of publicly available parental leave supports (Chapter 5). In the United States where such support is not available, only 12% of companies offered paid maternity leave (over and above income support by short-term disability payments in some States, Chapter 5). Paid maternity leave was taken by just over a quarter of working mothers, with a similar proportion taking unpaid leave. About 20% of mothers used paid annual leave, sick leave or disability benefits, while 25% of mothers quit their jobs (Catalyst, 2006a and 2006b). In Switzerland, a country where paid maternity insurance was only introduced in 2005, some large employers are increasingly aware that making paid work more attractive to mothers with very young children can keep them in their workforce. Some companies are considering an increase in the duration of maternity pay towards five months, as otherwise they find that many mothers decide not come back to work. In Switzerland, as in many other countries visited in the course of the OECD *Babies and Bosses* reviews, enterprises also try to strengthen workplace attachment among parental leave-takers by keeping them informed about workplace developments, through newsletters, regular meetings, etc. to increase the likelihood of return to the original employer when leave expires.

"Leave saving" is a hybrid of taking leave and working flexible hours. About a quarter of European enterprises report they have schemes which enable flexible working hours to be combined with compensation in the form of paid leave (EFILWC, 2006). In the Netherlands, arguably the OECD country where public involvement in time-related employment supports is most intensive, legislation allows holiday entitlements to be cumulated without loss over a period of five years, giving the possibility to build up extended paid leave periods. Employees can save earnings or leave worth up to 12% of gross annual earnings to use at a later stage for a period of at maximum one year, and the saved amount can be also be sold and paid out as salary during the period of leave. Often these arrangements are covered by industrial bargaining (11% of Australian Workplace Agreements include provisions for flexible use of paid annual leave, Australian government, 2006) or arranged informally at the workfloor. The practical importance of such measures is likely to be underestimated by the available statistics.

7.2.3. Enterprise childcare support

By its very nature only large companies are big enough to organise on-site childcare facilities. Only a few do so; about 3% of all companies in Japan with more than 30 employees; for the United States, Bond *et al.* (2005) report that 17% of large employers (1 000+ employees) offered childcare at or near the worksite, compared to 5% of small employers (50-99 employees). Across Europe, such support is limited, except for large enterprises (over 500 employees) of which 13% offered childcare facilities (EFILWC, 2006).

Of course, employers could help employees with their childcare costs or pool resources amongst each other (*e.g.* per industry or sector) to buy childcare places. This latter model is uncommon, except, in the Netherlands, where public policy aspires that the cost of formal childcare is paid in equal shares by parents, the public and employers for one-third each. Prior to recent childcare reform, about two-thirds of the industrial agreements included childcare support provisions for employees. Since 1 January 2005 employers were expected to contribute to the financing of the childcare support that is paid to working parents through the tax system, but as only 64.7% did so in May 2006 (and as it was deemed unrealistic to expect that 90% of employers would make this contribution by 2008), public authorities have moved to make employer contributions towards childcare support paid by the tax authorities mandatory since 1 January 2007. Employers are expected to cover at least one-sixth of the costs of childcare (this can be as stipulated in collective agreements), which translates into a contribution of 0.28% of gross wages up to an hourly maximum (Ministerie van Financiën, 2007).

7.3. The business case for family-friendly workplaces

There is potentially a "business case" for employers to introduce family-friendly policy measures. This is because such measures can contribute to the quality of the enterprise workforce by retaining some workers who would otherwise quit (and increase the likelihood that mothers return to the same firm upon expiry of maternity leave),[7] and by attracting those workers who value family-friendly workplace support. Both these factors contribute to a reduction in recruitment and training costs. Family-friendly support may diminish stress among working parents (Box 7.3), reduce absenteeism and improve worker loyalty; all these factors contribute to motivation, flexibility and productivity of the workforce (for example, Comfort *et al.*, 2003; Duxbury and Higgins, 2003; Gray, 2002; and Nelson *et al.*, 2004). Furthermore, policies

---

Box 7.3. **Stress in workplaces**

Sources of stress in the work and home environments have been found to negatively affect an individual's physical and psychological health and may, for example, lead to substance abuse, depression and gastrointestinal disorders, or, at the organisational level, increased employee absenteeism, high turnover, poor work performance, job dissatisfaction and low firm loyalty.

"Work/family stress" can be related to worries about child- and/or back-up care arrangements and their quality and parental after-school hours concerns (Barnett and Gareis, 2006). Stress frequently occurs due to the high psychological job demands (*i.e.* high output required) combined with low job decision latitudes or low perception of control. Non-professional and non-managerial workers with high demand/low control jobs (*e.g.* restaurant/hospitality work, data entry, assembly line, clerks, administrative support staff) are most likely to have a relatively high work life conflict (Duxbury *et al.*, 1999). In Canada, women reporting high work life conflict are much more likely to be unsatisfied with their jobs, have a higher rate of absenteeism, and have a higher level of perceived stress and experience burnout and depression. In the United Kingdom, nearly half of all long-term sick absences from work for non-manual workers are due to stress (CIPD, 2004).

Estimates suggest that, in 1995, stress-related absenteeism costs companies more than GBP 3.7 billion per year, but workers' perceived stress levels have more than doubled since that study was conducted (Hewitt, 2004). Canadian estimates of the direct and indirect costs of workers with high work-life conflict (*e.g.* absenteeism, inability to meet deadlines, temporary worker replacement of worker, reduced productivity) are between USD 3.9 billion and USD 8.7 billion per year (Duxbury and Higgins, 2003). Employers thus have a financial case for considering workload intensity of workers and management practices.

---

that enable women to reach management positions will help the employers to access a greater pool of skilled workers. It is also possible that parents may value provisions such as flexibility in working hours by more than the cost of employers of providing them, reducing total remuneration costs to those employers who provide them. All these possible outcomes will increase profitability, so assuming that the various theories reflect reality, employers should be falling over themselves to introduce family-friendly work practices voluntarily. That actually they are not suggests either that the theories are over-optimistic, or else that there are some other reasons why workplaces cause parents problems.

The various arguments suggest that the business case for more family-friendly workplace support is going to be strongest when workers are difficult and expensive to replace, so there are greater incentives to keep the workers that are *in situ*. The more skilled are workers, the greater the costs of replacing them. There is indeed evidence that women working in a technical or professional capacity do have more access to family-friendly workplaces. Furthermore, as it is mothers who have most difficulties in reconciling work and family life, the greater the proportion of women already employed in a business, the greater the potential gains from having a family-friendly workplace. There is also an issue of size: large companies find it easier to manage flexibility in hours than do, for example, many small and medium-sized enterprises, which do not have the financial and organisational capacity to implement family-friendly workplace practices.[8] So we might expect that large employers of high-skilled women are going to be in the vanguard when introducing family-friendly workplaces, with small employers of low-skilled men being laggards. Evidence (Edwards *et al.*, 2003) suggests that this is indeed the case.

Other than this, family-friendly workplaces might not exist as often as they should because of some form of market failure. For example, it could be that firms are *ignorant* of the potential benefits of such policies, a belief that has motivated many government-sponsored initiatives across the world, as will be described below. Further, it might be that prejudice (against women, or parents of children) blinds some people against implementing such measures. As possible evidence in favour of such an assertion are findings that firms with an avowed Equal Employment Opportunities policy and where there are a relatively high proportion of female managers are much more likely to implement family-friendly workplaces.

Another potential reason for the slow dissemination family-friendly work practices is that parent's preferences for such measures are not necessarily given voice by unions in negotiations. The *Babies and Bosses* reviews noted that unions (whose leadership has had a male dominance)[9] were often not particularly active in demanding family-friendly provisions. Even when such demands were on the table at the start of negotiations, they were often not pushed at crucial stages in the endgame of negotiation processes. Hence, progress in extending family-friendly work practices via collective negotiations has not been rapid. Indeed, sometimes conflict within the union movement has prevented progress. In Denmark, the union of metalworkers, with only a few female members, opposed a more general sharing of contributions to maternity insurance across the unionised workforce as this would increase the cost of such provisions to its own members.[10]

If market failures mean that potentially desirable opportunities for introducing family-friendly workplaces are not being exploited, it should be possible to identify this – companies which have such measures should, other things being equal, be more profitable than those which do not.

Empirical evidence on this is mixed and, as might be expected, differs according to the measure in question. Apart from additional costs generated by hiring (and training) replacement workers to maintain productivity and output levels, introducing flexible work schedules may be more expensive than existing (shift) production processes. Moreover, there is no "one-size-fits-all", as different measures fit better in different workplaces. For example, teleworking and working during school-terms obviously do not fit all production processes, and job-sharing fits better in one workplace than the other. This contributes to some ambiguity in the evidence on the use of some measures. For example, Meyer et al. (2001) found that job-sharing has a negative effect on profits because of the associated diseconomies of scale, Gray (2002) found that job-sharing can have a positive impact on enterprise productivity, but less so than measures (flexitime) which support a more visible and full-time workplace engagement of the worker. As shown above, revealed preferences for part-time work and flexible work-schedules have been most successful matching labour supply to shifting demand for labour, and allowing firms to tap (mainly female) labour supply.

Overall, hard-nosed evidence to support the business case for family-friendly policies is not overwhelming. Indeed, it appears that initial expectations on the effects of introducing work/life balance measures were overly optimistic. Bloom and van Reenen (2006a) find that there is a positive correlation between productivity and worklife balance, but when controlling for good management practices (Bloom and van Reenen, 2006b), the positive effect disappears so that the correlation between enterprise productivity and work/life balance policies is "essentially zero". There are a number of ways in which this evidence can be interpreted. The most straightforward is that the various claims of their being a business case for family-friendly work practices are overstated. An alternative is that the potential gains do exist, but there are also possible disadvantages – for example, some employees see flexibility in employment measures which are restricted to parents as unfair, because they may face additional work burdens because of parents taking advantage of measures to which they themselves are not entitled.

In sum, while it seems likely that some further increase in voluntary introduction of family-friendly workplaces will occur due to market pressures and bargaining between employers and unions, it is probably unrealistic to expect such practices to become quasi-universal. One possible response is to accept that the market is the ultimate arbiter of the worth of the case for family-friendly workplaces and to (continue to) leave this to unions and employers to regulate as they see fit. There are, however, two reasons why, even if the *business case* for family-friendly workplaces is unproven, governments may nevertheless wish to intervene to ensure their more widespread diffusion.

The first reason is that there may be "externalities" to the results of the bargaining process. For example, policy makers may be concerned about the decline in birth rates and demographic trends, but these issues are not of immediate interest to employers and unions and are thus unlikely to feature prominently in the industrial bargaining process. Similarly, institutions in male dominated sectors are likely to lack incentives to pursue gender equity objectives. However, governments are interested in giving both fathers and mothers sufficient time to spend at work and with their children because this helps to sustain birth rates, strengthens future labour supply and reduces child poverty risks.

The second reason why governments may wish to intervene in negotiations for family-friendly workplaces is to ensure that access to them is equitable. As described above, it is possible or even likely that only some employers will introduce such measures, for only some employees – particularly those who are high-skilled. If this is unacceptable to policy makers, then they may wish to ensure that workers with weak bargaining positions also gain access to some family-friendly measures to which they might otherwise not have had access.

The next section will discuss how governments might intervene in the bargaining process, but before turning to this issue it is worth considering what will happen if only some workplaces are family-friendly. Those workers who want to adjust working hours to match care commitments will gravitate towards working for family-friendly enterprises and/or sectors, which commonly provide certain types of support (flexible schedules, part-time employment, paid leave and care days to care for sick children). For example, Nielsen *et al.* (2004), illustrate that women "self-select" into public sector employment which has more favourable family-friendly working conditions and a lower wage penalty for having children. However, "signalling" of this sort may reduce maternal career advancement and earnings progression. For example, in the legal service sector in Canada (a sector with many female workers in an economy with a relatively high proportion of female managers, Chapter 3), half of the women who work flexible hours feel they pay for this in reduced career progression (Catalyst, 2006c).

7.3.1. Public intervention towards more work/life balance support in workplaces

Encouragement

Apart from setting standards in weekly working hours and paid annual leave and legislation protecting the employment conditions of part-time workers (see above), governments have a number of instruments through which they can influence the outcome of industrial bargaining process in order to promote family-friendly workplace policies.

One obvious way is to use their own powers as the largest employers in most OECD countries. Public-sector employers may lead by example, making it more likely that public sector employees have access to family-friendly workplace support than the average private sector employee. On the other hand, as described above, smaller, male-dominated, less-skilled private sector workplaces are often more hesitant to implement these practices.

Policy intervention towards more family-friendly workplace support often concerns initiatives to supporting non-controversial information campaigns and other non-binding initiatives to increase awareness of the merits of family-friendly policies, including prize winning award competitions for best practices in enterprises and/or provide some financial assistance to enterprises which make family-friendly support available. The Swiss authorities have gone so far as to prepare a comprehensive "Work and Family handbook" which outlines the business case, provides an overview of possible workplace measures, address issues as overcoming resistance to reform while presenting various examples of enterprise practices on the implementation of different family-friendly workplace measures (SECO, 2007).

An equally non-binding, but a more innovative approach pursued in some OECD countries involves measures (*e.g.* partial subsidisation) that promote the provision (on consultancy basis) of practical and tailored advice to improve workplaces practices. For example, the so-called Family and Work Audit in Austria provided financial incentives to participation with 90% of fees being reimbursed for companies with up to 20 employees, down to 25% for companies with over 500 employees. The Audit focuses on the needs of individual companies rather than setting benchmark standards for all companies. It looks at ten areas including working time, workplace practices, management competence, personnel development and support services. The strength of this initiative lies in its structured involvement of workers and management, and the possibility of regular follow-up, with an external auditor assessing achievements (the process can then be repeated to ensure the ongoing nature of the process). However, there is not much evidence that such initiatives have become widespread.[11]

Legal requirements

Therefore, in some countries, policy has moved beyond encouragement to extend access to family-friendly workplace support to many low-income workers whose bargaining position is relatively weak. Already in 1978 Swedish policy gave parents with children who are not yet in primary school (i.e. under eight) the legal right to work six hours a day (at pro-rated pay). Germany, for example, now grants the right to work part-time to employees in enterprises with 15 or more workers; while the Netherlands enacted the right to change working hours for employees in enterprises of ten of more workers. Belgium grants employees the right to work 80% of normal hours. In most cases, these regulations give employers the right to refuse the requested change in working hours on business grounds subject to judicial review.

There are other ways of using legislation to enhance family-friendliness in workplaces. Recognising that flexibility in workplaces is hard to legislate, the Japanese 2001 "Law on Childcare and Family Care Leave" stipulates that firms must take at least one measure out of five options (short-time working hours, flexitime, adjustment of time to start/end work, exemption of non-scheduled work, setting up and operation of a childcare centre) to assist employees who are bringing up a child not yet three years old.

UK legislation provides another option between encouragement and direct legislation of entitlements: it grants British parents with children under age six the legislated *right to request* flexible working hours. Legislation does not guarantee parents an *entitlement* to part-time work, although these requests are often granted. The law forces employees to motivate their request, while employers have to justify any refusal. This forces both parties to better explain their motives and thus enhances workplace communications, and is flexible enough to focus on measures that suit the workplace and the worker, but obviously involves costs to both parties when recourse to judicial proceedings is sought.

7.4. Conclusions

Family-friendly workplaces are essential for the reconciliation of work and family life. There is a potential business case for family-friendly measures as they may improve the quality of the enterprise-workforce, reduce recruitment and training costs, diminish stress among employees, reduce absenteeism and improve worker loyalty; thereby contributing to greater flexibility, productivity and profitability of the enterprise and its workforce.

The business case is strongest for enterprises that employ workers that are difficult and expensive to replace, that already employ many women, that are large, and public employers often taking a lead role.

However, the *Babies and Bosses* reviews found that while employers who had introduced such measures were enthusiastic about their effect, hard evidence on the positive effect of family-friendly policies on productivity is not overwhelming. As a result, access to family-friendly workplace support is unequal. The vast majority of firms have only introduced a limited set of family-friendly workplace practices, and beyond part-time work, flexible working schedules, days to care for sick children and some cases of employer-provided paid leave, the prevalence of other family-friendly practices, such as teleworking, employer-provided childcare support, school-time working is limited.

Governments are generally reluctant to override outcomes of industrial bargaining processes, but they may be compelled to do so, because of "externalities" to the bargaining process which hamper the pursuit of public policy objectives. For example, policy makers may be concerned about, for example, the decline in birth rates or demographic trends, but these issues are not of immediate interest to employers and employees and therefore did not feature prominently in the bargaining process, which determined workplace outcomes. Equity concerns about limited access among low-income workers to workplace supports may be another reason for government intervention to extend coverage of family-friendly measures.

The reluctance among governments to intervene in industrial bargaining processes means that in many countries, authorities often limit themselves to information campaigns or other initiatives to increase awareness on the merits of family-friendly policies. The *Babies and Bosses* reviews found that publicly supported "consultancy" initiatives which provide tailored advice to companies are an innovative way of fostering family-friendly workplace, especially when they included re-assessment to ensure long-term enterprise commitment. However, there is not much evidence that such initiatives have become widespread.

Some countries have started to formalise legally family-friendly practices which already existed in many workplaces. For example, Germany, the Netherlands and Sweden, have moved to legislate entitlements to changing working hours, Japanese law stipulates that firms must take at least one measure out of five options (most of which are working time related), and UK policy grants parents with children under age six the "right to ask" for flexible working hours.

All these initiatives can impose labour costs on individual employers. However, when family-friendly workplace support is provided by employers on a voluntary basis and/or after agreement with unions, access to such support is unequal, with many workers in a weak bargaining positions missing out. The "right to ask" is a middle way approach for consideration in other countries as it emphasises employer and employee involvement, does not involve a "one-size-fits-all" solution, and extends access to many low-income workers.

Notes

1. The OECD definition of part-time employment refers to persons who usually work less than 30 hours per week in their main job (OECD, 2007c).

2. Data from a different source for Japan show that 65% of male Japanese workers aged 25-54 worked more than 43 hours per week in 2001 (OECD, 2003a).

3. Chart 7.2 includes responses from *all* workers, not just working parents. Hence, at least part of the reason why some countries with low birth rates (Austria, Germany and Switzerland) have low conflict levels is purely statistical. A further explanation is that where mothers are in effect forced to give up their careers if they have children, there is by definition no conflict between working hours and family commitments.

4. Fagnani and Letablier (2004) report findings from a survey among French parents with young children about the impact of the 35-hour law on their ability to balance work and family (and annualised hours schemes are not uncommon in France). Almost two-thirds of employees with standard working schedules report that the 35-hour week has made it easier for them to reconcile work and family life while this is only half of those who work non-standard schedules (*i.e.*, evenings, nights, weekends).

5. Modern communications technology allows easier and faster communications between off-site employees and their enterprises. However, teleworking has not become as important as initially thought by its advocates, with the exception perhaps among enterprises in the communication services industry.

6. Bond *et al.* (2005) report that 79% of US employers say that they provide paid or unpaid time off for employees to provide elder care without risking their jobs, and this proportion is universally high across firms of all sizes.

7. For example, a large British avionics company which developed a human resources package consisting of home working, career breaks, part-time working, term-time working and job share was able to decrease stress-related absences by 15% and increase the number of mothers retuning from maternity leave by 35% (DTI, 2004).

8. Though small business may be more flexible in responding to the special needs of their workforce, reflecting the close proximity of owners/managers and employees.

9. Workplace practices and working-time policies operate in diverse institutional frameworks across the OECD (EIRO, 2007; and OECD, 2002a, 2003a, 2004a, and 2005a) but with increased decentralised bargaining, union membership has fallen in many countries over recent decades. Except in Nordic countries, unionisation among men is generally higher than for women. In Finland and Sweden, however, almost 80% of the female labour force is unionised compared to 70 to 75% of men. Part-time workers (predominantly female, Chapter 3) are less likely to be unionised (and even less likely to be active in a union), but a relatively rapid decline in male membership has reduced the gender unionisation gap,

although men still make up the majority of members in European countries with low to medium unionisation rates (Carley, 2005). In 2004, the US unionisation rate was 13.8% for men and 11.1% for women.

10. In Denmark, many employers provide maternity pay, which in effect makes employing women relatively more expensive. Some unions would like to arrange for employers to make collective provision for maternity pay, so that males as well as females contribute to the costs. Instead, the metalworkers union prefers to run a scheme for provision of maternity pay just for their members, and given that only 1-2% of the members of this union are women, the necessary levy is very low. Collective provision across industries would involve net transfers from male-dominated sectors to female-dominated sectors, so it is in the narrow interests of the members of the metalworkers union to provide relatively generous benefits to their female members at relatively low costs to their male members.

11. Other examples of governments supporting tailor made consultancy initiatives include the Work Life Challenge Fund in the United Kingdom which between 2000 and 2003 provided USD 22 million in financial assistance to more than 400 public and private companies for the employment of private human resources consultancies to develop and implement tailored work-life balance measures. In an evaluation, employers stated that the presence of specialist consultants facilitated acceptance and implementation of family friendly policies in the workplace (Nelson et al., 2004). The Canadian province of Québec supports companies with less than 2 000 employees by connecting them with Emploi Québec management consultants or private human resources specialists and providing employers with up to half of the cost so as to incite companies to develop work-life conciliation strategies for their employees.

ANNEX 7.A1

Some Quantitative Information on Work/Life Conflict Levels and Workplace Flexibility

The fourth European Working Conditions survey conducted in 2005 was carried out by the European Foundation for the Improvement of Living and Working Conditions, an autonomous EU agency based in Dublin (EFILWC, 2007). Almost 30 000 workers were interviewed in 31 countries. Results for 22 countries (OECD member states) are presented in Annex Table 7.A1.1. In most of those 22 countries (Luxembourg excluded) over 1 000 interviews took place after quality control.

In the survey, employees were asked if their job "fits in with their family or social commitments outside work" according to a four-point scale ("very well", "well", "not so well", and "not at all well"). This is described respectively in Annex Table 7.A1.1 as causing minimal, low, medium and high levels of work and life conflict. In order to focus upon the age group of workers most likely to be juggling work and care duties, the age group 30-44 years was chosen and unsurprisingly the highest levels of work-life conflict (23%) were recorded for those workers with weekly hours of 55 or more. At the other end of the scale, over 50% of part-time workers (those working less than 30 hours per week) stated that their "job-fit with family/social commitments outside work" caused minimal levels of work/life conflict.

Table 7.A1.1. **Work/life conflict among workers in European countries**

Degree of conflict between working hours and family and/or other social commitments, by number of weekly working hours, age group 30-44, 2005

		Minimal	Low	Medium	High
Austria	Less than 30 hours	54.4	40.5	3.4	1.6
	At least 30 hours but less than 45	48.1	42.5	7.1	2.2
	At least 45 hours and less than 55	12.2	79.0	4.8	4.0
	55 hours or over	16.5	12.2	16.3	55.0
Belgium	Less than 30 hours	40.2	44.0	9.2	6.7
	At least 30 hours but less than 45	30.8	50.3	14.7	4.2
	At least 45 hours and less than 55	25.9	64.5	9.6	0.0
	55 hours or over	9.0	4.8	60.8	25.4
Czech Republic	Less than 30 hours	65.9	19.9	14.2	0.0
	At least 30 hours but less than 45	29.6	61.3	8.0	1.1
	At least 45 hours and less than 55	13.3	47.7	26.4	12.5
	55 hours or over	12.7	47.4	39.9	0.0
Denmark	Less than 30 hours	49.7	40.2	8.1	2.0
	At least 30 hours but less than 45	59.1	30.7	9.4	0.8
	At least 45 hours and less than 55	37.4	42.3	12.0	8.3
	55 hours or over	14.2	59.8	18.2	7.8
Finland	Less than 30 hours	57.8	28.2	9.1	5.0
	At least 30 hours but less than 45	36.2	47.3	13.1	3.4
	At least 45 hours and less than 55	13.3	72.8	13.9	0.0
	55 hours or over	20.6	0.0	79.4	0.0
France	Less than 30 hours	37.5	31.7	28.1	2.7
	At least 30 hours but less than 45	34.5	45.8	16.7	3.0
	At least 45 hours and less than 55	20.4	49.8	29.8	0.0
	55 hours or over	16.6	43.0	26.6	13.8
Germany	Less than 30 hours	43.2	54.9	1.0	0.9
	At least 30 hours but less than 45	30.0	56.3	13.2	0.4
	At least 45 hours and less than 55	2.6	73.8	23.6	0.0
	55 hours or over	5.5	26.4	68.1	0.0
Greece	Less than 30 hours	44.1	32.4	12.0	11.5
	At least 30 hours but less than 45	35.5	36.3	18.3	9.8
	At least 45 hours and less than 55	9.4	38.8	37.6	14.2
	55 hours or over	7.4	29.4	19.6	43.6
Hungary	Less than 30 hours	60.8	27.0	7.4	4.8
	At least 30 hours but less than 45	16.7	61.7	17.9	3.7
	At least 45 hours and less than 55	11.3	36.4	38.5	13.9
	55 hours or over	1.9	32.2	37.4	28.5
Ireland	Less than 30 hours	60.6	32.0	7.4	0.0
	At least 30 hours but less than 45	35.5	44.8	15.6	4.1
	At least 45 hours and less than 55	13.5	50.4	34.8	1.2
	55 hours or over	0.0	18.2	76.8	5.0
Italy	Less than 30 hours	18.6	70.3	11.1	0.0
	At least 30 hours but less than 45	12.7	52.5	25.8	9.0
	At least 45 hours and less than 55	2.8	54.8	30.8	11.7
	55 hours or over	0.0	29.5	41.8	28.7
Luxembourg	Less than 30 hours	52.3	41.1	4.1	2.5
	At least 30 hours but less than 45	35.7	45.5	15.0	3.9
	At least 45 hours and less than 55	32.5	41.8	20.6	5.0
	55 hours or over	0.0	100.0	0.0	0.0

Source: EFILWC (2007).

Table 7.A1.1. **Work/life conflict among workers in European countries** (cont.)

Degree of conflict between working hours and family and/or other social commitments,
by number of weekly working hours, age group 30-44, 2005

		Minimal	Low	Medium	High
Netherlands	Less than 30 hours	51.8	36.2	11.7	0.3
	At least 30 hours but less than 45	28.5	55.4	13.4	2.7
	At least 45 hours and less than 55	20.3	52.3	24.5	3.0
	55 hours or over	0.0	0.0	14.9	85.1
Norway	Less than 30 hours	56.3	27.1	14.7	1.9
	At least 30 hours but less than 45	48.7	39.6	10.0	1.7
	At least 45 hours and less than 55	36.0	42.7	21.3	0.0
	55 hours or over	31.8	42.2	0.0	26.0
Poland	Less than 30 hours	47.8	35.3	12.8	4.1
	At least 30 hours but less than 45	22.5	55.0	18.5	4.0
	At least 45 hours and less than 55	15.6	36.1	35.3	13.0
	55 hours or over	10.1	42.0	28.9	18.9
Portugal	Less than 30 hours	43.2	29.5	25.2	2.1
	At least 30 hours but less than 45	21.4	63.4	11.4	3.7
	At least 45 hours and less than 55	22.4	49.3	22.1	6.3
	55 hours or over	8.9	56.3	32.3	2.6
Slovak Rep.	Less than 30 hours	61.2	34.7	0.0	4.1
	At least 30 hours but less than 45	17.8	62.0	16.4	3.8
	At least 45 hours and less than 55	7.4	54.1	34.7	3.8
	55 hours or over	7.3	38.3	40.1	14.2
Spain	Less than 30 hours	54.5	45.5	0.0	0.0
	At least 30 hours but less than 45	29.3	54.1	12.4	4.2
	At least 45 hours and less than 55	3.7	49.2	39.0	8.1
	55 hours or over	4.9	55.9	2.9	36.4
Sweden	Less than 30 hours	52.6	34.9	10.1	2.4
	At least 30 hours but less than 45	34.8	43.6	16.2	5.5
	At least 45 hours and less than 55	27.5	41.9	24.7	6.0
	55 hours or over	19.9	43.8	12.9	23.4
Switzerland	Less than 30 hours	57.9	36.3	5.2	0.6
	At least 30 hours but less than 45	38.9	47.7	10.3	3.1
	At least 45 hours and less than 55	20.9	61.8	17.2	0.0
	55 hours or over	11.2	49.1	34.0	5.7
Turkey	Less than 30 hours	29.4	40.6	11.5	18.5
	At least 30 hours but less than 45	25.5	40.2	33.1	1.3
	At least 45 hours and less than 55	20.8	61.3	12.6	5.3
	55 hours or over	5.4	44.4	19.4	30.9
United Kingdom	Less than 30 hours	70.1	26.8	1.7	1.4
	At least 30 hours but less than 45	46.9	34.8	14.6	3.8
	At least 45 hours and less than 55	26.6	43.7	22.0	7.6
	55 hours or over	0.0	23.9	28.2	47.8
EU22 average	Less than 30 hours	50.5	36.8	9.4	3.3
	At least 30 hours but less than 45	32.7	48.7	15.1	3.6
	At least 45 hours and less than 55	18.0	52.0	24.3	5.6
	55 hours or over	9.3	36.3	31.8	22.7

Source: EFILWC (2007).

ANNEX 7.A2

Selected National Information on the Prevalence of Employer-provided Workplace Support

Table 7.A2.1. **Flexible workplace practices in Australia**

Work/family provisions in Australian Workplace Agreements (AWAs), 2004

	Working parents (%)	Working mothers (%)
AWAs contain provisions for:		
Paid family leave	59	. .
Other (paid) leave for caring purposes	40	. .
Flexible use of annual leave	11	. .
Flexible working hours[1]	41	44
Permanent part-time work[1]	25	35
Work from home arrangements[1]	16	17

1. Applies to families where at least one parent is employed.
Source: Australian Bureau of Statistics and the Department of Employment and Workplace Relations (DEWR).

Table 7.A2.2. **Canadian flexible workplace practices**

Percentage of Canadian employer provision and percentage of employee take-up
of selected family-friendly policies, 1998-99

| | Employer provision | | | Employee take-up | | | |
| | Part-time work[1] | Childcare services[2] | | Flexible hours | | Teleworking | |
	Total	Women	Men	Women	Men	Women	Men
All workplaces	57	6	6	36	44	5	5
Company size							
Less than 10	53	2	1	42	53	7	6
10-49	68	3	2	35	48	4	5
50-99	74	3	3	41	39	5	4
100-499	72	4	4	34	37	4	4
500-999	86	9	12	34	39	5	6
1 000+	91	23	24	30	39	4	7
Collective bargaining status							
No coverage in workplace	57	3	3	38	48	6	6
Some coverage in workplace	57	12	11	32	36	3	4
Employment status							
Full-time				35	44	5	6
Part-time				41	42	6	3
Permanent				36	43	5	5
Non-permanent				37	54	8	4

Definitions: **Part-time:** Less than 30 working hours per week. **Childcare services:** Category includes a variety of support services, such as information and referral services and assistance with external suppliers or on-site centres. **Flexible hours:** Employee has no set start or finish time but a required number of hours per week. In some cases, specific core hours might be required. **Teleworking:** Arrangement to work at home for some of regularly scheduled hours.
1. The proportion refers to employees who have used the policy.
2. Denotes percentage of workplaces employing part-time workers.
3. The proportion refers to employees who have knowledge of employer offering policy.
Source: Comfort *et al.* (2003).

Table 7.A2.3. **Flexible workplace practices in Japan**

Workplace measures for employees with young children, 1999

	Percentage of companies[1]
Total proportion of firms providing measures	59.6
Proportion of firms providing:	
Short-time working hours	70.6
Flexitime	17.5
Adjustment of time to start/end work	46.1
Exemption of non-scheduled work	51.5
Providing childcare centre	2.7
Financial aid for childcare	3.3

1. For companies with more than 30 employees.
Source: MOL and JIWE (2000).

Table 7.A2.4. **Trends in flexible working practices in the United Kingdom**

Flexible working and leave arrangements for non-managerial employees in continuing workplaces, 1998 and 2004

	Percentage of workplaces	
	1998	2004
Employer/manager responses:[1]		
Switching from full-time to part-time hours	46	64
Flexitime	19	26
Job-sharing	31	41
Homeworking	16	28
Term-time only	14	28
Annualised hours	8	13
Zero hours contracts	3	5
Employee responses:[2]		
Switching from full-time to part-time hours	. .	32
Flexitime	32	38
Job-sharing	15	19
Homeworking	9	14
Term-time only	. .	14

1. Base: All continuing workplaces with ten or more employees in 1998 and 2004. Figures are weighted and based on responses from at least 847 managers.
2. Depending upon the arrangement, between 16 and 37% of employees did not know if these flexible working arrangements were available and so could not respond to the questions.
Source: 2004 Workplace Employment Relations Survey (WERS), "Inside the Workplace: First findings".

Table 7.A2.5. **Employer-provided leave arrangements in the United Kingdom**

Extra-statutory leave arrangements to support employees with caring responsibilities by sector in the United Kingdom, 2004

	Percentage of workplaces		
	Private sector	Public sector	All workplaces
Fully-paid maternity leave[1]	51	84	57
Fully-paid paternity leave[1]	49	84	55
Paid parental leave	21	47	25
Special paid leave for family emergencies	43	80	49
Leave for carers of older adults	4	16	6

Note: Base: All continuing workplaces with ten or more employees in 2004. Figures are weighted and based on responses from at least 1 928 managers
1. All workplaces with at least some female employees (to calculate maternity leave) and male employees (to calculate paternity leave).
Source: B. Kersley, C. Alpin, J. Forth, A. Bryson, H. Bewley, G. Dix and S. Oxenbridge (2005), Inside the Workplace: First findings from the 2004 Workplace Employment Relations Survey (or WERS 2004), Routledge.

Table 7.A2.6. **Employer-provided leave arrangements in the United States**

Summary of leave practices and levels of replacement pay during leave
in the United States, 2005

	Percentage of employers who provide:				
	< 12 weeks leave	12 weeks leave	> 12 weeks leave	Some payment	> 6 weeks replacement pay
Maternity leave	22	50	29	46	7
Paternity leave	29	52	19	13	..
Adoption, foster care	22	58	19	..	..
Leave to care of seriously ill children	21	59	19	..	..

Note: Companies interviewed are mandated to comply with the federal Family and Medical Leave Act (FMLA, 1993) which requires that at least 12 weeks of unpaid, job-guaranteed leave is available for childbirth, adoption and foster care if employee has worked at least 1 250 hours in the preceding year.
Source: Bond *et al.* (2005).

ISBN 978-92-64-03244-6
Babies and Bosses: Reconciling Work and Family Life
A Synthesis of Findings for OECD Countries
© OECD 2007

Bibliography

ABS (2007), "Labour Force Statistics and Family Characteristics, series 6224.0.55.001" (FA4 – Families by Couple and One Parent family type, Age of parents, Age group of dependents, Labour force status), Australian Bureau of Statistics, Canberra.

Adema, W. (2006a), "Towards Coherent Care and Education Support Policies for New Zealand Families", *Social Policy Journal of New Zealand*, Vol. 28, Ministry of Social Development, Wellington, pp. 46-76, July.

Adema, W. (2006b), "Social Assistance Policy Development and the Provision of a Decent Level of Income in Selected OECD Countries", OECD Social, Employment and Migration Working Papers, No. 38, OECD, Paris, *www.oecd.org/els/workingpapers*.

Adema, W. and M. Ladaique (2005), "Net Social Expenditure, 2005 edition", OECD Social, Employment and Migration Working Papers, No. 29, OECD, Paris, *www.oecd.org/els/workingpapers*.

Adema, W., D. Gray and S. Kahl (2003), "Social Assistance in Germany", OECD Labour Market and Social Policy Occasional Papers, No. 58, OECD, Paris, *www.oecd.org/els/workingpapers*.

Adsera (2004), *Labor Market Performance and the Timing of Births. A Comparative Analysis across European Countries*, Population Research Center, University of Chicago, *www.spc.uchicago.edu/prc/pdfs/adsera03.pdf*.

Ahn, N. and P. Mira (2002), "A Note on the Changing Relationship between Fertility and Female Employment Rates in Developed Countries", *Journal of Population Economics*, Vol. 15(4), pp. 667-682.

AIHW (2006), *Australia's Welfare 2005*, Canberra, Australia.

Albrecht, J., A. Björklund and S. Vroman (2001), "Is There a Glass Ceiling in Sweden?", IZA Discussion Paper, No. 282, Forschungsinstitut zur Zukunft der Arbeit (Institute for the Study of Labour), Bonn.

Algemene Rekenkamer (2003), "Alleenstaande ouders in de bijstand", Tweede Kamer der Staten-Generaal, vergaderjaar 2002-03, 28875, Nrs. 1-2, SDU Uitgevers, "s-Gravenhage (the Hague)", the Netherlands.

Algemene Rekenkamer (2005), *Terugblik 2005, elf onderzoeken nader beschouwd*, SDU Uitgevers, "s-Gravenhage (the Hague)", the Netherlands.

Araki, T. (2002), "Re-Examining the Role of Labor Unions in the Era of the Diversified Workforce", *Japan Labor Bulletin*, Vol. 41, No. 5, Japan Institute of Labour, Tokyo, pp. 6-14.

Arulampalam, W., A.L. Booth and M.L. Bryan (2006), "Is There a Glass Ceiling over Europe?", Exploring the Gender Pay Gap across the Wage Distribution, *Industrial and Labor Relations Review*, Vol. 60, No. 2, The Berkeley Electronic Press.

Aughinbaugh, A. and M. Gittleman (2003), "Maternal Employment and Adolescent Risky Behaviour", BLS Working Papers, No. 366, US Department of Labor, Bureau of Labor Statistics, February.

Australian Government (2006), "Work and Family, The Importance of Workplace Flexibility in Promoting Balance between Work and Family", Paper prepared by the Minister for Employment and Workplace Relations, September, *www.workplace.gov.au/ workplace/Individual/Employee/WorkFamily.*

Baker, M., J. Gruber and K. Milligan (2005), "Universal Childcare, Maternal Labour Supply and Family Well-Being", NBER Working Paper No. 11832, National Bureau of Economic Research, Cambridge, MA, December, *www.nber.org/papers/w11832.*

Bardasi, E. and J. Gornick (2002), "Explaining Cross-National Variation in Part-Time/ Full-Time Wage Differentials Among Women", Paper presented at the workshop on Comparative Political Economy of Inequality, Cornell University, New York.

Barnett, R. and K. Gareis (2006), "Antecedents and Correlates of Parental After-school Hours Concerns: Exploring a Newly Identified Work-family Stressor", *American Behavioral Scientist*, Vol. 49, pp. 1382-1399.

Batljan, I. (2001), "Focus on Fertility: From a Population Policy to a Child Friendly Society", Ds, Vol. 57, Fritzes public publications, Stockholm.

Baum, C.L. (2003), "Does Early Maternal Employment Harm Child Development? An Analysis of the Potential Benefits of Leave taking", *Journal of labor Economics*, Vol. 21, No. 2, University of Chicago, pp. 408-448.

Becker, G. and H.G. Lewis (1973), "On the Interaction between the Quantity and Quality of Children", *Journal of Political Economy*, Vol. 81, pp. 279-288.

Behrman, J.R., S.W. Parker and P.E. Todd (2005), "Long-Term Impacts of the Oportunidades Conditional Cash Transfer Program on Rural Youth in Mexico", Ibero-America Institute for Economic Research (IAI) Discussion Papers, No. 122, Georg-August Universität, Göttingen, Germany.

Belsky, J. (2005), "childcare and its Impact on Young Children (0-2)", in R.E. Tremblay, R.G. Barr and R. de V. Peters (eds.), *Encyclopedia on Early Childhood Development* [on line], Centre of Excellence for Early Childhood Development, Montreal, Province of Québec, Canada, pp. 1-6.

Belsky, J., E. Melhuish, J. Barnes, A.H. Leyland, H. Romaniuk and the National Evaluation of Sure Start Research Team (2006), "Effects of Sure Start Local Programmes on Children and Families: Early Findings from a Quasi-experimental, Cross Sectional Study", *British Medical Journal*, 16 June.

Bennett, F. and J. Millar (2005), "Making Work Pay", *Benefits*, Vol. 13, No. 1, Colchester, United Kingdom, pp. 28-33.

Berger, E., D. Chauffaut, C. Olm and M-O. Simon (2006), "Les bénéficiaires du Complément de libre choix d'activité : une diversité de profiles", *Études et résultats*, No. 510, Direction de la Recherche, des Études, de l'Évaluation et des Statistiques (DREES), ministère des Affaires sociales, Paris, August, *www.sante.gouv.fr/drees/ etude-resultat/er510/er510.pdf.*

Blanpain, N. (2005), "Accueil des jeunes enfants et coûts des modes de garde en 2002", *Études et Résultats*, No. 422, Direction de la Recherche, des Études, de l'Évaluation et des Statistiques (DREES), ministère des Affaires sociales, Paris, August, *www.sante.gouv.fr/drees/etude-resultat/er422/er422.pdf.*

Blau, F.D. and J. Currie (2004), "pre-school, Daycare, and Afterschool Care: Who is Minding the Kids", National Bureau of Economic Research Working Paper, No. 10670, Cambridge, MA.

Blau, F.D. and L.M. Kahn (2001), "Understanding International Differences in the Gender Pay Gap", *Journal of Labor Economics*, Vol. 21, pp. 106-144.

Bloom, N. and J. van Reenen (2006a), "Management Practices, Work-Life Balance, and Productivity: A Review of Some Recent Evidence", *Oxford Review of Economic Policy*, Vol. 22, No. 4, Oxford University Press.

Bloom, N. and J. van Reenen (2006b), "Measuring and Explaining Management Practices across Firms and Countries", Centre for Economic Performance Discussion Paper, No. 716, London School of Economics Research on Line, April, *http://eprints.lse.ac.uk/archive/00000733*.

Blossfeld, H-P. (1995), "Changes in the Process of Family Formation and Women's Growing Economic Independence: A Comparison of Nine Countries", in H.P. Blossfeld (ed.), *The New Role of Women-Family Formation in Modern Societies*, Westview Press, Oxford.

Bond, J.T., E. Galinsky, S.S. Kim and E. Brownfield (2005), *2005 National Study of Employers*, The Families and Work Institute, New York.

Bradshaw, J. and N. Finch (2002), "A Comparison of Child Benefit Packages in 22 Countries", Department for Work and Pensions Research Report, No. 174, Leeds.

Brewer, M. and A. Shephard (2004), *Has Labour Made Work Pay?*, Joseph Rowntree Foundation, York.

Brewer, M., A. Duncan, A. Shephard and M.J. Suarrez (2003), "Did Working Families' Tax Credit Work? Analysing the Impact of In Work Support on Labour Supply and Programme Participation", Inland Revenue Working Paper, No. 2, London.

Brooks-Gunn, J. (2003), "Do You Believe in Magic? What We Can Expect From Early Childhood Intervention Programs", *Social Policy Report*, Vol. XVII, No. 1, Society for Research in Child Development, Washington DC, *www.srdc.org/spr.html*.

Burda, M., D.S. Hamermesh and P. Weil (2007), "Total Work, Gender and Social Norms", NBER Working Paper No. 13000, National Bureau of Economic Research, Cambridge, MA, March, *www.nber.org/papers/w13000*.

Butz, W. and M. Ward (1979): "The Emergence of Countercyclical US Fertility", *American Economic Review*, Vol. 69, No. 3, pp. 318-328, June.

Calhoun, C.A. and T.J. Esenshade (1988), "Childbearing and Wives' Foregone Earnings", *Population Studies*, Vol. 42, No. 1, pp. 5-37, March.

Carley, M. (2005), "Industrial Relations in the EU, Japan and USA, 2003-04", *European Industrial Relations Observatory*, EIRO on Line, *www.eurofound.europa.eu/eiro/2005/02/feature/tn0502102f.html*.

Carley, M. (2006), "Working Time Developments", *European Industrial Relations Observatory*, EIRO on Line, *www.eurofound.europa.eu/eiro/2006/08/update/tn0608101u.html*.

Catalyst (2006a), "Quick Takes, Maternity Leave", updated 9-6-06, *www.catalystwomen.org*.

Catalyst (2006b), "Quick Takes, Working parents", updated 8-30-06, *www.catalystwomen.org*.

Catalyst (2006c), "Beyond a Reasonable Doubt: Lawyers State their Case on Job Flexibility", *Catalyst*, New York, *www.catalyst.org/files/full/BeyondReasDoubtJobFlexibility.pdf*.

CBS (2007), "Aantallen sociale uitkeringen en percentages ziekteverzuim", Centraal Bureau voor de Statistiek, Voorburg/Heerlen, the Netherlands, *statline.cbs.nl.*

Chapman, B., Y. Dunlop, M. Gray, A. Liu and D. Mitchell (2001), "The Impact of Children on the Lifetime Earnings of Australian Women: Evidence from the 1990s", *Australian Economic Review*, Vol. 34, No. 4, pp. 373-389.

CIPD (2004), *Employee Absence 2004: A Survey of Management Policy and Practice*, Chartered Institute of Personnel and Development, London.

Claassen, R. (2007), "Kindertijdwerk: Pleidooi voor een dertigurige werkweek", *Socialisme en Democratie*, Nr. 1/2, Jaargang 64, pp. 57-67.

Cleveland, G. and M. Krashinsky (2003), *Fact and Fantasy: Eight Myths about Early Childhood Education and Care*, Childcare Resource and Research Unit, University of Toronto, Toronto.

Comfort, D., K. Johnson and D. Wallace (2003), *Part-Time Work and Family-Friendly Practices in Canadian Workplaces*, The Evolving Workplace Series, Human Resources Development Canada and Statistics Canada, Ottawa.

CSO (2006), *Quarterly National Household Survey, Childcare, Quarter 1-2005*, Central Statistics Office, Dublin, 31 May.

Cummings, C., A. Dyson and L. Todd (2004), "Evaluation of the Extended Schools Pathfinder Projects", DfES Research Report No. 530, Department for Education and Skills (DfES) and University of Newcastle upon Tyne, *www.dfes.gov.uk/research/data/uploadfiles/RR530.pdf.*

Cummings, C., A. Dyson, I. Papps, D. Pearson, C. Raffo, L. Tiplady and L. Todd (2006), "Evaluation of the Full Service Extended Schools Initiative, Second year: Thematic papers", DfES Research Brief No. RB795, Department for Education and Skills (DfES), September.

Currie, J. (2001), "Early Childhood Education Programs", *Journal of Economic Perspectives*, Vol. 15, No. 2, pp. 213-238, Spring.

Currie, J. (2004), "Viewpoint: Child Research Comes of Age", *Canadian Journal of Economics*, Canadian Economics Association, Vol. 37, No. 3, Montreal, pp. 509-527.

D'Addio, A.-C. and M. Mira d'Ercole (2005), "Trends and Determinants of Fertility Rates in OECD Countries: The Role of Policies", OECD Social, Employment and Migration Working Papers, No. 27, OECD, Paris, *www.oecd.org/els/workingpapers.*

DARES (2004), "La difficile conciliation entre vie professionnelle et vie familiale", *Premières synthèses*, n° 50.3, ministère de l'Emploi, du Travail et de la Cohésion sociale, Paris, December.

Datta Gupta, N. and N. Smith (2002), "Children and Career Interruptions: the Family Gap in Denmark", *Economica*, Vol. 69, No. 276, pp. 609-629.

Datta Gupta, N, R. Oaxaca and N. Smith (2003), "Swimming Upstream, Floating Downstream: Comparing Women's Relative Wage Positions in the US and Denmark", IZA Discussion Paper, No. 756, Bonn.

Deding, M.C., M. Lausten and A. Rosenstjerne Andersen (2007), "Starting School: The Effect of Early Childhood Factors on Child Well-Being", SFI Working Paper No. 2:2007, Danish National Institute of Social Research, Copenhagen.

Del Boca, D. (2003), "Low Fertility and labour Force Participation of Italian Women: Evidence and Interpretations", OECD Labour Market and Social Policy Occasional Papers, No. 61, OECD, Paris, *www.oecd.org/els/workingpapers.*

Dex, S. and K. Ward (2007), "Parental Care and Employment in Early Childhood", Equal Opportunities Commission Working Papers Series, No. 57, Institute of Education, University of London/Equal Opportunities Commission, London.

DfES (2004), *Every Child Matters: Next Steps*, Department for Education and Skills, London.

Dingeldey, I. (2001), "European Tax Systems and Their Impact on Family Employment Patterns", *Journal of Social Policy*, Vol. 30, Cambridge University Press, Cambridge, pp. 653-672.

DREES (2005), " Les bénéfiaires de l'Allocation parentale d'éducation: trajectoires d'activité et retour à l'emploi ", *Études et Résultats*, n° 399, ministère de l'Emploi, du Travail, et de la Cohésion sociale, Direction de la recherche, des études, de l'évaluation et des statistiques, Paris, May.

DTI (2004), "Achieving Best Practice in Your Business: Maximising Potential through Work-life Balance. Case Studies from the IT, Electronics & Communications Industries", Department of Trade and Industry, London.

Duxbury, L. and C. Higgins (2003), *Work-Life Conflict in Canada in the New Millennium: A Status Report*, prepared for Health Canada, October, *www.phac-aspc.gc.ca/publicat/ work-travail/pdf/rprt_2_e.pdf*.

Duxbury, L., C. Higgins and K. Johnson (1999), *An Examination of the Implications and Costs of Work Life Conflict in Canada*, submitted to Health Canada, *www.phac- aspc.gc.ca/dca-dea/publications/duxbury_e.html*.

Dwyer, G. (2005), *Dissecting the Working for Families Package*, New Zealand Business Roundtable, Wellington.

Edwards, P., M. Ram and J. Black (2003), "The Impact of Employment Legislation on Small Firms: A Case Study Analysis", *Employment Research Series*, No. 20, Department of Trade and Industry, London.

EFILWC (2004), *Fertility and Family Issues in an Enlarged Europe*, European Foundation for the Improvement of Living and Working Conditions, Dublin.

EFILWC (2006), *Working Time and Work-life Balance in European Companies: Establishment Survey on Working Time 2004-05*, European Foundation for the Improvement of Living and Working Conditions, Dublin, *www.eurofound.europa.eu*.

EFILWC (2007), *Fourth Survey on European Working Conditions 2005*, European Foundation for the Improvement of Living and Working Conditions, Dublin, *www.eurofound.europa.eu*.

Einarsdóttir, Þ. with G.M. Pétursdóttir (2004), *Culture, Custom and Caring: Men's and Women's Possibilities to Parental Leave*, Centre for Gender Equality, Centre for Women's and Gender Studies, Akureyri, Iceland.

EIRO (2007), *Industrial relations developments in Europe 2006*, European Industrial Relations Observatory, European Foundation for the Improvement of Living and Working Conditions, Dublin.

Engelhardt, H., T. Kögel, and A. Prskawetz (2001), "Fertility and Women's Employment Reconsidered: A Macro level Time Series Analysis for Developed Countries, 1960-2000", MPIDR Working Paper, No. WP 2001 021, Max Planck Institute for Demographic Research (MPIDR), Rostock.

Engström, P., P. Hesselius and M. Persson (2007), "Excess Use of Temporary Parental Benefit", IFAU Working Paper, No. 19, Institute for Labour Market Policy Evaluation, Uppsala, Sweden.

Ermish, J. and M. Francesconi (2001), "The Effects of Parents' Employment on Children Lives", Joseph Rowntree Foundation, Family Policy Studies Center, York.

Evangelou, M., G. Brooks, S. Smith and D. Jennings (2005), *The Birth to School Study: A longitudinal Evaluation of the Peers Early Education Partnership (PEEP) 1998-2005*, Department of Education and Sciences, DfES Publications, Nottingham, United Kingdom, *www.dfes.gov.uk/research*.

Eydoux, A. and M-T Letablier (2007), "Les familles monoparentales en France", Centre d'études de l'emploi, rapport de recherche, n° 36, Juin.

FaCSIA (2006), "childcare", Department of Family, Community Services and Indigenous Affairs, Canberra, *www.facs.gov.au/internet/facsinternet.nsf/childcare/nav.htm*.

Fagnani, J. and M-T. Letablier (2004), "Work and Family Life Balance: The Impact of the 35-hours Laws in France", *Work, Employment and Society*, Vol. 10, No. 3, pp. 551-572.

Families and Work Institute (2004), *Generation & Gender in the Workplace*, American Business Collaboration, New York.

Federal Labour Standards Review (2006), *Fairness at Work, Federal Labour Standards for the 21st Century*, Human Resources and Skills Development Canada, Gatineau, Québec, Canada.

Ford, R., D. Gyarmati, K. Foley, D. Tattrie and L. Jimenez (2003), *Can Work Incentives Pay for Themselves? Final Report on the Self Sufficiency Project for Applicants*, Social Research and Demonstration Corporation, Ottawa.

Förster, M. and M. Mira d'Ercole (2005), "Income Distribution and Poverty in OECD Countries in the Second Half of the 1990s", OECD Social, Employment and Migration Working Papers, No. 22, OECD, Paris, *www.oecd.org/els/workingpapers*.

Fitzgerald, J. and T. Maloney (2007), "The Impact of Changes in Family Assistance on partnering and Women's Employment in New Zealand: A preliminary Look", Paper presented at the New Zealand Association of Economists Annual Conference 2007, 25 June.

Francesconi, M. and W. van der Klaauw (2007), "The Socioeconomic Consequences of 'In Work' Benefit Reform for British Lone Mothers", *Journal of Human Resources*, Vol. XLII, No. 1, pp. 1-31.

Freud, D. (2007), *Reducing Dependency, Increasing Opportunity: Options for the Future of Welfare to Work – An Independent Report to the Department of Work and Pensions*, HMSO, London.

Galtry, J. (2003), "The Impact on Breastfeeding of Labour Market Policy and Practice in Ireland, Sweden and the USA", *Social Science and Medicine*, Vol. 57, Elsevier, the Netherlands, pp. 167-177.

Gauthier, A.H. and J. Hatzius (1997), "Family Benefits and Fertility: An Econometric Analysis", *Population Studies*, Vol. 51, No. 3, pp. 295-306.

Gíslason, I.V. (2007), *Parental Leave in Iceland, Bringing the Fathers in*, Jafnréttisstofa, Reykjavik, Iceland.

Gornick, J. and A. Heron (2006), "The Regulation of Working Time as Work-Family Reconciliation Policy: Comparing Europe, Japan and the United States", *Journal of Comparative Analysis*, Vol. 8, No. 2, pp. 149-166, June.

Gornick, J. and M. Meyers (2003), *Families that Work: Policies for Reconciling Parenthood and Employment*, Russell Sage Foundation, New York.

Government of Ireland (2006), *Government Discussion Paper: Proposals for Supporting Lone Parents*, Department of Social and Family Affairs, Dublin, Ireland.

Gray, H. (2002), "Family Friendly Working: What a Performance! An Analysis of the Relationship between the Availability of Family Friendly Policies and Establishment Performance", Centre for Economic Performance, Discussion Paper, No. 529, London School of Economics, London.

Gray, M. and B. Chapman (2001), "Foregone Earnings from Child Rearing: Changes Between 1986 and 1997", *Family Matters*, No. 58, pp. 4-9, Autumn.

Gregg, P. and L. Washbrook (2003), "The Effects of Early Maternal Employment on Child Development in the UK", CMPO Discussion Paper, No. 03/70, Leverhulme Centre for Market and Public Organisation, University of Bristol.

Grubb, D., J.-K. Lee and P. Tergeist (2007), "Addressing Labour Market Duality in Korea", OECD Social, Employment and Migration Working Papers, OECD, Paris, *www.oecd.org/els/workingpapers*, forthcoming.

Gustafsson, S.S., E. Kenjoh and C.M.M.P. Wetzels (2002), "Postponement of Maternity and the Duration of Time Spent at Home after First Birth: Panel Data Analysis Comparing Germany, Great Britain, the Netherlands and Sweden", OECD Labour Market and Social Policy Occasional Papers, No. 59, OECD, Paris, *www.oecd.org/els/workingpapers*.

Hagoort, K., M. Hersevoort and M. Goedhuys (2007), "De arbeidsmarkt- en inkomenspositie van moeders met jonge kinderen in 2004", Centraal Bureau voor de Statistiek, Voorburg/Heerlen, the Netherlands.

Hewitt, P. (2004), *Unfinished Business: The New Agenda for the Workplace*, Institute for Public Policy Rresearch (IPPR), London.

HM Treasury (2004), *Choice for Parents, The Best Start for Children: A Ten Year Strategy for Childcare*, Her Majesty's Treasury, London.

Hofferth, S. and S. Curtin (2003), "The Impact of Parental Leave on Maternal Return to Work after Childbirth in the United States", OECD Social, Employment and Migration Working Papers, No. 7, OECD, Paris, *www.oecd.org/els/workingpapers*.

Hullen, G. (2000), "The Effects of Education and Employment on Marriage and First Birth", FFS Flagship Conference; Partnership and Fertility – A Revolution, Brussel, May 29-31.

Immervoll, H., H.J. Kleven, C.T. Kreiner, and E. Saez (2005), "Welfare Reform in European Countries: A Microsimulation Analysis", OECD Social, Employment and Migration Working Papers, No. 28, OECD, Paris, *www.oecd.org/els/workingpapers*.

INEGI (1996), "Encuesta Nacional de Ingresos y Gastos de los Hogares – ENIGH" (Results from the National Income and Expenditure Household National Survey), Instituto Nacional de Estadistica Geografia e Informatica, Mexico.

INEGI (2002), "Encuesta Nacional de Ingresos y Gastos de los Hogares – ENIGH" (Results from the National Income and Expenditure Household National Survey), Instituto Nacional de Estadistica Geografia e Informatica, Mexico.

INEGI (2004), "Encuesta Nacional de Ingresos y Gastos de los Hogares – ENIGH" (Results from the National Income and Expenditure Household National Survey), Instituto Nacional de Estadistica Geografia e Informatica, Mexico.

INSP (2006), "Encuesta Nacional de la Salud y Nutricion – ENSANUT" (Results from the Health and Nutrition National Survey), Instituto Nacional de la Salud Publica, Mexico.

Jaumotte, F. (2003), "Female Labour Force Participation: Past Trends and Main Determinants in OECD Countries", OECD Economics Department Working Papers, No. 376, OECD, Paris.

Jeon, S. H. (2004), "The Impacts of the 1988 Tax Reform on Married Women's Labour Supply in Canada", Department of Economics Working Paper, Vol. 19, McMaster University, Hamilton, Ontario.

Joshi, H. (1990). "The Cash Opportunity Costs of Childbearing: An Approach to Estimation Using British Data.", *Population Studies*, Vol. 44, No. 1, pp. 41-60.

Joshi, H. and H. Davies (1992), "Child Care and Mothers' Lifetime Earnings: Some European Contrasts", Discussion Paper No. 600, Centre for Economic Policy Research, London, January.

Joshi, H. and H. Davies (2002), "Women's Incomes over a Synthetic Lifetime", in E. Ruspini and A. Dale (eds.), *The Gender Dimension of Social Change*, The Policy Press, Bristol, pp. 111-131.

Kamerman, S., M. Neuman, J. Waldfogel and J. Brooks-Gunn (2003), "Social Policies, Family Types and Child Outcomes in Selected OECD Countries", OECD Social, Employment and Migration Working Papers, No. 6, OECD, Paris, *www.oecd.org/els/workingpapers.*

Kapsalis, C. and P. Tourigny (2002), *Profiles and Transitions of Groups at Risk of Social Exclusion: Lone Parents*, Human Resources Development Canada, November.

Kezuka, K. (2000), "Legal Problems Concerning Part-time Work in Japan", *Japan Labor Bulletin*, Vol. 39, No. 9, Japan Institute of Labour, Tokyo.

KNSO (2005), *Social Indicators in Korea – 2005*, Korean National Statistical Office, Seoul, Korea.

Kögel, T. (2001), "Did the Association Between Fertility and Female Employment Within OECD Countries Really Change its Sign?", MPIRD Working Paper, No. 34, Max Planck Institute for Demographic Research, Rostock, Germany.

Kohler, H.P. and J. A..Ortega (2002), "Tempo-adjusted Period Parity Progression Measures, Fertility Postponement and Completed Cohort Fertility", *Demographic Research*, Vol. 6, Article 6.

Koutzis, G. and L. Kretzos (2003), "Annualised Hours in Europe", *European Industrial Relations Observatory,* EIRO on line, *www.eurofound.europa.eu/eiro/2003/08/study/tn0308101s.html.*

Lanfranchi, A, J. Gruber and J. Gay (2003), "Succès scolaire des enfants d'immigrés: effets des espaces transitoires destinés à la petite enfance", *Programme National de Recherche 39*, Centre Suisse de Coordination pour la Recherche en Éducation, Aarau, Switzerland.

Langen, A. van and M. Hulsen (2001), *Schooltijden in het basisonderwijs: feiten en fictie*, ITS, Nijmegen.

La Valle, I.S., C. Arthur, J. Scott Millward and M. Clayden (2002), "The Influence of Atypical Working Hours on Family Life", *Findings*, No. 982, Joseph Rowntree Foundation, York, United Kingdom, *www.jrf.org.uk/knowledge/findings/socialpolicy/982.asp.*

Lefebvre, P. and P. Merrigan (2002), "The Effect of Childcare and Early Education Arrangements on Developmental Outcomes of Young Children", *Canadian Public Policy*, Vol. 28, No. 2, University of Toronto Press, Downsview, Ontario, pp. 159-186.

Lei, Y. and C. Michalopoulos (2001), *SSP Plus at 36 Months: Effects of Adding Employment Services to Financial Work Incentives*, Social Research and Demonstration Corporation, Ottawa.

Ludwig, J. and D. A. Phillips (2007), "The Benefits and Costs of Head Start", NBER Working Paper No. 12973, National Bureau of Economic Research, Cambridge, MA, March, *www.nber.org/papers/w12973*.

Lutz, H. (2003), "Auswirkungen der Kindergeldregelung auf die Beschäftigung von Frauen mit Kleinkindern", Austrian Institute of Economic Research (WIFO), Vienna.

Manning, A. and B. Petrongolo (2004), *The Part-Time Pay Penalty*, Department of Trade and Industry, London.

Meyer, C.S., S. Mukerjee and A. Sestero (2001), "Work Family Benefits: Which Ones Maximize Profits?", *Journal of Managerial Issues*, Vol. 13, No. 1, Pittsburgh State University, Pittsburgh, pp. 28-44.

Michalopoulos, C., D. Tattrie, C. Miller, P.K. Robbins, P. Morris, D. Gyarmati, C. Redcross, K. Foley and R. Ford (2002), *Making Work Pay: Final Report on Long Term Welfare Recipients in the Self-sufficiency Project*, Social Research and Demonstration Corporation, Ottawa.

Millar, J. and K. Gardiner (2004), *Low Pay, Household Resources and Poverty*, Joseph Rowntree Foundation, York, United Kingdom.

Mincer, J. (1985), "Inter-Country Comparisons of Labor Force Rrends and of Related Developments: An Overview", *Journal of Labor Economics*, Vol. 3, pp. 1-32.

Ministerie van Financiën (2007), "Werkgeversbijdrage in de kosten van kinderopvang", Ministry of Finance, "s-Gravenhage (the Hague)", the Netherlands, *www.minfin.nl/nl/onderwerpen,belastingen/belastingplannen/belastingplan-2007/werkgeversbijdrage-kinderopvang/index.html*.

Ministry of Internal Affairs and Communication (2001), *Survey on Time Use and Leisure Activities*, Tokyo, *www.stat.go.jp/english/data/shakai/2001/shousai/yoyaku.htm*.

MOL and JIWE (2000), *Employment Management Study Group on Part-time Work Report*, Ministry of Labor (Women's Bureau), Tokyo and Japan Institute of Workers' Evolution, Tokyo.

Morishima, M. (2002), "Pay Practices in Japanese Organizations: Changes and Non-changes", *Japan Labor Bulletin*, Vol. 41, No. 4, Japan Institute of Labour, Tokyo, pp. 8-13.

Morris, P. and C. Michalopoulos (2000), *The Self-Sufficiency Project at 36 Months: Effects on Children of a Program that Increased Parental Employment and Income*, Social Research and Demonstration Corporations, Ottawa.

Moss, P. and M. O'Brien (2006), "International Review of Leave Policies and Related Research 2006", Employment Relations Research Series, No. 57, Department of Trade and Industry, London, Crown copyright.

NAO (2004), *Early Years: Progress in Developing High Quality Childcare and Early Education Accessible to All*, National Audit Office, London.

Nelson, A., K. Nemec, P. Solvik and C. Ramsden (The Tavistock Institute, 2004), "The Evaluation of the Work Life Balance Challenge Fund", Employment Relations Research Series, No. 32, Department of Trade and Industry, London.

New Zealand Ministry of Education (2006), *Growing Independence: A Summary of the Key Findings from the Competent Learners @ 14 Project*, Ministry of Education, Wellington, New Zealand.

NICHD Early childcare Research Network (2005), *Childcare and Child Development – Results from the NICHD Study of Early Childcare and Youth Development*, National Institute of Child Health and Human Development, the Guilford Press, New York/ London.

Nielsen, H., M. Simonsen and M. Verner (2004), "Does the Gap in Family-Friendly Policies Drive the Family Gap?", *Scandinavian Journal of Economics*, Vol. 106, No. 4, Oxford, pp. 721–744.

Nishi, F. and M. Kan (2006), "Current Situation of Parasite-singles in Japan (Summary)", Statistical Research and Training Institute, Ministry of Internal Affairs and Communication, Japan, March, *www.stat.go.jp/training/english/reseach/r-index.htm*.

NOSOSCO (2005), *Social Protection in the Nordic Countries 2005*, Nordic Social Statistical Committee, Copenhagen, Denmark.

NS (2006), "Work and Worklessness among Households", National Statistics, First Release, 28 July 2006, London.

OECD (1984), *The Tax/Benefit Position of Production Workers, 1979-83*, OECD, Paris.

OECD (1997), *The Tax/Benefit Position of Employees, 1995-96*, OECD, Paris.

OECD (1999a), *OECD Historical Statistics, 1960-97*, OECD, Paris.

OECD (1999b), *The Battle Against Exclusion, Vol. 2: Social Assistance in Belgium, the Czech Republic, the Netherlands and Norway*, OECD, Paris.

OECD (1999c), *The Battle Against Exclusion, Vol. 3: Social Assistance in Canada and Switzerland*, OECD, Paris.

OECD (2001a), *Employment Outlook*, OECD, Paris.

OECD (2001b), *Starting Strong: Early Childhood Education and Care*, OECD, Paris.

OECD (2002a), *Babies and Bosses: Reconciling Work and Family Life, Vol. 1: Australia, Denmark and the Netherlands*, OECD, Paris.

OECD (2002b), *Employment Outlook*, OECD, Paris.

OECD (2003a), *Babies and Bosses, Reconciling Work and Family Life, Vol. 2: Austria, Ireland and Japan*, OECD, Paris.

OECD (2003b), *Taxing Wages, 2001-02*, OECD, Paris.

OECD (2004a), *Babies and Bosses: Reconciling Work and Family Life, Vol. 3: New Zealand, Portugal and Switzerland*, OECD, Paris.

OECD (2004b), *Learning for Tomorrow's World, First Results from PISA 2003*, OECD, Paris.

OECD (2004c), *Benefits and Wages*, OECD, Paris.

OECD (2005a), *Babies and Bosses: Reconciling Work and Family Life, Vol. 4: Canada, Finland, Sweden and the United Kingdom*, OECD, Paris.

OECD (2005b), *Extending Opportunities: How Active Social Policies Can Benefit Us All*, OECD, Paris.

OECD (2005c), *Taxing Wages, 2003-04*, OECD, Paris.

OECD (2005d), *Economic Surveys: New Zealand*, OECD, Paris.

OECD (2006a), *Education at a Glance*, OECD, Paris.

OECD (2006b), *Education Policy Analysis: Focus on Higher Education, 2005-06 edition*, OECD, Paris.

OECD (2006c), *Women and Men in OECD Countries*, OECD, Paris.

OECD (2006d), *Revenue Statistics, 1965-2005*, OECD, Paris.

OECD (2006e), *Starting Strong II: Early Childhood Education and Care*, OECD, Paris.

OECD (2006f), *Taxing Wages, 2004-05*, OECD, Paris.

OECD (2007a), *Social Expenditure Database, 1980-2003*, OECD, Paris, *www.oecd.org/els/social/expenditure*.

OECD (2007b), *Society at a Glance, OECD Social Indicators*, OECD, Paris, *www.oecd.org/els/social/indicators*.

OECD (2007c), *Employment Outlook*, OECD, Paris.

OECD (2007d), *Facing the Future: Korea's Family, Pension and Health Policy Challenges*, OECD, Paris.

OECD (2007e), *Taxing Wages, 2005-06*, OECD, Paris.

OECD (2007f), *Benefits and Wages*, OECD, Paris.

OECD (2007g), *Economic Surveys: Hungary*, OECD, Paris.

OECD (2008), *Child Well-being and Child Policy across the OECD (working title)*, OECD, Paris, forthcoming.

Ogawa, T., C.-F. Ko and K.Y.-M. Oh (2004), "Implications of Population Ageing in East Asia: An Analysis of Social Protection and Social Policy Reforms in Japan, Korea and Taiwan", Paper presented at the Conference of the International Sociological Association, Ageing Societies and Ageing Sociology: Diversity and Change in a Global World, United Kingdom.

Oliveira M., J, F. Gonand, P. Antolin, C. de la Maisonneuve and K.-Y. Yoo (2005), "The Impact of Ageing on Demand, Factor Markets and Growth", OECD Economics Department Working Papers, No. 420, OECD, Paris.

Oreopoulos, P. (2003), "The Long-Run Consequences of Living in a Poor Neighbourhood", *Quarterly Journal of Economics*, Vol. 118, MIT Press, Cambridge, MA, pp. 1533-1575.

Osawa, M. (2001), "People in Irregular Modes of Employment: Are they really not subject to discrimination", *Social Science Japan Journal*, Vol. 4, No. 2, pp. 183-199.

Parker, S. (2003), "Evaluation of Impact of Oportunidades Program on School Registration, School Failure and School Leaving" (Title in Spanish), Centro de Investigación y Docencia Económicas (CIDE).

Perry, B. (2004), "Working For Families: The Impact on Child poverty", *Social Policy Journal of New Zealand*, Vol. 22, July.

Prognos (2005), *Betriebswirtschaftliche Kosten-Nutzen-Analyse familienfreundlicher Unternehmenspolitik*, Kasimir Meyer AG, Wohlen, Switzerland, *www.seco.admin.ch*.

Puide, A. (2001), *Recipients and Social Assistance Dependency*, STAKES, Helsinki, Finland.

Riele, S. (2006), "Gebruik van kinderopvang", *Sociaal-economische Trends*, aflevering 3, Centraal Bureau voor de Statistiek, Voorburg/Heerlen, the Netherlands.

Riesenfelder, A, C. Sorger, P. Wetzel and B. Willsberger (2006), *Evaluierung der Einfuhrung des Kinderbetreuungsgeldes*, Lechner, Reiter und Riesnfelder Sozialforschung OEG, Wien, Austria.

Robertson, J. (2007), *Parental Decision Making in Relation to the Use of Early Childhood Education Services*, Ministry of Education, Wellington, New Zealand.

Román, A.A. (2006), *Deviating from the Standard: Effects on Labor Continuity and Career Patterns*, Proefschrift aan de Universiteit van Utrecht, Dutch University Press, Amsterdam, the Netherlands.

Roy, L. and J. Bernier (2007), *Family Policy, Social Trends and Fertility in Québec: Experimenting with the Nordic Model?*, ministère de la Famille, des Aînés et de la Condition féminine, Québec, Canada.

Ruault, M. and A. Daniel (2003), "Les modes d'accueil des enfants de moins de 6 ans : premiers résultats de l'enquête réalisée en 2002 ", *Études et Résultats*, n° 235, Direction de la recherche, des études de l'évaluation et des statistiques (DREES), ministère des Affaires sociales, Paris, avril, *www.sante.gouv.fr/drees/etude-resultat/ er235/er235.pdf*.

Ruhm, C. (1998), "The Economic Consequences of Parental Leave Mandates: Lessons From Europe", *Quarterly Journal of Economics*, Vol. 113, pp. 285-317.

Ruhm, C.J. (2004), "How Well do Parents with Young Children Combine Work and Family Life", NBER Working Paper, No. 10247, National Bureau of Economic Research, Cambridge, MA.

Sceviour, R. and R. Finnie (2004), "Social Assistance Use: Trends in Incidence, Entry and Exit Rates", *Canadian Economic Observer*, Statistics Canada, Ottawa, August.

SECO (2007), *KMU-Handbuch "Beruf und Familie" – Massnahmen zur Vereinbarkeit von Beruf und Familie in kleine und mittleren Unternehmen*, Eidgenössisches Volkswirtschaftsdepartment EVD, Staatssekretariat für Wirtschaft, SECO, Bern, *www.seco.admin.ch*.

Sigle-Rushton, W. and J. Waldfogel (2006), "Motherhood and Women's Earnings in Anglo American, Continental European and Nordic Countries", Paper presented for the Conference on Cross-National Comparisons of Expenditures on Children, Princeton University, 7-9 January, Princeton.

Sleebos, J. (2003), "Low Fertility Rates in OECD Countries: Facts and Policy Responses", OECD Social, Employment and Migration Working Papers, No. 15, OECD, Paris, *www.oecd.org/els/workingpapers*.

Spiess, C.K, and K. Wrohlich (2006), "The Parental Leave Benefit Reform in Germany: Costs and Labour Market Outcomes of Moving Towards the Scandinavian Model", IZA Discussion Paper, No. 2372, Bonn, *www.iza.org*.

Statistics Bureau (2006), "Report on the Annual Report on the Labour Force Survey", Table 15, Ministry of Internal Affairs and Communications, Tokyo, *www.stat.go.jp*.

Statistisches Bundesamt (2005), "Tabellenband, Kinderlosigkeit von Frauen", Statistisches Bundesamt Deutschland, Berlin, *www.destatis.de*.

Stevens, J., J. Brown and C. Lee (2004), "The Second Work Life Balance Study: Results from the Employees' Survey", Department of Trade and Industry, Employment Relations Research Report, No. 27, London.

Stevenson, B. and J. Wolfers (2007), "Marriage and Divorce: Changes and their Driving Forces", NBER Working Paper No. 12944, National Bureau of Economic Research, Cambridge, MA, March, *www.nber.org/papers/w12944*.

Sutherland, H., T. Sefton and D. Piachaud (2003), *Poverty in Britain: The Impact of Government Policy Since 1997*, Joseph Rowntree Foundation, York, United Kingdom.

Sylva, K., E. Melhuish, P. Sammons, I. Sirja-Blatchford and B. Taggart (2004), "The Effective Provision of Pre-School Education Project: Final Report Results", DfES, November, London, *www.ioe.ac.uk/projects/eppe*.

SZW (2006), *Beleidsdoorlichting arbeid en zorg, September 2006*, Ministerie van Sociale Zaken en Werkgelegenheid, "s-Gravenhage (the Hague)", the Netherlands.

Thibault, F., F. Legendre, J-P Lorgnet and R. Mahieu (2004), "De l'APE à la PAJE: Comment appréhender les effets sur l'emploi des femmes?", *Revue de l'OFCE*, Vol. 90, pp. 276-282.

Torres, A., T. Monteiro, F. Vieira da Silva and M. Cabrita (2000), "Men and Women between Family and Work in Portugal", Work and Organisation Research Center, Tilburg, the Netherlands.

Tougas, J. (2002), "Reforming Quebec's Early Childhood Care and Education: the First Five Years", Centre for Urban and Community Studies Occasional Paper, No. 17, University of Toronto, Canada.

Valdimarsdóttir, F.R. (2006), *Nordic Experiences with Parental Leave and its Impact on Equality Between Women and Men*, Nordic Council of Ministers, Copenhagen.

Weichselbaumer and Winter-Ebmer (2005), "A Meta-Analysis on the International Gender Wage Gap", *Journal of Economic Surveys*, Vol. 19, No. 3, pp. 479-511.

Weichselbaumer and Winter-Ebmer (2007), "International Gender Wage Gaps", *Economic Policy*, April, pp. 235-287.

Whiteford, P. and W. Adema (2007), "What Works Best in Reducing Child Poverty: A Benefit or Work Strategy?", OECD Social, Employment and Migration Working Papers, No. 52, OECD, Paris, *www.oecd.org/els/workingpapers*.

Willis, R.J. (1973), "A New Approach to the Economic Theory of Fertility Behavior", *Journal of Political Economy*, pp. 14-64, March.

Woodland, S., N. Simmonds, M. Thornby, R. Fitzgerald and A. McGee (2003), "The Second Work Life Balance Study: Results from the Employers' Survey", National Center for Social Research, Department of Trade and Industry, Employment Relations Research Report, No. 22, London.

Woolley, F. (2004), "Why Pay Child Benefits to Mothers?", *Canadian Public Policy*, Vol. XXX, No. 1., pp. 47-69.

World Values Survey Association (2004), *World Values Survey*, Stockholm.

OECD PUBLICATIONS, 2, rue André-Pascal, 75775 PARIS CEDEX 16
PRINTED IN FRANCE
(81 2007 09 1 P)   ISBN 978-92-64-03244-6 – No. 55775   2007